NATIONAL GEOGRAPHIC

LONDON
BOOK
OF LISTS

→ **THE CITY'S BEST,
WORST, OLDEST,
GREATEST, & QUIRKIEST**

Tim Jepson & Larry Porges

NATIONAL GEOGRAPHIC

Washington, D.C.

CONTENTS

There are older and larger cities than London. Other cities with sublime sights and monuments, superb food and nightlife. But there are no cities that come close to London's medley of art, culture, history, tradition, excitement, cosmopolitan élan, contemporary flair—and flair for quirkiness.

In the *National Geographic London Book of Lists* we have tried to capture something of what makes London London. You'll find some of our own guidebook favorites—restaurants with superb views, the city's best curries, the oldest stores.

But it also delves deeper, listing strange old laws still on the statute books; the arcane slang of London's taxi drivers; the best places for pie, mash, and eels; the jobs you might apply for at Buckingham Palace; the capital's lost rivers and ghost Tube stops; and more than 130 other lists that we hope create a more eclectic picture of this most fascinating of cities.

The lists are organized with a minimum of organization, but we've grouped some of the broader subjects—pubs, taxis, crime, food, music, and other themes—so that you can either dip into the book or read it cover to cover. Either way, you'll find a mixture of the historical and the present day, of intriguing facts and statistics, as well as details and insights into lesser known aspects of the city.

As with any book of lists, there is plenty that we didn't have room to cover, and plenty with which you might take issue or that you would have liked to see included. But visit National Geographic's Facebook page (Nat Geo Books), our Twitter handle (@NatGeoBooks), and our Travel website *(travel.nationalgeographic .com)*—we'll be posting additional lists and soliciting feedback and London lists of your own.

A last word on "facts" in the book, many of which are necessarily hard or impossible to confirm—the exact height of old St. Paul's Cathedral before it burned in 1666, for example. Others are contentious, with sources often in disagreement. But we stand by our assertions, while being prepared to entertain rival or more recent claims.

It's been immense fun to compile our London labor of love—we hope you'll enjoy it, too.

Big Ben & the Elizabeth Tower

MOST VISITORS—and many Londoners—believe Big Ben is the tower at the end of the Houses of Parliament. Actually, it's the nickname for the Great Bell near the top of the tower. The tower itself is called the Elizabeth Tower, renamed after the 2012 Diamond Jubilee of Queen Elizabeth II. Before that it was known as the Clock Tower.

Height 315 ft (96 m)

Steps 334 plus another 59 to the lantern (or Ayrton Light)

Time to build 34 years

Completed 1859

Lean 9.1 in (230 mm) to the northwest

Lean caused by new Jubilee Line Tube Tunneling $^3/_4$ in (22 mm)

Weight of Great Bell 15.1 tons (13.7 tonnes)

Size of Great Bell 9 ft (2.75 m) across and 7.5 ft (2.28 m) high

Great Bell's first chime July 11, 1859

Time to wind clock Wound by hand until 1913, when it took two men 32 hours every week

Accuracy To within about a second a day

Adjustments One old (pre-1971) British penny on the balance produces a two-fifths of a second gain over 24 hours

Diameter of each clock face 23 ft (7 m)

Pieces of glass in each clock face 312

Length of pendulum 14 ft 9 in (4.5 m)

Weight of pendulum 683 lb (310 kg)

Beat of pendulum Every 2 seconds

Length and weight of minute hand 13 ft 9 in (4.2 m), 220 lb (100 kg) of copper sheet

Distance traveled by minute hand annually 118 mi (190 km)

Length and weight of hour hand 8 ft 10 in (2.7 m), 661 lb (300 kg) of gun metal

London-Born Movie Stars

London's exports throughout the years have included many top-notch stars, including some—such as Bob Hope and Stewart Granger—that many might have thought were native-born Americans.

- **Boris Karloff** 1887, *in Camberwell*
- **Charlie Chaplin** 1889, *in Walworth*
- **Noël Coward** 1899, *in Teddington*
- **Bob Hope** 1903, *in Eltham*
- **Stewart Granger** 1913, *in Kensington*
- **Roger Moore** 1927, *in Stockwell*
- **Elizabeth Taylor** 1932, *in Hampstead*
- **Michael Caine** 1933, *in Rotherhithe*
- **Oliver Reed** 1938, *in Wimbledon*
- **Helen Mirren** 1945, *in Chiswick*
- **Daniel Day-Lewis** 1957, *in Greenwich*

- **Emma Thompson** 1959, *in Paddington*
- **Kiefer Sutherland** 1966, *in Paddington*
- **Helena Bonham Carter** 1966, *in Golders Green*
- **Damian Lewis** 1971, *in St. John's Wood*
- **Sacha Baron Cohen** 1971, *in Hammersmith*
- **Benedict Cumberbatch** 1976, *in Hammersmith*
- **Robert Pattinson** 1986, *in Barnes*
- **Daniel Radcliffe** 1989, *in Fulham*

•Movie Locations You Can Visit•

Alfred Hitchcock was among the first to make extensive use of the capital's landmarks in his films—see Tower Bridge in *The Man Who Knew Too Much*, from 1934. Whether the real thing or a version re-created on a distant studio lot, the capital has been a protagonist from the early days of film through the Ealing comedies of the fifties, to dozens of films set in Swinging London of the sixties. London also features in some of the biggest movies of recent years. (See also Tube Movies, p. 164.)

Blow-Up's **Maryon Park**

• *Blow-Up* (1966), **Pottery Lane**
The studio of the fashion photographer played by David Hemmings in Michelangelo Antonioni's dissection of Swinging London is on Pottery Lane, Holland Park (W11). The scene in which Hemmings photographs what may be a murder was shot in Maryon Park in the Royal Borough of Greenwich: Antonioni was unhappy

The Coronet Cinema makes a cameo in the 1999 film *Notting Hill*.

with the park's grass and had it painted a more vivid green.

• The Bond movies
Sotheby's on New Bond Street, W1, in *Octopussy* (1983), where the Fabergé egg is auctioned; the College of Arms, Queen Victoria Street, EC4 (*On Her Majesty's Secret Service*, 1969), where Bond researches his ancestry; The Reform Club, 104 Pall Mall, SW1 (*Quantum of Solace*, 2008), to which M is summoned for a

meeting with the minister, all play supporting roles. The Reform is also the setting for "Blades" club, scene of the fencing duel in *Die Another Day* (2002); the same film uses a security booth at the southern end of Westminster Bridge as the entrance to the fictitious Vauxhall Cross Tube station.

• *Performance* (1970), Powis Square
Mick Jagger plays the role of a declining rock

star in the film directed by Nicolas Roeg. The exterior of Jagger's home in the film is in Notting Hill, at 25 Powis Square, off Colville Terrace.

• *Notting Hill* (1999)
Multiple west London (W11) locations appear in this movie starring Hugh Grant as a bookseller and Julia Roberts as the film star with whom he improbably falls in love. Grant's bookshop is still there at 13 Blenheim Crescent (though it is

no longer a travel bookshop), as is the entrance to Grant's flat at 280 Westbourne Park Road (opposite Nu-Line builders' merchants); Portobello Road market also features in the film, as does the Coronet Cinema at Notting Hill Gate; Rosmead Gardens (closed to the public) is the garden square in which Roberts and Grant share a nocturnal tryst.

• *Harry Potter and the Philosopher's Stone* (2001), **Leadenhall Market** A building in Bull's Head Passage in Leadenhall Market, EC3, was the setting for the Leaky Cauldron, which leads to the magical arcade of shops known as Diagon Alley. Harry Potter fans should also visit Platform 9¾, the departure point for the Hogwarts Express, which actually exists at King's Cross railroad station.

Cockney Rhyming Slang

It works like this: You replace a word with a rhyming phrase and then, usually, remove all but the first word, the others remaining implied. For example, **Stairs** → *Apples and pears* → **Apples**. Although "Cockney" implies parts of east London, the slang was found across much of the capital. These are some of the better known examples:

- Believe it → *Adam and Eve it*
- Hair → *Barnet Fair* → **Barnet**
- Face → *Boat race* → **Boat**
- Money → *Bread and honey* → **Bread**
- Dead → **Brown bread**
- Row → *Bull and cow* → **Bull**
- Look → *Butcher's hook* → **Butcher's**
- Mate → *China plate* → **China**
- Balls (Testicles) → *Cobbler's awls* → **Cobbler's**
- Head → *Crust of bread* → **Crust**
- Boots → **Daisy roots**
- Phone → **Dog and bone**

- Word → *Dickey bird* → **Dickey**
- Drunk → *Elephant's trunk* → **Elephant's**
- Road → *Frog and toad* → **Frog**
- Watch (from fob) → *Kettle and hob* → **Kettle**
- Eyes → *Mince pies* → **Mincies**
- Alone → *Tod Sloan* (a jockey) → **On your tod**
- Stink → **Pen and ink**
- Lies → *Pork pies* → **Porkies**
- Hat → *Tit for tat* → **Titfer**
- Wife → **Trouble and strife**
- Wigs → *Syrup of figs* → **Syrup**
- Tea → *Rosie Lee* → **Rosie**

·London's Population: 2,000 Years of Up, Down . . . and Up·

Britain's first census was held in 1801; one has followed every decade since, except for a break in 1941. Attempts to count London's inhabitants before 1801 run up against a lack of statistics. Moreover, times of rapid expansion and shifting administrative boundaries have often made statistics obsolete by the time they are published. Here, though, are some snapshots of London's approximate population during the centuries, with figures that are minimum estimates before 1801.

• **A.D. 60: 20,000**
The population of Roman Londinium can be estimated from, among other things, figures given by the Roman historian Tacitus for casualties suffered during the revolt led by Queen Boudicca in A.D. 60.

• **A.D. 150: 45,000**
Extrapolating from the A.D. 60 figure, many historians suggest a peak population in the vicinity of 45,000 for Roman London in the second and third centuries. No other English town would reach that number for another 1,500 years.

• **400: 5,000**
Full Roman withdrawal from Britain began in 383 and was effectively complete after 410. People may have initially remained in the city, seeking sanctuary within the walls.

• **500: 300**
Rome's collapse had a catastrophic effect on London. While the city was probably never abandoned, the population shrank dramatically.

• **700: 5,000**
Bede (ca 673-735), the great British chronicler, described London in the seventh century as a "mart of many peoples" and an important trading center.

• **900: 8,000**
The reign of King Alfred (849-899) and his

restoration of London after the depredations of the Vikings produced a period of relative stability that encouraged a steady or increasing population.

• 1100: 14,000
Following the Norman Conquest, the building of the Tower of London, Westminster Hall, and other edifices underlined—and furthered—the city's growth and importance.

• 1300: 45,000
Population approached a peak not seen since Roman times following a century of prosperity and expansion beyond the city walls. London was three times as big as York and Bristol, England's next largest cities.

• 1340: 50,000
London accounted for only 1.4 percent of the country's overwhelmingly rural population. London's population was a quarter that of Paris, with 200,000 inhabitants, and half that of Venice, Naples, and Milan.

• 1350: 25,000
The death toll exacted by the Black Death (1348-1350) is disputed, but by 1350 London's population may have dropped by a third or a half.

• 1500: 50,000

• 1600: 200,000
The fourfold increase in population in Tudor times had dramatic effects. Suburbs extended south and east and into Westminster. Overcrowding and fear of contagion grew.

• 1650: 350,000
Unskilled workers continued to pour in from the countryside, challenging craftsmen and the apprentice system, and increasing the numbers of London's poor.

• 1700: 575,000
Trends that began in early Tudor times grew more pronounced and established patterns that survive to this day. The poor spread along the Thames to the east, while the rich sought refuge from the old city by moving west.

• 1750: 750,000
London was 20 times larger than the next biggest English town, dwarfed all other western European cities, and contained more than 10 percent of the country's population.

• 1801: 959,300
London's population was 11 times that of England's next largest city, the booming port of Liverpool, and twice that of Paris, Europe's next most populous city.

• 1851: 2,363,263
London was six times the size of Liverpool, seven times that of Manchester, and ten times that of Birmingham. Newcomers, mostly from southeastern England, poured into London, helping to make it the world's largest city.

• 1891: 5,572,012
Population increase occurred in the outer areas of the city for the first

Londoners en masse celebrate the 2011 wedding of Prince William and Kate Middleton.

time: London was also the seat of an empire with a population estimated at more than 372 million.

• 1901: 6,506,954
Immigration by Jews and others from the Continent, as opposed to newcomers from elsewhere in Britain and Ireland, increased, but so did migration from the city, resulting in a slowing of the rate of population growth.

• 1911: 7,160,525

• 1939: 8,615,245
No census was taken in 1941 because of World War II, but the National Registration Act of 1939, which legislated the introduction of identity cards for all, made population figures available nonetheless.

• 1951: 8,196,978

• 1971: 7,452,520

• 1991: 6,829,300

• 2001: 7,322,400

• 2011: 8,173,941
As of the latest census, depending on how you define your terms, London is the world's 19th largest metropolis with a fixed metropolitan limit (by other measures, London is the 20th or 23rd largest). London is the third largest in Europe after Istanbul (13,854,740) and Moscow (11,689,048). Yet London's population is still below its 1939 peak. In addition, the lowest population in a single district is found in the City of London itself, the original capital—still there, and still within its ancient borders, but now with only 7,400 inhabitants.

FAST FACT

London was probably the first western city to exceed a million inhabitants. It was the world's largest city from 1831 to 1925, when it was overtaken by New York City and then Tokyo.

·Monarchs Who Reigned Most Briefly·

Finding consensus on Britain's briefest serving monarchs is a bit of a challenge. Some of the royals with a secure spot on the commonly accepted list of English rulers were proclaimed king or queen but were never actually crowned or anointed (a critical step in the process) . . . but then there are those usually omitted from the list who are in the same boat. We're adopting a "more the merrier" approach and including all pretenders.

• Lady Jane Grey (1553)
Lady Jane Grey tops the list with a reign of only nine days. Proclaimed queen after the death of young Edward VI, Jane (a Protestant) was quickly supplanted by Edward's half sister Mary (a Catholic). A victim of religious and power politics, Lady Jane Grey was executed in February 1554.

Lady Jane Grey

• Edgar Aetheling (1066)
Edgar was proclaimed king by the remnants of the Anglo-Saxon nobility after Harold II's death at the hands of William the Conqueror. The Norman army wasn't impressed, and Edgar was brushed aside two months later.

• Edward V (1483)
Twelve-year-old Edward's three-month reign ended abruptly when Richard III, his uncle and official Protector, assumed the throne. Edward and his younger brother, the famous Princes in the Tower, were locked away in the Tower of London and were never heard from again. We fear the worst.

• Harold II (1066)
After only a nine-month rule, Harold II took an arrow in the eye and was killed at the Battle of Hastings. (Yes, we know that he may not have actually been killed in that exact fashion, but it's hard to shake these traditional stories.) Thus began the Norman era and "modern" England.

• Edward VIII (1936)
Edward abdicated the throne in 1936 to marry his American/commoner/twice-divorced mistress, Wallis Simpson. His reign lasted a little more than ten months before he was succeeded by his brother, George VI—father of Queen Elizabeth II.

• Richard III (1483-1485)
The much-maligned Richard usurped the crown from his nephew, Edward V, in 1483. After a contentious two-year reign, future King Henry VII defeated his forces at the Battle of Bosworth. Though he fought bravely, Richard was killed and his name was (perhaps slightly unfairly) besmirched

The ill-fated Edward V

forever by the Tudor propaganda machine.

• Harthacnut (1040-1042)

One of the myriad pre-Norman monarchs with hard-to-pronounce names, Harthacnut reigned during the period of Danish Viking rule over most of England. Rare for the time (it was quite a nasty and violent age), Harthacnut appears to have died a natural death while overindulging at a wedding feast after two years as king.

FIRST PERSON

❝Alas, I rather hate myself, for hateful deeds committed by myself. I am a villain.❞
~**Richard III,** *from William Shakespeare's play of the same name*

London Gardens: The Big Five

Green-fingered enthusiasts will find much to detain them in London, especially at Kew, one of the world's greatest city gardens, but also in four of the capital's other big standouts.

• **Royal Botanic Gardens, Kew** *(kew.org).* London's greatest gardens boast 250 years of history, 30,000 plants, and 300 acres (121 ha) of grounds.

• **Kensington Gardens** *(royalparks.org.uk/parks/kensington-gardens).* Extending across 242 acres (98 ha) the Gardens host, among other things, the Albert Memorial, Peter Pan statue, and Serpentine Gallery.

• **Hampton Court Palace Gardens** *(hrp.org.uk/hamptoncourtpalace).* The 60 acres

(24 ha) of garden around this immense palace date from the time of Henry VIII.

• **Eltham Palace and Gardens** *(english-heritage.org.uk).* Medieval, art deco, and other horticultural elements combine in this 19-acre (7 ha) garden.

• **Syon House and Gardens** *(syonpark.co.uk).* The majestic Great Conservatory is the centerpiece of a 40-acre (16 ha) garden, landscaped by the celebrated "Capability" Brown (1716-1783).

Seven Best Small Parks and Gardens

London's big public parks—Hyde Park, The Regent's Park, Green Park, Holland Park, Greenwich Park—are widely celebrated. Here are some of the best of the city's smaller and less well-known green spaces.

Chelsea Physic Garden *(chelseaphysicgarden.co.uk).*
A Londoners' favorite, this delightful walled garden was founded in 1673, making it the United Kingdom's second-oldest botanic garden after Oxford's.

Fenton House and Garden *(nationaltrust.org.uk/fenton-house).*
The walled garden of this fine 17th-century Hampstead merchant's house features a 300-year-old apple orchard, kitchen garden, formal lawns, and historic rose garden.

Geffrye Museum Garden *(geffrye-museum.org.uk).*
The Period Gardens of this museum of historic domestic interiors reflect how town gardens have changed over 400 years. There is also a large herb garden and the Front Garden, which frame the museum's fine historic buildings.

Kyoto Garden *(rbkc.gov.uk).*
This restful, perfectly realized Japanese-style garden is easily missed in Holland Park, itself one of the city's finest small parks.

The Phoenix Garden *(thephoenixgarden.org).*
Despite its proximity to one of the West End's busiest junctions (Shaftesbury Avenue and Charing Cross Road), this is among the quietest community gardens in central London.

Postman's Park *(cityoflondon.gov.uk).*
The park was named for postmen from the former General Post Office who lunched here, and it is known for the Watts gallery of plaques celebrating "heroic men and women" who gave their lives to save others.

Westminster Abbey Gardens *(westminster-abbey.org).*
When you visit the Abbey church, spend some time in its three historic gardens: the Garth, Little Cloister, and College Garden, which have been cultivated for more than 900 years.

Ten Extreme Weather Events

It's true: Londoners, like most Britons, really do like to discuss the weather. Here are ten weather events that were really worth talking about.

Hottest day

London's highest temperature since reliable records began was 100.6°F (38.1°C), measured on August 10, 2003, at the Royal Botanic Gardens, Kew. This is merely mild compared to the world record of 134°F (56.7°C) recorded in Death Valley, California, in 1913.

Coldest day

In December 1796, a temperature of -6°F (-21.1°C) was recorded at Greenwich.

Earliest snow

According to official U.K. Met Office records, London's earliest snowfall occurred on September 25, 1895.

Latest snow

On June 2, 1975, the *Guardian* newspaper reported that snow had fallen at Lord's Cricket Ground, beating London's previous latest snowfall (in May 1821). When readers took the paper to task over the claim, an inquiry found in the paper's favor: It had snowed in London in June.

Worst winter

January 1205 was so cold that wine and ale froze and was sold by weight rather than volume. The coldest year ever was probably 1684 (see Worst Years, p. 229), while 1963 was London's coldest recent winter, with an average January temperature of 23.7°F (-4.6°C) and ice so thick at the Thames at Shepperton that two men could sit midstream on armchairs.

Heaviest rainfall

Almost 7 inches (17.8 cm) of rain fell in two hours on Hampstead on August 14, 1975. Despite a reputation for dismal weather, however, London actually receives relatively little rain. Even Rome, which receives an average of 33 inches (83.4 cm) annually, gets more than London's average yearly total of 23.3 inches (59.2 cm). According to Met Office averages from 1981 to 2010, the capital's wettest months are October and November; the driest, February and July.

Worst storm

Many Londoners remember the Great Storm of October 15-16, 1987—a once in 200-year event, and famously not predicted by the BBC and Met Office. Winds reached 94 miles an hour (151 kph), and a third of all trees in Kew Gardens were destroyed. The storm of November 26-27, 1703, however, was worse. The lead roof was blown off Westminster Abbey, and 700 ships were heaped together in the docks below London Bridge. Writer Daniel Defoe observed of the tempest: "No pen could describe it, nor tongue express it, nor thought conceive it."

Thickest fog

The great fog of 1952 is infamous (see Worst Years, p. 229), but 1873 saw several record-breaking weeks of smoky fog, resulting in a death rate 40 percent higher than normal.

Last flood

The Thames last flooded in London on January 6-7, 1928, breaching the Thames and Chelsea embankments. Fourteen people drowned and more than 4,000 were left homeless. Heavy rain and a sudden thaw that swelled the river's headwaters were compounded by high spring tides, a storm surge up the Thames estuary, and the dredging of the river after 1909, which made it easier for tidal water to flow upstream. A level of 18 feet 3 inches (5.55 m) above the datum line, a foot (30 cm) higher than the previous record, was recorded.

Tornado

The "London Tornado" of October 1091 was the first recorded in the United Kingdom. It killed two people, razed 600 houses, and destroyed the wooden London Bridge. Chroniclers described how, at the church of St. Mary-le-Bow, four dislodged rafters 26 feet (7.9 m) long were driven so hard into the ground that only 4 feet (1.2 m) protruded.

FIRST PERSON

"I'm leaving because the weather is too good. I hate London when it's not raining."
~Groucho Marx

·Seven of Our Favorite London Ghosts·

If ghosts existed, London could lay claim to being one of the most haunted cities in the world. (We're not officially taking a position on whether ghosts are or aren't real.) For now, let's pretend they do exist and list a few of the city's best-known and best-loved apparitions.

• **Anne Boleyn**
Henry VIII's second wife was beheaded in the Tower of London in 1536. Her ghost is said to walk between the Tower's Queen's House and the Chapel—and in a nice spooky twist, she's evidently holding her severed head under her arm. Cool.

• **John Bradshaw**
Although he died in 1659, the body of the judge

William Terriss (pre-ghost)

who ordered the execution of King Charles I in 1649 was exhumed from his Westminster Abbey grave in 1661, after the monarchy was restored, and his corpse hanged and decapitated. His specter is reported to walk around Westminster Abbey's Triforium.

• **Henry VI**
In May 1471, the deposed king was stabbed to death by an unknown assailant while praying in the Tower of London's Wakefield Tower chapel. Something claiming to be Henry's ghost has been seen wandering the Tower property.

• **The Laughing Cavalier**
An unknown specter has been seen in the old cellar of The George, a pub on the Strand. The apparition is said to look like a royalist cavalier from the 17th-century English Civil War.

• **Sir Walter Raleigh**
Raleigh was imprisoned in the Tower of London for more than a decade,

FIRST PERSON

"Whether Raleigh's ghost or some other phenomenon is responsible, several yeoman warders and their wives have changed housing at the Tower because of strange incidents.**"**
~**Employee at the Tower of London,** *who wished to remain anonymous*

although his 1618 execution was at the Palace of Westminster. His ghost, said to haunt one of the houses of Tower Green, is evidently quite troublesome: He throws mugs around, and women staying alone at the Queen's House have reported getting tossed out of bed.

• **William Terriss**
In 1897, an actor named William Terriss was murdered outside the stage door of the Adelphi Theatre by a jealous rival, Richard Prince. His supposed ghost is frequently seen there.

• **Sarah Whitehead (aka "The Black Nun")**
In 1811, Philip Whitehead—an employee at the Bank of England—was charged with forgery: He was hanged in 1812. His sister, Sarah Whitehead, frequently visited the bank after his death, dressed all in black, convinced that the Bank governors were keeping an immense fortune from her. By 1818, the governors gave her a large sum of money on condition she stay away. During her natural life she kept her promise, but her ghost is less true to her word and has been spotted by passersby, or so it's said.

•Nine Great Aristocratic Houses•

Scattered in and around London are several sumptuous aristocratic mansions, surviving vestiges of an era of slightly ostentatious home building that peaked in the 18th century.

• **Apsley House**
(149 Piccadilly, Hyde Park Corner, W1, english-heritage.org.uk)
Once home to the Duke of Wellington (hero of the Napoleonic Wars), and still home to his descendants, Apsley House enjoys pride of place on Hyde Park Corner. The stately 18th-century mansion, including the Duke's impressive art collection, is open to visitors.

• **Burlington House**
(Piccadilly, W1, royal academy.org.uk)
Richard Boyle, the Third Earl of Burlington, renovated his family home on the north side of Piccadilly into a light, Palladian-style house in the early 18th century. Later, it was expanded, and today it houses the Royal Academy of Arts as well as five academic societies. The courtyard is open to the public, and works from the academy's collection are displayed in one of the original reception rooms.

• **Chiswick House**
(Burlington Lane, Chiswick, W4, chgt.org.uk)
Lord Burlington—a true connoisseur of the arts—built Chiswick House in 1729. The west London Palladian villa was designed for the purpose of displaying Burlington's art collection and

FAST FACT

Queen Elizabeth, the Queen Mother, called Clarence House home from 1953—when her husband died and her daughter became queen—until her passing in 2002.

entertaining his friends, rather than as a home (he also owned a London town house). The expansive rolling gardens have an informal air and are perfect for rambling.

• **Clarence House**
(St. James's Palace, SW1, royalcollection.org.uk)
Clarence House, just off of St. James's Park, was built in the 1820s and is the official London residence of the Prince of Wales, the Duchess of Cornwall, and Prince Harry. Visits (offered only in summer) include a guided tour of five ground-floor rooms and access to the gardens.

• **Ham House and Garden**
(Ham Street, Ham, Richmond, Surrey, TW10, nationaltrust.org.uk)
One of London's earliest grand houses, Ham House and its 18 acres

(7 ha) of formal gardens have been fully restored to their original 17th-century appearance.

• **Marble Hill House**
(Richmond Road, Twickenham, TW1, www.english-heritage.org.uk)
Built in the 1720s, Marble Hill is an elegant restored house originally built for George II's mistress Henrietta Howard. The white Palladian villa and park overlook the Thames in bucolic western London between Twickenham and Richmond.

• **Osterley Park**
(Jersey Road, Isleworth, Middlesex, TW7, nationaltrust.org.uk)
A masterpiece of the 18th-century architect and designer Robert Adam, Osterley Park was converted from a 16th-century redbrick house into a grand mansion for

the Child banking family. The house and gardens appear as they would have looked when the house was first completed in the 1780s.

• **Spencer House**
(27 St. James's Pl., SW1, spencerhouse.co.uk)
The ancestral home of Diana, Princess of Wales, Spencer House was built in 1756-1766 for John, First Earl of Spencer. The house's eight state rooms (which display artwork lent by the Queen) are open to the public on Sundays or by appointment.

• **Syon House**
(Brentford, TW8, syonpark.co.uk)
Magnificent Syon House is another work of Robert Adam, who remodeled it in the 1760s for Sir Hugh Smithson, First Duke of Northumberland. Most of Adam's original design work survives.

·Abbey Road's Most Significant Recordings·

The obligatory march across Abbey Road's famed crosswalk (zebra crossing)

Let's play a game: We say a phrase, and you say the first thing that comes into your mind. Here we go: Abbey Road.

If you didn't conjure up an image of the Beatles crossing the street in the late 1960s, you're not playing this game correctly. It's nearly impossible not to link the famous Abbey Road Studios with the four lads from Liverpool (as demonstrated by the legions of fans who linger at all hours to try out the crosswalk). And while the association with the Beatles is richly deserved, there have been many other important records created at Abbey Road, one of the world's first great recording studios.

• **Sir Edward Elgar, "Land of Hope and Glory," November 1931**

FIRST PERSON

❝The regal 'pomp and circumstance' which Elgar set to music … now assumes the proportions of a world première.**❞**

~**Maynard Owen Williams,** National Geographic *magazine, May 1937*

(on the coronation of King George VI)

The first recording ever made at Abbey Road was by composer Sir Edward Elgar, THE rock star of 1931 English classical music. Elgar conducted the London Symphony Orchestra as they played his classic British patriotic opus, "Land of Hope and Glory," known better in the United States as "Pomp and Circumstance" (a standard at many graduation ceremonies).

• **Glenn Miller Orchestra, Recordings of October/ November 1944**
Big-band legend Glenn Miller made one of his last recordings at Abbey Road, leading his Army Air Force Band in a session with singer Dinah Shore. In December, Miller left England for Paris to play for troops in France, but his plane was lost without a trace over the English Channel. The Abbey Road recordings stayed in dry dock until the copyright expired half a century later and

were finally released as Miller's *Lost Recordings* album in 1996.

• **Max Bygraves, "Cowpuncher's Cantata," 1952**
The tongue-in-cheek song "Cowpuncher's Cantata," by comedian and singer Max

To the studio's inner sanctum

Bygraves, was the first Abbey Road recording to hit the U.K. singles charts, where it reached number 11.

• **Eddie Calvert, "O Mein Papa," 1954**
This trumpet instrumental—a cover of a 1930s German

song—became the first Abbey Road recording to hit the top spot in the U.K. singles charts.

• **Ruby Murray, "Softly Softly," 1955**
Ruby Murray was a smash sensation in 1955. With seven top-ten hits in just that one year, the Northern Irish singer was in the U.K. pop charts for a total of 80 weeks. "Softly, Softly" was her first number-one song.

• **Cliff Richard and the Drifters, "Move It," 1958**
One of the United Kingdom's most successful pop music stars of all time, Cliff Richard recorded the single "Move It" at Abbey Road as part of his 1959 debut album *Cliff*. The song climbed to number two on the British charts, and established Richard as one of Britain's first true rock stars.

• **The Beatles, "Love Me Do," September 1962**
And then, in June

"All You Need Is Love" was actually very much a work in progress at the time of the *Live From Abbey Road* performance, and much of it was improvised.

1962, a band from Liverpool made its first demo at Abbey Road. The executives at EMI recording company were impressed, and the Beatles came back in September to record their first single, "Love Me Do." The song was one of 14 released the following year on the group's inaugural album, *Please Please Me*, and Beatlemania was born.

• The Beatles, *Live From Abbey Road*, 1967
This live television production was viewed by nearly 400 million people worldwide, at the time the largest audience ever for a single televised event. It wasn't solely a Beatles concert (there were artists representing 19 countries), but the live performance of John Lennon's "All You Need Is Love" capped off and stole the show.

• The Jeff Beck Group, *Truth*, 1968
Jeff Beck's album *Truth* was the guitarist's first solo effort after two years with the Yardbirds and helped launch popular music's shift toward the hard rock/heavy metal sound of the 1970s. Beck's career move in part inspired fellow Yardbird guitarist Jimmy Page to break away from the group and form Led Zeppelin.

• The Beatles, *Abbey Road*, 1969
You knew it was coming. The Beatles recorded their final album at Abbey Road and released their most successful LP to date (no mean feat) in 1969. *Abbey Road* included the singles "Something" and "Come Together." EMI astutely changed the name of the recording studio to Abbey Road Studios after the album's release and success.

• Pink Floyd, *Dark Side of the Moon*, 1973
Recorded in 1972-1973, Pink Floyd's eighth album helped further the music world's movement away from clean-cut pop and rock. Among the songs on the experimental/progressive album, which has sold more than 50 million copies worldwide, are "Money" and "Time."

• Radiohead, *The Bends*, 1995
Radiohead's seminal album *The Bends* was completed at Abbey Road in 1994. The alternative/Britpop band's album stayed on the British charts for 160 straight weeks. Singles from the album included "High and Dry" and "Fake Plastic Trees." In 2000, it was ranked by Virgin Records as the second-best album of all time (after the Beatles' *Revolver*).

·The Beatles' London·

The Beatles' 1969 Savile Row rooftop gig—their last live performance

Liverpool was The Beatles' home city, of course, but once they'd gained success, much of their recording and domestic life revolved around London, which is dotted with locations associated with the Fab Four.

• **Abbey Road, NW8,** of course: the "zebra" crossing; the parked Volkswagen (now in a German museum); and the passing tourist, American Paul Cole, who only realized he'd been photographed months later. We're not forgetting the music and the recording studio at 3 Abbey Road (see Abbey Road, p. 25).

• The roof at **3 Savile Row, W1,** headquarters of The Beatles' Apple Corps business (*apple, core, corps:* It was a joke), was the scene of the group's last live performance, on January 30, 1969. The last time all four Beatles were in a room together as a band was in the same building in September of the same year.

• The Beatles lived in the Hotel President in **Russell Square, WC1,** in the summer of 1963 after moving from Liverpool to London. They then moved into an apartment at **57 Green Street, W1,** near Hyde Park, in the fall of the same year; it was the only true "home" shared by all four Beatles.

• The Apple boutique opened at **94 Baker Street, W1,** in 1967. It was decorated in psychedelic colors until neighbors complained, and then the building was painted white. The business collapsed after eight months.

• Recording company Decca famously failed to sign the band after they failed an audition on January 1, 1962, at the Decca Studios at **165 Broadhurst Gardens, NW6.**

• Paul lived or often stayed at **57 Wimpole Street, W1,** home of the parents of his girlfriend, Jane Asher. He wrote several songs there, including "Eleanor Rigby,"

"Michelle," and "I Want to Hold Your Hand," the last with John.

• Paul bought the house at **7 Cavendish Avenue, NW8,** in 1965, and it remained his London base for many years. Songs such as "Penny Lane," "Getting Better," and "Hey Jude" were written here, and visitors included Andy Warhol and Mick Jagger.

• John first met Yoko in November 1966, at an exhibition of her art at the Indica Gallery at **6 Mason's Yard, SW1.** She handed him a card on which was written simply, "Breathe."

• John and Yoko first lived together at **34 Montagu Square, W1,** in a flat owned by Ringo. Paul wrote several songs there, and it was the scene of John and Yoko's

October 1968 drug bust and the place their nude *Two Virgins* album cover was shot.

• The cover of *Please Please Me,* the group's first album, was shot in February 1963, at the old EMI record company headquarters at **20 Manchester Square, W1.** The famous stairwell—also used for two greatest hits albums of 1973—is now preserved in offices in Hammersmith.

• The celebrated sleeve for the *Sergeant Pepper's Lonely Hearts Club Band* album was shot and composed at **4 Chelsea Manor Studios, 1 Flood Street, SW3,** in Chelsea.

• Trident Studios was located at **17 St. Anne's Court, Soho, W1.** The Beatles recorded "Hey Jude" and several *White Album* tracks there in 1968.

For a time, Jimi Hendrix also rented the flat at 34 Montagu Square—John and Yoko's first home—but was evicted for painting the walls black.

Musicians Who Died in London

London offers some of the world's finest and most varied popular music. But what the city gives, it can also take away. Here are some of the many musicians who died in the capital before their time.

- **Jimi Hendrix, 27** Singer and guitarist, *dead on arrival at St. Mary Abbot's Hospital, Kensington, September 18, 1970.*

- **"Mama" Cass Elliot, 32** Singer *with The Mamas & The Papas, July 29, 1974, at 9 Curzon Place, Mayfair.*

- **Marc Bolan, 29** Lead singer *with T-Rex, killed in a car crash on Barnes Common, September 16, 1977.*

- **Keith Moon, 31** Drummer *with The Who, September 7, 1978, at 9 Curzon Place—the same apartment building as "Mama" Cass Elliot.*

- **Billy Fury, 42** Singer, *January 28, 1983, at St. Mary's Hospital, Paddington.*

- **Freddie Mercury, 45** Singer *with Queen, November 24, 1991, at Garden Lodge, Kensington.*

- **Amy Winehouse, 27** Singer and songwriter, *July 23, 2011, at Camden Square.*

- **Robin Gibb, 62** Singer and songwriter *with the Bee Gees, May 20, 2012, in Chelsea.*

· The Ten Best Small Venues for Live Music ·

London has perhaps the most dynamic live music scene of any city in the world. Every night you can choose between hundreds of shows in any number of genres. The big and historic venues—the O2, Royal Albert Hall, Forum, Eventim Apollo, Brixton Academy, and Shepherd's Bush Empire—are well known. Here are the best of the smaller spaces:

- **Bush Hall** *(bushhall music.co.uk).* A dance hall in the Roaring Twenties, a soup kitchen in World War II, a bingo hall, and a rehearsal space for The Who, Bush Hall was also a snooker club before being renovated as a beautiful performance space. It punches above its weight, having hosted, among others, Adele, Laura Marling, Nick Cave, R.E.M., and The Killers.

- **Cecil Sharp House** *(cecilsharphouse.org).* Cecil James Sharp's (1859-1924) documentation of traditional folk songs and dances helped ensure their survival. This historic venue dates from 1930 and was named in his honor. Programs include the best of British and other folk and traditional dance.

- **Green Note** *(greennote .co.uk).* It typifies the small, cozy, candlelit music club only locals know about. James Studholme, singer with regulars Police Dog Hogan, is a fan: "London has surprisingly few venues like this; the vibe and intimate atmosphere are spot on. Any night you know you are going to hear something interesting and often exceptional."

• **The Half Moon** *(halfmoon.co.uk)*. This is a superb historic pub in its own right, with fine food and a range of local and other beers, but its intimate back room has been celebrated since 1963 for its music, hosting the likes of The Who, The Rolling Stones, U2, Van Morrison, Bo Diddley, and Kasabian.

• **Kings Place** *(kingsplace .co.uk)*. This modern complex contains stores, cafés, restaurants, and the offices of *The Guardian* newspaper. The two small theaters lack the heritage of other venues, but they have pitch-perfect acoustics and provide a great platform for performers and listeners alike.

• **The Old Queen's Head** *(theoldqueens head.com)*. A classic of its type: The big London pub with a

welcoming room upstairs has long hosted live folk, blues, semi-acoustic, and other genres. The free weekly Sunday Social is a lazy afternoon of roast lunches, newspapers, board games, and live music.

• **Ronnie Scott's Jazz Club** *(ronniescotts.co.uk)*. Scott opened a Soho basement for musicians to jam in 1959. The likes of Count Basie, Sarah Vaughan, and Miles Davis were soon checking in. Ronnie has gone to the great gig in the sky and the venue has moved, but the emphasis on the finest musicians—Wynton

Lucky Thompson at Ronnie Scott's, 1962

Marsalis, Kurt Elling, Cassandra Wilson—endures.

• **The Roundhouse** *(roundhouse.org.uk)*. Larger than some in our list (1,700 capacity), it nevertheless has an intimate air and is a wonderful place to listen to music, thanks in part to its unusual setting—a historic railroad turning shed dating from 1847.

• **Union Chapel** *(union chapel.org.uk)*. As the name suggests, the striking Gothic Revival building (built 1874-1890) functions as a working church and charity drop-in center, as well as a peerless performance space that *Time Out*, London's best listings source, has voted the city's finest.

• **The Vortex Jazz Club** *(vortexjazz .co.uk)*. First stop for jazz enthusiasts, especially those who lean toward modern jazz, urban sounds, improvisation, and the avant-garde.

London in Song

Dozens—hundreds—of songs reference London or parts
of London. These are some of the most famous:

"Baker Street," Gerry Rafferty (1978)

Windin' your way down on Baker Street
Light in your head and dead on your feet.

"Burlington Bertie," Harry B. Norris (1900)

What price Burlington Bertie,
The boy with the Hyde Park drawl . . .
The boy with the Bond Street crawl?

"A Foggy Day (In London Town)," George & Ira Gershwin (1937)

A foggy day, in London town
Had me low, had me down
I viewed the morning with much alarm
The British Museum had lost its charm.

"The Lambeth Walk," Furber, Rose & Gay (1937)

Lambeth you've never seen,
The skies ain't blue, the grass ain't green.

"A Nightingale Sang in Berkeley Square," Maschwitz & Sherwin (1939)

There were angels dining at the Ritz
And a nightingale sang in Berkeley Square.

"Up the Junction," Squeeze (1978)

I never thought it would happen
With me and the girl from Clapham.

"Waterloo Sunset," The Kinks (1967)

As long as I gaze on Waterloo sunset, I am in paradise.

"Werewolves of London," Warren Zevon (1978)

I saw a werewolf with a Chinese menu in his hand
Walkin' through the streets of Soho in the rain.

·London Rock Locations·

London is dense with locations that feature large in the history of popular music. Some survive only in the mind's eye or remembered lyrics; some remain to be visited under your own steam or on one of the "rock tours" offered by a variety of tour operators.

• The album cover for **David Bowie**'s *The Rise and Fall of Ziggy Stardust and the Spiders From Mars* (1972) was shot outside 23 Heddon Street, W1.

• The cover image for *The Clash* (1977), the first album by **The Clash,** was photographed on (surviving) steps at The Stables Market in Camden Town. The band's early auditions and rehearsals were held in the basement at 113–115 Praed Street, W2.

• The famous clip of **Bob Dylan** throwing away cards with the words to "Subterranean Homesick Blues," shot in 1965, was made behind the Savoy hotel (where Dylan stayed and sang with Joan Baez, who helped write the cards) at the intersection of Savoy Hill Road and a dead-end alley, Savoy Steps. The site is little changed.

• **Elvis** famously never performed in Britain and it was long believed the nearest he got was during his Army service, when his military DC-7 touched down in March 1960, to refuel in Scotland. But now it seems he toured London's sights in 1958—never leaving his car—with singer Tommy Steele. When a friend let the secret out, Steele commented: "I swore never to divulge publicly what took place and I regret that it has found some way of 'getting into the light.' I can only hope he can forgive me."

• **Jimi Hendrix** played his first London gig in 1966 at the now-vanished Bag O' Nails club at

9 Kingly Street, Soho. He lived on the top floor of 23 Brook Street, W1. At the time of his death in 1970—at or near the Hotel Samarkand, 21-22 Lansdowne Crescent, W11—he was staying at the Cumberland Hotel, Marble Arch, W1.

• **Iron Maiden** made its London debut in 1976 at the Cart and Horses pub, still in business (and offering live music) at 1 Maryland Point, E15.

• According to many accounts, **Bob Marley** lived at 34 Ridgmount Gardens, WC1, during his "first" visit to London in 1972, but a year earlier he had stayed at a B&B at 12a Queensborough Terrace, W2. With success came two years in a smart Chelsea town house at 42 Oakley Street, SW3, in 1977-1978.

• **Oasis** shot the cover of *(What's the Story) Morning Glory?* (1995) near 34 Berwick Street, W1.

• In 1966, **Pink Floyd**'s Syd Barrett lived and wrote many of the group's early songs at

David Bowie/Ziggy Stardust in 1973

2 Earlham Street, Soho, WC2. The cover of the band's *Animals* (1977) album features a pig flying over Battersea Power Station.

• **Keith Richards** lived at 3 Cheyne Walk, SW3, in Chelsea, from 1968-1978. The house at #4

once belonged to the novelist George Eliot (1819-1880)—an unlikely juxtaposition.

• **The Rolling Stones** recorded their first album in early 1964 on a "two-track Revox in a room insulated with egg cartons," according to Keith Richards, at the then Regent Sounds Studio at 4 Denmark Street, WC2. Mick Jagger, Richards, and Brian Jones shared an apartment at 102 Edith Grove, SW10, in 1962-1963.

• **The Sex Pistols** lived at 6 Denmark Street for a year, but left when they couldn't afford the £4 ($6.50) a week rent. Their first single, "Anarchy in the U.K.," was recorded at Lansdowne Studios on Lansdowne Road, W11 (which has since been converted to apartments).

·Grand Old Railway Hotels·

As railroads came to dominate travel in Britain during the 19th century, the great railway companies built lavish hotels at strategic termini to house the burgeoning number of train travelers. Many have recently been refurbished to reflect their former glory.

The refurbished Great Northern Hotel reopened in 2013.

• Andaz Liverpool Street Hotel
(40 Liverpool St., EC2, london.liverpoolstreet .andaz.hyatt.com)
The Andaz came into this world as the Great Eastern Hotel in 1884. The hotel, now part of the Hyatt family and handily adjacent to Liverpool Street station, was renovated and modernized in 2007.

• Charing Cross Hotel
(The Strand, WC2, guoman.com)
Centrally located off Trafalgar Square, the 1865 Charing Cross Hotel was refurbished in 2011 into a luxury boutique hotel.

• Great Northern Hotel at King's Cross
(Pancras Rd., N1, gnhlondon.com)
London's first railway hotel, originally built in 1854, reopened as a boutique hotel in 2013. Though only the facade remains from the original 19th-century building, it is again welcoming long-distance train travelers: It stands directly across the street from the Eurostar terminus at St. Pancras International Station.

• Hilton London Paddington
(146 Praed St., W2, hilton.com)
The Great Western Royal Hotel (now the Hilton London Paddington) opened just three weeks after the Great Northern did in 1854. The hotel connects via a footbridge to Paddington Station and its zippy express train to Heathrow airport.

• Grosvenor Hotel
(101 Buckingham Palace Rd., SW1, guoman.com)

Charing Cross and its eponymous railway hotel, ca 1900

The Grosvenor was built in 1862, just off Victoria Station; its annex went up in 1907. This was the first London hotel to use elevators, or lifts—called "ascending rooms"—which were powered by water pressure.

• **The Landmark London Hotel**
(222 Marylebone Rd., NW1, landmarklondon.co.uk)

Next to Marylebone Station, the 1899 Landmark (then called the Great Central Hotel) was the last of London's railway hotels built during the Victorian golden age of train travel. The restored hotel, with 300 rooms and suites, boasts an impressive soaring atrium that is home to its main restaurant (see Afternoon Teas, p. 64).

• **St. Pancras Renaissance Hotel**
(Euston Rd., NW1, marriott.co.uk)
Competing with the nearby Great Northern, this lovely Gothic hotel (formerly the 1873 Midland Grand Hotel) resides directly within St. Pancras International Station. The 2011 renovation added 207 rooms, tucked along the platform.

FAST FACT

By 1880, more than 500 million passengers were taking to Britain's rails annually—an increase of 700 percent from 1850.

The River Thames

Where would London be without the Thames? Not in this location, certainly—the Romans established the city at the spot where the river stopped being tidal and could most easily be forded. Two thousand years on, the crowds of commuters and pleasure boaters plying its waters attest to its continuing importance.

Length from the source to the sea 215 miles (346 km)

Source of the river Thames Head, in Gloucestershire's Cotswold Hills

Direction of river flow West to east

Body of water into which the river discharges The North Sea

Ancient Celtic word for the river from which the name most likely derives Tamesas

Rank among English rivers in length First (The Severn is longer but runs into Wales.)

Number of bridges crossing the Thames 215 and counting

Number of islands 190

Of these, number of islands with any human habitation 45

Best island name Magna Carta Island at Runnymede (It's unknown if the Magna Carta was actually signed on this island, but we do know it was signed somewhere at Runnymede.)

Number of main tributaries 38

Perhaps surprising river wildlife Dolphins, seals, seahorses, porpoises, and water voles, in addition to fish and eels, which count as less surprising

Number of different fish species At least 125

Number of rowing clubs More than 200

Year of the world's first underwater tunnel (connecting Rotherhithe and Wapping) 1843

Number of tunnels under the river today 17

Harrods lords over Brompton Road in 1910, when Brompton Road was slightly less congested.

Twelve Harrods Facts

Harrods *(harrods.com)* has a storied retail history that goes back more than 165 years. Here are some lesser known facts about one of the world's most well-known stores.

Harrods offers safe deposit boxes on the lower ground floor for customers to stash their cash, jewelry, and other valuables. The service started in 1896 and is still available today.

In 1898, Harrods installed Britain's first escalator, or "moving staircase," to the amazement of the public (see London Firsts, p. 80).

Harrods once had its own embalming and funeral service, established in 1900. Some of its "clients" included psychologist Sigmund Freud (d. 1939) and British prime minister Clement Attlee (d. 1967).

In the early 1900s, Harrods had its own Ladies Club, where female customers could write letters, leave messages for each other, or simply relax in luxury.

By 1902 Harrods was selling yachts, and eventually making them to order.

The store opened a livestock department in 1917, initially offering live poultry and goats. Later, it began to concentrate on unusual and exotic pets. The part of the store now known as Pet Kingdom became a favorite with kids.

The most famous teddy bear in the world—Winnie, the inspiration for Winnie the Pooh—was bought in 1921 from Harrods by author A. A. Milne for his son, Christopher Robin.

A memorial to the staff members who were killed in World War I stands near Door 3 (leading to Basil Street).

Beginning in 1919, Harrods sold airplanes (and flying lessons, too). While you can no longer purchase airplanes from them, you can charter a flight through their aircraft service, Harrods Aviation.

During World War II some areas of the store were used for military purposes. Outside of normal business hours, parachutes, uniforms, and aircraft parts were all manufactured on the premises, and the Royal Canadian Air Force was given a base.

More than 11,000 lights illuminate the store each night. This practice began in 1959 when Harrods started dressing itself up for Christmas.

In 2007, Harrods hired a live Egyptian cobra to guard a £62,000 ($100,000)* pair of haute couture ruby-, sapphire-, and diamond-encrusted sandals.

* Here and throughout the book we're using an approximate exchange rate of 1.6 U.S. dollars to the British pound.

London's Most Popular Attractions

Visit London, the capital's official visitor board *(visitlondon.com)*, keeps track of the city's most visited attractions. Here is its list of the top ten:

1. British Museum	6. Victoria & Albert Museum
2. Tate Modern	7. Science Museum
3. National Gallery	8. Tower of London
4. Natural History Museum	9. Madame Tussauds
5. London Eye	10. Royal Museums Greenwich

·Accounts of the Great Fire of London, 1666·

London's Great Fire of 1666 destroyed most of the wood-built City.

Starting on September 2, 1666, the Great Fire, fueled by a strong easterly wind, raged for four full days, destroying about 80 percent of wood-built London, including 13,200 houses and 87 churches. Having suffered horribly during the Great Plague the previous year, Londoners could be excused for thinking that the end of the world was nigh. Numerous contemporary accounts of the catastrophic event survive.

• "The streets full of nothing but people and horses and carts loaden with goods, ready to run over one another ... we saw the fire as only one entire arch of fire from this to the other side [of] the bridge, and in a bow up the hill, for an arch of above a mile long; it made me weep to see it."
—*Samuel Pepys's diary entry of September 2, 1666, as he watched the fire from the South Bank.*

• "And now the doleful, dreadfull, hideous note / Of Fire, is scream'd out with a deep strain'd throat; / Horror, and fear, and distracted cries / Chide Sloth away, and bid the Sluggard rise; / Most direfull acclamations are let flye / From every Tongue, tears stand in every Eye."
—A Short Description of the Burning of London,

by Samuel Wiseman, 1666. Little is known about Wiseman save that he was a resident of Fleet Street.

• "There hapned to break out a sad deplorable fire in Pudding Lane, neer New Fish Street, which . . . in a quarter of the town so close built with wooden pitched houses, spread itself so far before day, and with such distraction to the inhabitants and neighbours, that care was not taken for the timely preventing the further diffusion of it, by pulling down houses, as ought to have been; so that this lamentable fire in a short time became too big to be mastred by any engines or working neer it."
—Extract from the official narrative of the Great Fire, published in The London Gazette, *no. 85, September 3-10, 1666.*

• "[The Fire began in Pudding Lane, near Thames Street], the lodge of all combustibles, Oyl, Hemp, Flax, Pitch, Tar, Cordage, Hops, Wines, Brandies, and other materials favourable to Fire . . . where narrow Streets, old Buildings all of Timber, all contiguous each to other, all stuffed with aliment for the Fire, all in the very heart of the Trade and Wealth of the City."
—Edward Waterhouse's A short narrative of the late dreadful fire in London *(1667). Waterhouse was a Fellow of the Royal Society who saw the fire as divine judgment.*

• "The streets were crowded with People and Carts, to carry away what Goods they could get out: And they that were most active, and befriended (by their Wealth) got Carts, and saved much; and the rest lost almost all."
—Richard Baxter's Reliquiae Baxterianae *(1696). Baxter was a Puritan priest and theologian.*

• "In five or six miles of traversing about, I did not see one loade of timber . . . nor many stones but what were calcind white as snow, so as the people who now walked about the ruines, appeard like men in some dismal desart, or rather in some greate Citty, lay'd wast by an impetuous & cruel Enemy."
—John Evelyn's diary entry of September 7, 1666, recording his walk from Whitehall to London Bridge, examining the wreckage of the city.

FAST FACT

The Great Fire began in a bakery on Pudding Lane. The Monument, a 1677 column memorializing the event, is 202 feet (61 m) tall—and located that exact distance from the site of the fire's first spark.

• "There was great distress among the people, and countless poor persons with nothing but a stick in their hands, who had formerly been prosperous and well-placed, were scattered here and there in the fields where they had built huts for themselves."
—*From the autobiography (ca 1719) of Francisco de Rapicani, an Italian visiting London in 1666 as confidential secretary to Queen Christina of Sweden.*

• "The ignorant and deluded mob, who upon the occasion were hurried away with a kind of phrenzy, vented forth their rage against the Roman Catholics and Frenchmen; imagining these incendiaries . . . had thrown red-hot balls into the houses."
—*From the autobiography of William Taswell, an eyewitness of the fire as a child attending the Westminster School.*

• "Those that had a house to-day were the next glad of an hedge or a pigstie or stable."
—*From the autobiographical writings of Anthony Wood, an antiquarian based in Oxford.*

• "Much terrified in the nights nowadays, with dreams of fire and falling down of houses."
—*Samuel Pepys's diary entry of September 15, 1666.*

• "Men, women, and children, of all ages and of all ranks, ran through the streets, their backs loaded with their most precious goods; and among them were carried many sick and disabled persons, who had been driven from their houses by the fire. As they ran they made a heart-rending murmur."
—*Extract from an Italian account, author unknown, of the Great Fire entitled* Relatione esattissima del' Incendio Calamitoso della villa di Londa *(Padua, 1666).*

• "Methinks it is an ill prospect, and a ghastly sight, for those that look from the balconies or tops of their stately new houses, to see ashes and ruinous heaps on every side of them—to see ten private houses (besides churches and public halls) in the dust for one that is raised again."
—*Samuel Rolle's* London's Resurrection or the Rebuilding of London, *published in 1668, describing the rebuilding of London. Rolle was a minister, most likely born in London, who spent much of his career just outside the city in Middlesex.*

FAST FACT

The heat from the fire was so intense that the lead roof of St. Paul's Cathedral melted. There are reports of molten lead flowing down nearby streets.

·London's Ten Oldest Football League Soccer Clubs·

The 1965-1966 edition of Queen's Park Rangers (aka QPR)—one of London's oldest teams

Soccer is by far the most played and most watched of the capital's main sports. Clubs proliferate in a multitude of leagues—some teams are even older than those on the list below, which includes only those currently playing in the game's professional leagues.

• Fulham 1879
Founded as a church team—"Fulham St. Andrew's Church Sunday School F.C.," at Star Road, West Kensington—it turned professional in 1898.

• Leyton Orient 1881
It was founded by members of Glyn Cricket Club and became Orient Football Club in 1888, possibly at the request of a player, Jack Dearing, who worked for the Orient Shipping Company.

• Barnet 1882
Barnet began as Woodville F.C., a club founded by students from two local schools, Cowley College and Lyonsdown Collegiate School; it became Barnet F.C. in 1888.

• Tottenham Hotspur 1882
The team was founded

FAST FACT

Chelsea was founded in March 1905, making it London's 12th oldest club. It was voted into the Football League in the same year— the only team to join the league without having first played a match.

by a combination of members of the local Hotspur cricket club and grammar-school pupils at the Bible class of All Hallows Church, N17.

• **Millwall 1885**
Millwall was founded by workers at J. T. Morton, a cannery and food-processing factory on the Millwall Dock on the Isle of Dogs.

• **Queen's Park Rangers 1886**
St. Jude's (1884) combined forces with Christchurch Rangers (1882) to form Queen's Park Rangers, so called because

most of the players came from the Queen's Park area of northwest London.

• **Arsenal 1886**
Originally called Dial Square, the team was founded by workers at the Woolwich Arsenal Armament factory—hence "Gunners," the club's nickname. In 1891, it was the first London club to become professional.

• **Brentford 1889**
Members of Brentford Rowing Club founded a club to have something to do in winter when they weren't rowing.

• **Wimbledon 1889**
Wimbledon Common provided a place for the Wimbledon Old Centrals to play soccer. The team is now known as MK Dons after a controversial move out of the capital to Milton Keynes in 2003.

• **West Ham United 1895**
Workers at the Thames Ironworks and Shipbuilding Co. Ltd. founded the team that became West Ham United F.C. in 1900; it's still known as "The Irons" or "Hammers," after its origins.

London's Ten Most Watched Soccer Teams*

• Arsenal	60,079	• Queen's Park Rangers	17,779
• Chelsea	41,462	• Crystal Palace	17,280
• Tottenham	36,065	• Millwall	10,559
• West Ham United	34,719	• Brentford	6,302
• Fulham	25,394	* Average weekly home-game attendance, 2012-2013 season	
• Charlton	18,499		

Bespoke Shirts & Suits

London is full of shops helpfully willing to sell you high-end, bespoke (custom-made) clothes and accessories. Jermyn Street in St. James's and nearby Savile Row in Mayfair are the most well-known epicenters for shirtmakers (some have been serving the discerning dresser since the 18th century) and purveyors of custom-made suits.

Benson & Clegg
9 Piccadilly Arcade, SW1, tel 020 7491 1454, bensonandclegg.com

Budd Shirtmakers
3 Piccadilly Arcade, SW1, tel 020 7493 0139, buddshirts.co.uk

Dege & Skinner
10 Savile Row, W1, tel 020 7287 2941, dege-skinner.co.uk

Harvie & Hudson
77 & 96-97 Jermyn St., SW1, tel 020 7839 3578, harvieandhudson.com

Henry Herbert Shirts
9-10 Savile Row, W1, tel 020 7837 1452, henryherbert.com

Hilditch & Key
37 & 73 Jermyn St., SW1, tel 020 7734 4707, hilditchandkey.co.uk

King & Allen
206-210 Bishopsgate, EC2, tel 0800 027 4430, kingandallen.co.uk

New & Lingwood
53 Jermyn St., SW1, tel 020 7493 9621, newandlingwood.com

Roderick Charles
90 Jermyn St., SW1, tel 020 7930 4551, roderickcharles.com

Turnbull & Asser
71-72 Jermyn St., SW1, tel 020 7808 3000, turnbullandasser.co.uk

·Six Surviving London Windmills·

Locals unhappy with the flour quality from nearby mills built Wimbledon windmill in 1817.

The Greater London area once had more than 300 windmills, including mills in locations as unlikely as Mayfair (in Bond Street), Chelsea (Tothill Fields), and The Strand. These are the best surviving mills:

• **Arkley Mill**
This well-preserved mill in the Borough of Barnet, with four sails intact, dates from 1823 and was a working mill until 1918; it was restored in 1930.

• **Brixton Mill, SW2**
This four-sailed mill in south London was extensively restored in 2011 and is open to the public. It began functioning in 1816 as a wind-driven mill, was converted to steam in 1902, and finished its working days in 1934 (*brixtonwindmill.org*).

• **The Old Mill, Plumstead Common, SW18**
This mill near Greenwich dates from the early 1800s, but was converted as early as 1848 as part of a brewery. Today, its distinctive four-story tower survives.

FAST FACT

Modern-day Millbank on the Thames and Great Windmill Street in the West End took their names from former working mills.

• **Shirley Windmill**

Croydon's windmill dates from 1808, though it was damaged by fire and rebuilt on several occasions. Like many similar mills, it was eventually put out of business by steam-powered "roller" mills that produced finer, whiter flour. Extensive restoration took place after 1996 (*shirleywind mill.org.uk*).

• **Wimbledon Windmill, SW19**

The windmill has been a landmark of Wimbledon Common since 1817, when it was built to serve local residents. The mill ceased working in 1864 and was given over to residential use, housing six families, but today it is a working mill once more, complete with a

museum (*wimbledon windmill.org.uk*).

• **The Windmill on Wandsworth Common, SW18**

A hexagonal black tower without sails is all that survives of this windmill, built in 1837 to pump water from a nearby railway cutting and into the ornamental pond on Wandsworth Common.

· Some Curious Street Names and How They Came About ·

London town is full of intriguing street names, many derived from derivations of derivations . . . but always somehow managing to end up sounding charming or antiquated or gruesome.

• **Birdcage Walk**

Running along the southern length of St. James's Park, Birdcage Walk marks the former site of the Royal Aviary, built by James I in the early 17th century to

house the royal hunting falcons and hawks. For 200 years, only members of the royal family and the Hereditary Grand Falconer were allowed to ride alongside the Aviary in carriages. Until 1828, all others had to walk (hence the name).

• **Bleeding Heart Yard**

Legend has it that the body of Lady Elizabeth Hatton, brutally murdered in 1626, was found in Farringdon—her heart,

torn from her body, was still beating nearby. Skeptics who frown on this urban legend claim the street was actually named after an old pub located there.

• **Cheapside Market streets**

Cheapside—"cheap" broadly meaning "market" in medieval English— is the former site of one of the principal markets in London. The names of several streets in the area derive from the ancient

Poultry, one of many old streets near Cheapside

businesses plied there, making it pretty clear what was sold on Wood Street, Poultry, Milk Street, Honey Lane, and Bread Street, all located on or near Cheapside. Less obvious is the origin of Friday Street's name, until we learn that it led directly to the market's fishmongers.

• Cockpit Steps

In Westminster, a walkway named Cockpit Steps, running south of Birdcage Walk, marks the former site of royal cockfights. For much of London's history,

cockfighting (and betting on cockfighting) was a popular pastime among the upper classes. The old Royal Cockpit was built in the 1700s. While this structure no longer exists, the steps remain, reminding travelers—for better or worse—of the old sport.

• Fetter Lane

Fetter Lane (running north of Fleet Street) was apparently a place where medieval vagabonds congregated to feign diseases and other afflictions to evoke the pity of (and open the

pocketbooks of) passersby. The name may be derived from the Middle English word *faitour,* which by medieval times had come to mean "false beggars."

Flask Walk

This Hampstead lane was the location of several taverns that sold flasks of water— from a medicinal spring nearby—to London's eating houses and others in the rapidly expanding 17th- and 18th-century city.

• Houndsditch

Houndsditch, at the east end of London, was the medieval final resting place for the city's deceased dogs and the rubbish disposed with them. Ironically, Jeremy Bentham—philosopher, legal and social reformer, and champion of animal rights—was born on the street in 1748.

• Mount Pleasant

Mount Pleasant was the tongue-in-cheek name

for the medieval dumping ground of household refuse, ashes, and other trash, along the banks of the woefully polluted Fleet River in Clerkenwell (before the river was buried underground—see Lost Rivers, p. 211). The street name remains, though the irony is lost.

• Old Jewry

Old Jewry, a one-way street near the present-day Guildhall, was a Jewish settlement in Anglo-Saxon times. Soon after the Norman Conquest, William the Conqueror encouraged Jews to come to England, and many ended up settling on or around Old Jewry in the city's Jewish quarter.

• Pall Mall

Pall Mall's name is derived from the popular game of the same name that was imported from France and Italy in the 16th and 17th centuries. The game, in which a mallet was used to hit a ball through a hoop hanging aboveground, was commonly played there. Today Pall Mall serves as the address of choice for London's most celebrated and exclusive gentlemen's clubs.

• Pudding Lane

Belying its charming-sounding name, "pudding" was actually the medieval term for animal guts, and Pudding Lane was a riverside street that housed many a butcher shop. Animal innards were tossed out the overhanging windows; gravity, time, and the occasional broom would funnel the "pudding" down the sharply pitched street to the flowing waste removal system known as the Thames. But Pudding Lane is most notorious as the site where the Great Fire of London started in 1666.

• Rotten Row

The story goes that Rotten Row, the mile-long (1.6 km) bridle path running along the southern edge of Hyde Park, derives its name from "Route du Roi," French for the King's Road, as this was the path William III built to travel to and from Kensington Palace. Debate prevails on the truth of this oft-repeated explanation . . . but let's just go with it.

• Sherborne Lane

Running south of King William Street in the City, Sherborne Lane was formerly known as Shiteburne Lane: The street was a longtime public privy.

FAST FACT

London needed quite a few Sherborne Lanes: The human and animal inhabitants of medieval London produced 50 tons (45 tonnes) of excrement a day.

Fish and Chips

ritons don't eat as many portions of fish and chips as they did, but the quantities consumed are still big enough to generate some pretty impressive statistics.

Fish and chip shops in the U.K. 10,500

McDonald's in the U.K. 1,200

Kentucky Fried Chicken outlets in the U.K. 850

Portions of fish and chips eaten annually 382 million

**Money spent annually on
fish and chips** £1.2 billion ($1.9 billion)

**Number of annual servings for every
U.K. man, woman, and child** 6

**Percentage of British people who visit a
chippie at least once a year** 80

**Percentage of British people who visit a
chippie at least once a week** 22

**Percentage of British people who buy fish and
chips to eat in the home as a family meal** 56

**World's largest portion of fish and chips, served at Fish
& Chips, Enfield, London, July 2012** 103 pounds (47 kg)

**Largest portion of chips in a single box, at Adventure
Island, Southend, in 2011** 988 pounds (448 kg)

**Fastest British chip, from unpeeled
potato to serving** 222 seconds

**British-grown potatoes that become chips
every year** 1.38 million tons (1.25 million tonnes)

**Estimated number of fish and chip shops in
the U.K. in 1927, the peak year** 35,000

·The Best Fish and Chip Shops·

Fish and chip shops, or "chippies," first sprang up because they offered cheap and relatively nutritious food for the masses. Refrigeration and the railways—which brought fresh North Sea fish to the capital—led to their proliferation in the late 19th century.

Fish, chips, and a pub—almost heaven

• **Golden Hind** *(73 Marylebone Lane, W1U, tel 020 7486 3644)* has been serving fish and chips to Marylebone locals since 1914. The lines and the extension of their premises merely underline the fact that they know what they're doing.

• **Kerbisher & Malt** *(164 Shepherd's Bush Road, W6, tel 020 3556 0228, kerbisher.co.uk)*. Old-time fryers might turn over in their graves, but

attention to detail such as double-frying the chips makes this new made-to-look-old place (white tiles, long shared wooden tables) in Hammersmith one of the best in town.

• If you're in Westminster and fish and chips is what you need, head for **The Laughing Halibut** *(38 Strutton Ground, SW1, tel 020 7799 2844)*. Don't expect frills: Most

chippies are known as fish and chip *shops*, not restaurants, for a reason.

• **Poppies** *(6-8 Hanbury St., E1, tel 020 7247 0892, poppiesfishandchips .co.uk)*. Poppies dates from 1945 and overdoes the British kitsch—jukebox, mini red phone box, pictures of Cliff Richard—but stick to fish (fried or grilled),

FAST FACT

British soldiers identified each other during the D-Day landings by calling out "fish" to which the response or password was "chips."

albeit at higher prices than old-school chippies, and you should have no complaints.

• The fish and chips at **Rock & Sole Plaice** *(47 Endell St., WC2, tel 020 7836 3785, rock andsoleplaice.com)* are not bad, but this Covent Garden establishment's main claim to fame is that it is one of central London's oldest surviving chippies, dating from 1871.

• **Toff's** *(38 Muswell Hill Broadway, N10, tel 020*

The main event

8883 8656, toffsfish .co.uk). Unless you're on a mission, it's unlikely you'll make the trip as far north as Muswell Hill, but if you do, you'll find the establishment that many rate London's best fish and chip restaurant.

The majestic sticky toffee pudding to finish provides more carbs if you're still hungry.

• When it comes to chippies, "follow the cabbie" is a good adage. London's taxi drivers swear by **The Fryer's Delight** *(19 Theobald's Rd., WC1, tel 020 7405 4114)*, where boss Giuseppe has been frying for more than 45 years, and **Masters Super Fish** (191 Waterloo Rd., SE1, tel 020 7928 6924), which is known for its gargantuan portions as well as its quality.

• Traditional Places to Eat Pie, Mash & Eels •

Gone are the days when a meal out for many Londoners meant fish and chips or pie, "mash" (mashed potatoes), and eels. But a handful of "pie and mash" shops survive—most are in the East End, close to the Thames, once the source of the eels, which were both cheap and able to survive the river's polluted waters.

When eel stocks dwindled, cheap beef and mutton pies came to the fore.

• **Arments** *(7-9 Westmoreland Rd., SE17, tel 020 7703 4974, armentspie andmash.com)* is a family-run concern in operation since 1914. Arments has been selling pie, mash, eels, and all the classic trimmings—notably "liquor," a green,

parsley-based sauce for the pies—from no-nonsense premises and at absurdly low prices.

• **F. Cooke** *(150 Hoxton St., N1, tel 020 7729 7718).* Pie, mash, and eels shops tend to run in families, and the Cookes are no exception. Current owner Joseph Cooke's family has been in the business since 1862. The welcome

The East End had more than 500 street vendors selling hot eels, pies, and pea soup in 1851. Dutch eel ships had to top up the Thames' stocks to meet demand.

here is warm; the experience authentic; and the interior—all marble, tiles, and mirrors—a delight.

• **G. Kelly** *(526 Roman Rd., E3, tel 020 8980 3165, gkellypieandmash.co.uk)* was established in 1937, but the Kellys have been selling pie and eels around Bethnal Green since 1915.

• **L. Manze** *(76 Walthamstow High St., E17, tel 020 8520 2855)* was awarded historic status in 2013 in recognition not only of its glorious 1929 interior, but also as an East End institution that survived the Blitz and redevelopment. David Beckham is one of many fans.

• **M. Manze** *(87 Tower Bridge Rd., SE1, tel 020 7407 2985, manze.co.uk)*. The Manze family came to the East End from Italy in 1878. In time they established a chain of pie 'n' mash shops, starting with this outlet in 1902 (L. Manze, above, was #14). It's still there, still in the family, and still making pies from the original recipes.

• **Manze's** *(204 Deptford High St., SE8, tel 020 8692 2375, manzepieandmash .com)*. A third surviving Manze institution, run by George, great-great-grandson of the original Italian immigrants: classic pies and "liquor," plus traditional chili vinegar and hot or cold sarsaparilla to wash it all down.

• **Maureen's** *(6 Market Way, Chrisp Street Market, E14, tel 07956 381216)*. Maureen Paterson, who set up this restaurant in the 1950s, has passed the reins to her son, Jason, but it remains a treasure. Users of London's Docklands Light Railway have voted it the East End's "number one hidden gem."

F. Cooke's pie and mash shop in East London

·Nine Drinks, Dishes, and Treats Invented in London·

ondon's food and cooking have long been reviled, often with justification—although these days its restaurants include some of the world's best and most varied. London has also come up with a handful of drinks and foodstuffs that have made the world a better culinary place.

• Buck's fizz

This combination of Champagne and orange juice (and occasionally grenadine) was reputedly invented in 1921 by Pat McGarry, a bartender at Buck's Club at 18 Clifford Street (largely the inspiration for comic writer P. G. Wodehouse's Drones Club). The idea was to allow patrons an excuse to start drinking early. The "true" recipe, which contains more than Champagne and juice, is still a secret known only to Buck's Club bartenders.

• Chelsea buns

This spiral of dough rolled into a square and flavored with currants, cinnamon, and lemon peel was first created in the Chelsea Bun House

The time-honored Chelsea bun

on the corner of Pimlico Road and Lower Sloane Street (demolished in 1839). It was a great favorite of King George II and other royal visitors.

• Fish and chips

In 1968, the National Federation of Fish Fryers weighed in on the long-running dispute about who first paired chipped potatoes with fried fish, the latter a London staple since its introduction to the city by 17th-century Jewish refugees from Spain and Portugal. It was, the Federation declared, one Joseph Malin, a Jewish émigré of Cleveland Way, Whitechapel, who opened the first chippie around 1860.

• London buns

The ancient origins of this elongated bun, covered in sugar icing, are obscure, though some claim it was invented in the same place as the Chelsea bun. The original version, sometimes with added currants and caraway seeds, is now much rarer in the capital—superseded by the round, icing-topped Bath bun—but it is still popular in Australia, where it is known as a finger or candlegrease bun.

• Omelette Arnold Bennett

The Savoy created this haddock-, Parmesan-, and cream-filled omelet as a quick snack for writer Arnold Bennett (1867-1931), who was a regular visitor to the hotel's dining rooms, especially after attending nearby theaters in his role as drama critic. Bennett's novel *Imperial Palace* is set in the hotel, and the dish remains on the menu to this day.

Omelette Arnold Bennett, a Savoy hotel creation

• Pêche Melba

There are several versions of how this dish came into being. One of the most popular is that Auguste Escoffier (1846-1935), chef at the Savoy, created a dessert of peaches and vanilla ice cream (and later raspberry sauce) at an 1892 dinner held in honor of the Australian opera singer Dame Nellie Melba (1861-1931). Escoffier also created Melba toast in London for the singer, probably in 1897, when she became ill and the dry, crisp, thinly toasted bread, served with soup and salad, or topped with cheese or pâté, became a staple of her diet.

• The Scotch egg

A hardboiled egg wrapped in sausage meat and breadcrumbs and then deep-fried is not the slightest bit Scottish, but was supposedly invented in 1738 by staff at Fortnum & Mason in Piccadilly (see Oldest Stores, p. 104). They may have based the dish on *nargisi kofta,* a traditional Mughal delicacy of egg, spices, and ground lamb.

FAST FACT

Charles Dickens's *A Tale of Two Cities*, published in 1859, mentions "Husky chips of potatoes, fried with some reluctant drops of oil," one of the first literary references to "chips," or French fries.

• **Tom Collins**
Americans would have this as their cocktail, after the first recorded recipe in 1876 from the father of U.S. mixology, Jerry Thomas. But a virtually identical drink, the John Collins—consisting of lemon juice, soda water, sugar, and Holland gin—has existed in London since at least the 1860s. Too many cocktails have been enjoyed over the years for the history of the tipple to be clear, but it probably originated even earlier, devised by a barman at Limmer's Hotel and Coffee Shop on Conduit Street, possibly in the 1790s.

• **Wedding cakes**
The tradition of the white, tiered wedding cake is said to derive from the late 18th century, when William Rich, an apprentice baker, set up on Ludgate Hill near St. Paul's and fell in love with his master's daughter. Hoping to impress her, he accompanied his proposal of marriage with a large cake, the inspiration for which came from the distinctive tiered spire of the nearby church of St. Bride's.

·London's Best Curry Houses·

London's curry houses are hardly a recent phenomenon. City taverns have offered curried dishes since at least the 17th century, and the first Indian-owned curry house opened in 1809 (see London Firsts, p. 77).

Today, most visitors are sent to Brick Lane (Curry Mile) in the East End—not what it was—or to Southall, a district with some of the city's largest and longest established Indian communities. But the city center also has some upscale, if less "authentic" options. Curry houses come and go, and reputations change, but these are some of the hottest recommendations of the moment:

• **The Cinnamon Club** *(30-32 Great Smith St., SW1, tel 020 7222 2555, cinnamonclub.com)* is the doyen of white table-cloth London Indian restaurants. Housed in the fine Old Westminster Library building, it is a favorite of MPs from the nearby Houses of Parliament. High prices and refined food place it a long way in every sense from Southall and Brick Lane. A more recent offshoot, **Cinnamon Soho** *(5 Kingly St., W1, tel 020 7437 1664, cinnamon soho.com)*, is also recommended.

• **Brilliant** *(72-76 Western Rd., UB2, tel 020 8574 1928, brilliantrestaurant.com)* is one of Southall's stalwarts, known for its Punjabi and south Indian dishes (butter chicken, egg curry, kebabs, wonderful pickles). However, note that the restaurant is out toward Heathrow, a long way from the city center.

• Brick Lane hasn't completely lost its curry-making mojo—try **Sheba** at #136 *(tel 020 7247 7824, shebabricklane.com)*. But these days it pays to venture away from the menu touts to somewhere like the **Needoo Grill** *(87 New Rd., E1, tel 0207 247 0648, needoogrill.co.uk)*, which specializes in Pakistani grilled dishes; the slow-cooked lamb on the bone on Sundays is a treat.

• Purists may scoff, but the upscale **Chutney Mary** *(535 King's Rd., SW10, tel 020 7351 3113, chutneymary.com)*, with its gloriously gaudy dining room and orange tree conservatory, is a Chelsea fixture that has been offering fine Indian and European crossover dishes since 1990.

Brick Lane, traditional home of some of London's best curry houses

• **Dishoom** has two incarnations: the east London Shoreditch version *(7 Boundary St., E2, tel 020 7420 9324, dishoom.com)*, which affects the warm, vibrant, homey feel of a Bombay-style café, and the more central and polished Covent Garden outlet *(12 Upper St. Martin's Lane, WC2, tel 020 7420 9320)*. Both sell food from breakfast to dinner.

• It barely registers in London eating guides, but the dining room at the **Indian YMCA** *(41 Fitzroy Square, W1, tel 020 7387 0411, indian ymca.org)* off Tottenham Court Road is open to all and is popular with Indian locals and visitors. It's simple to a fault, but central and inexpensive.

• City center curry houses invariably have upscale settings and much higher prices than their Southall cousins, but the food can still be authentic, if toned down, as the theater district's **Moti Mahal** proves (*45 Great Queen St., WC2, tel 020 7240 9329, moti mahal-uk.com*).

• **Tayyabs** (*83-89 Fieldgate St., E1, tel 020 7247 8521, tayyabs.co.uk*) is sometimes called a hidden gem, but it really isn't (and knows it), as the sometimes three-hour lines suggest (do make reservations, and even then be prepared to wait). The food, especially the grilled fare, is great, but the atmosphere is hectic and noisy; the service brisk and brusque.

• **Veeraswamy** (*Mezzanine Floor, Victoria House, 99-101 Regent St., W1, tel 020 7734 1401, veeraswamy.com*) may not have the best food in the capital, but it is an institution—in business since 1926 and the city center's oldest Indian restaurant still in business. The elegant dining room—Bollywood meets Mayfair—is all carpets and polished wood, and the food is refined. Try for a window table and stick to the set menus to keep costs down.

•Menu Items at a Medieval Royal Feast•

For pure calorie consumption and general overexcess, somewhere between the food orgies (among other orgies) of the Romans and the all-you-can-eat buffets of Las Vegas stand the gluttonous feasts of Henry VIII and other late medieval monarchs. But what could you actually expect to find on the menu at a royal court?

• **Roasted meat**
Spit-roasted meat was eaten at every festive meal; options included pork, boar, beef, veal, mutton, kid, lamb, rabbit, poultry, and venison. No side veggies with that; vegetables were considered peasant fare and were frowned upon by the aristocracy.

• **Roasted peacock**
Peacocks were cooked and presented with much flair. The bird was first plucked, cooked whole to taste, and then served with its colorful feathers carefully replaced and its beak shimmering with gold leaf. Another show dish you might expect, especially at Christmas, was boar's heads. The heads were elaborately garnished and given pride of place at the center of the table.

• Roasted swan

Swans have long been given special treatment in English society; to this day, all unmarked mute swans in England are property of the Crown (see Antiquated Traditions, p. 198). Roasted swan was therefore eaten only on special occasions, although baby swans (cygnets) were often baked into tasty pies (see Recipes, p. 68).

Spit-roasted meats were staples of medieval feasts.

• Internal organs and other offal

The pendulum keeps swinging back and forth. Sometimes organ meats and entrails are in vogue for the upper classes, and sometimes they are reserved for the serfs among us. In late medieval times, beef lungs, spleen, ears, pig snouts and tails, and udders were considered real delicacies.

• Fish

Because of the many fast days when meat was forbidden, fish was an important (though expensive) element of the medieval diet. A meal might include herring, mullet, sole, flounder, salmon, trout, mackerel, oysters, or eels. Or all of the above, if you were the king.

• Black pudding

Black pudding was (and is) sausage made by mixing pork blood and oatmeal, and then cooking it in pig's intestine until it's all congealed. It's tastier than it sounds.

• Whale meat

Whale meat was considered an allowable protein source for Fridays and other fast days. At the time, whale was fairly plentiful and affordable because of the robust supply off England's shores. Sturgeon and porpoise were other seafood treats for the aristocratic classes.

• Marzipan and jelly

Marzipan was occasionally served at the end of a meal, although desserts weren't common in England until the 18th century. Henry VIII, however, seems to have been enamored with jelly ypocras (a molded sweet jelly made with spiced hippocras wine and served with cream of almonds).

• Wine and ale

Wine, stored by the barrel and served in jugs, was a drink reserved for the wealthy. Ale and beer were usually brewed onsite and also consumed in large quantities.

Where to Eat the Best Breakfasts

Breakfast can be the best meal of the day in London, especially if you go for the classic "full English"—a cholesterol-laden medley that includes some combination of fried eggs, bacon, sausage, baked beans, mushrooms, fried tomatoes, fried bread, and black pudding, washed down with a mug of dark, strong builders' tea. Dine in style at one of the following:

The Tate Modern gallery has its own café, but if you want the best alternative nearby, **Albion Neo Bankside** *(Pavilion B, Holland St., SE1, tel 020 7827 4343, albioncafes.com)* is a contemporary, glass-fronted café from designer Terence Conran that serves breakfast starting at 8 a.m. (9 a.m. on Sunday).

Balthazar *(4-6 Russell St., WC2, tel 020 3301 1155, balthazarlondon.com)* created a stir when it opened a London brasserie-style companion to its celebrated New York operation, but it has delivered, especially with its breakfasts.

The cozy and buzzing wood-paneled dining rooms at the **Dean Street Townhouse** *(69-71 Dean St., W1, tel 020 7434 1775, deanstreettownhouse.com)* make a perfect setting for any style of breakfast, whether it's romantic coffee *à deux* or a solo "full English" to aid recovery from the night before.

The Delaunay *(55 Aldwych, WC2, tel 020 7499 8558, thedelaunay.com)* comes from the people who launched The Wolseley and it is every bit as good: a glorious room, a lively and mixed crowd, and consistently fine food with a *Mitteleuropa* edge.

High above the city, the **Duck & Waffle** *(Heron Tower, 110 Bishopsgate, EC2, tel 020 3640 7310, duckandwaffle.com)* has some of the best views in London (see also Views, p. 135), and, in the glass-sided external elevator that whisks you to its 40th-floor premises, one of the best free rides in the capital.

Portobello Road has plenty of café options, but the **Electric Diner** *(191 Portobello Rd., W11, tel 020 7908 9696, electricdiner.com)* is the biggest and most animated.

The Middleton family stayed at **The Goring** hotel *(15 Beeston Pl., SW1, tel 020 7396 9000, thegoring.com)* and ate their wedding-day breakfast here before their daughter Kate married Prince William. Discretion, tradition, and a sense of occasion make dining here a treat at any time.

The Goring hotel—a hop, skip, and a jump from Buckingham Palace

City businesspeople favor the **Hawksmoor Guildhall** *(10 Basinghall St., EC2, tel 020 7397 8120, thehawksmoor.com)*, where it's about steak, hash browns, and eggs; Manx kipper with poached eggs; or a "full English," which, as one diner put it, "would fill an elephant."

If you need a change of breakfast, then go Japanese at Soho's **Koya Bar** *(50 Frith St., W1, no phone or reservations, koyabar.co.uk)*.

A former luxury car salesroom provides a grand but never stuffy setting for **The Wolseley** *(160 Piccadilly, W1, tel 020 7499 6996, thewolseley.com)*, which for years has maintained its combination of perfect service, eclectic clientele, convivial atmosphere, and perfectly prepared British classics such as kedgeree, haggis, and Omelette Arnold Bennett.

FAST FACT
Under perfect conditions, English breakfasts would be consumed in a "greasy spoon," a fast-disappearing breed of cheap, cramped, simple, and steam-filled cafés.

·London's Oldest Restaurants·

Knowing where a pub ends and a restaurant begins makes naming London's oldest restaurants a contentious business (see Historic Pubs, p. 175). The word "restaurant" only appeared in the capital around the 1820s, though before that there were plenty of taverns (pubs) and hundreds of street stalls that sold food. A handful of dining places known as "French ordinaries" appeared in Soho after 1685 with the first wave of Huguenot immigrants. Otherwise, dining out was seen as a masculine and rather louche affair until the 1890s. Here's a selection of venerable eating places that are still in business:

• 1742
Wiltons (55 Jermyn St., SW1, tel 020 7629 9955, wiltons.co.uk) was established as an oyster stall in Haymarket. It has changed location several times since—most recently in 1964—but still specializes in seafood.

• 1757
Thomas Simpson opened **Simpson's Tavern** (Ball Court, 38½ Cornhill, EC3, tel 020 7626 9985, simpsonstavern.co.uk), London's oldest remaining chophouse.

• 1798
The oldest restaurant in London on its original site, **Rules** (35 Maiden Lane, WC2, tel 020 7836 5314, rules.co.uk) opened as an oyster bar and is now known both for its lovely dining room and classic British cuisine.

• 1828
Simpson's-in-the-Strand (100 Strand, WC2, tel 020 7836 9112, simpsonsinthestrand.co.uk) was a coffeehouse, chess club, and smoking room for 20 years before becoming known for its classic British food.

• 1867
Still a Soho institution and pre-theater favorite, **Kettner's** (29 Romilly St., W1, tel 020 7734 6112, kettners.com) was opened by a chef to Napoleon III at a time when French food was becoming fashionable in the capital.

• 1874
These days the food at the **Criterion** (224 Piccadilly, W1, tel 020 7930 0488, criterionrestaurant.com) receives mixed reviews, but chances are that you'll spend so much time being dazzled by the opulent dining room—arguably London's most spectacular—that you may not even notice what you're eating.

FIRST PERSON

❝A restful temple of food.**❞**

~**P. G. Wodehouse,** *describing the staid but charming dining room at Simpson's-in-the-Strand*

• 1889
The City's skyscrapers bristle on all sides, but **Sweetings** *(39 Queen Victoria St., EC4, tel 020 7248 3062, sweetings restaurant.com)* remains a throwback, its listed building having survived both bombs and developers. The food—almost entirely fish—is also still much as it was a century ago (lunch only).

• 50-plus
Two dining places that have passed the half-century mark are **Mon Plaisir** *(19-21 Monmouth St., WC2, tel 020 7836 7243, monplaisir .co.uk)*, which claims to be London's oldest French restaurant, and **Greig's** *(26 Bruton Place, W1, tel 020 7629 5613, greigs.com)*, a traditional steakhouse in Mayfair.

· The Best Afternoon Teas ·

Afternoon tea is different from high tea, which is more substantial. The latter, or just "tea," might refer to the evening meal in much of the north of England and elsewhere. Its name is derived from the fact that it is taken later ("higher") in the day or because afternoon tea was taken informally at low, not high, tables with comfortable chairs.

A full afternoon tea—involving plenty of food as well as tea—is still a feature of many of London's classic hotels. Here are some of the

Tea with all the trimmings

best places to indulge: All are popular, so be sure to book.

• **The Berkeley**
(Wilton Place, SW1, tel 020 7235 6000, the-berkeley.co.uk)

This luxury hotel makes a play for the fashionable shoppers of Knightsbridge with its Prêt-à-Portea menu, a "designer" afternoon tea "with a fashionista twist inspired by the themes and colors of the fashion world." The menu changes seasonally.

• **Brown's Hotel**
(Albemarle St., W1, tel 020 7518 4155, browns hotel.com)
Two "tea sommeliers" are on hand to guide you in this hotel's English Tea Room, which combines traditional wood paneling, fireplaces, a

Jacobean plaster ceiling with contemporary Paul Smith lighting, fashionable fabrics, and original artworks. A "Tea-Tox"—that is, a low-cal "healthy" version of the afternoon tea—is also available.

• **Claridge's**
(Brook St., W1, tel 020 7629 8860, claridges .co.uk)
Claridge's hotel offers a genteel and quintessentially English experience in a fine art deco setting, with a choice of 40 teas, dainty finger sandwiches, pastries, scones, cream, jam, and more. Children's and Champagne teas are also available.

• **The Dorchester**
(53 Park Lane, W1, tel 020 7629 8888, the dorchester.com)
Along with Claridge's

The Landmark's Winter Garden

and the Ritz, the Dorchester hotel is a touchstone for traditional afternoon tea in the capital: The napery is crisp, the silver polished, the scones are made according to a 50-year-old recipe, and the surroundings are both sumptuous and soothing.

• **The Landmark London Hotel**
(222 Marylebone Rd., NW1, tel 020 7631 8188/8000, landmark london.co.uk)
Traditional, Champagne, and decadent Chocolate afternoon teas are offered in the Winter Garden restaurant, part of the wonderfully light and airy eight-story atrium at the heart of this hotel in the ever more fashionable Marylebone district.

• **The Ritz**
(150 Piccadilly, W1, tel 020 7300 2345, the ritzlondon.com)
Tea at the Ritz is an institution, and it's hard to think of a more elegant and traditional setting than the hotel's splendid Palm Court—all chandeliers, fountains, gilded statues, and extravagant floral displays. Be sure to look the part because there is a dress code, with jacket and tie required for men.

FAST FACT

The United Kingdom Tea Council and Tea Guild (tea.co.uk) gives awards for the best teas in London. There are 16 categories, including the appearance, flavor, and staff knowledge of the teas.

❝There are few hours in life more agreeable than the hour dedicated to the ceremony known as afternoon tea.**❞**

~**Henry James,** The Portrait of a Lady, *1881*

• **Sanctum Soho**
(20 Warwick Street, W1, tel 020 7292 6102, sanctumsoho.com)
Expect unabashed gender separation at this Soho hotel, which offers a Gents' Afternoon Tea and High Tea for High Heels. The male tea includes a poached oyster, a "tankard" of Jack Daniels, and a Villiger Export cigar; the women's supposedly daintier fare includes cocktails, caviar, and quails' eggs.

• **Sanderson London**
(50 Berners St., W1, tel 020 7300 1400, morgans hotelgroup.com)
Book here for a light-hearted Mad Hatter's Tea: menus hidden inside vintage books; napkins wrapped with riddles; teapots adorned with kings and queens; and sandwich plates featuring zebras, birdcages, carousels, and ticking clocks. The menu includes marshmallow mushrooms and a "Tick Tock" traditional Victoria sponge clock.

Time for Tea

Following are some of the dishes deemed acceptable at afternoon tea in 1936 from *Cookery Illustrated and Household Management* by Elizabeth Craig.

• Brown Bread and Butter, Potted Salmon Sandwiches, Pikelets Rock Cakes, Scotch Jam Sandwich, Hot Buttered Toast, Mustard and Cress Sandwiches, French Biscuits, Maids of Honour, Dundee Cake, Milk Bread and Butter, Whitstable Sandwiches, Rice Buns, Ginger Snaps, Caramel Layer Cake, Kentish Oatcakes, White Bread and Butter, Blackberry Jelly, Cornish Splits, Ginger Biscuits, Chocolate Cream Cake, Scones (note: serve scones buttered hot, or split, buttered and spread with greengage jam), Bloater Cream Sandwiches, Lemon Cheese, Rice Biscuits, Meringues, Canadian Layer Cake, Egg and Anchovy Sandwiches, Northumberland Griddle Cakes, Ayrshire Shortbread, Bath Buns, Marshmallow Layer Cake, Buttered Irish Barmbrack, Abernathy Biscuits, Windsor Cake, Fudge Layer Cake, Cucumber Sandwiches, Nut and Raisin Bread, Bread and Butter, Plum Jam, Spiced Raisin Cake, Eccles Cakes, Gingerbread, Ballater Scones, Damson Cheese, American Doughnuts, Chocolate Nougat Cake, Carievale Nut Bread and Butter, Balmoral Tartlets, Chelsea Buns, Raisin Slab Cake, Quince Marmalade, Lemon Cheese Cake, Coffee Cake, Black Currant Jam, Sponge Sandwich with Whipped Fruit Filling, Scotch Lawn Tennis Cake.

Tea for Two (Billion)

Never mind that tea wasn't introduced to Britain until the mid-17th century, or that coffee actually preceded it to the scepter'd isle and is now making a roaring comeback: It's hard to beat a nice warm cuppa tea on a rainy London afternoon. And, apparently, lots of people in Britain agree.

Number of cups of tea consumed daily in Britain 165 million

Number of cups of tea consumed annually in Britain 60.2 billion

Approximate cost to produce one cup of tea 3p (5 cents)

Number of tea-growing nations 30

Approximate number of tea varieties in the world 1,500

Average British tea consumption per capita (age ten and up) 3 cups per day

Percentage of British tea drinkers who take milk in their tea 98

Percentage of total British milk consumption attributed to taking milk with tea 25

Percentage of tea consumed in tea bags 95

Percentage of British people who take sugar with their tea 45

Percentage of sales growth of green teas in Britain from 2010 to 2012 83

Quantity of tea served nightly to Underground Blitz sleepers 2,400 gallons (10,910 liters)

·A Sampling of Recipes From Days Past·

Behold a few recipes you can envision London's housewives toiling over through the centuries. Our lawyers told us we had to try out these recipes before printing them. We didn't do that (sorry, we've been really busy ... plus the unicorn one in particular has hard-to-find ingredients), so don't try them at home. Especially the one with pennyroyal.

Preparing apples for a dumpling recipe

• **Apricot jumballs**
From Charles Elmé Francatelli's *The Cook's Guide, and Housekeeper's & Butler's Assistant,* 1855

"Take ripe apricocks [apricots], pare, stone, and beat them small, then boil them till they are thick, and the moisture dry'd up, then take them off the fire, and beat them with searc'd sugar, to make them into pretty stiff paste, roll them, without sugar, the thickness of a straw; make them up in little knots in what form you please; dry them in a stove or in the sun. You may make jumballs of any sort of fruit the same way."

• **Pennyroyal dumplings**
From *The Lady's Assistant,* 1773

(Nota bene: Pennyroyal is an herb similar in taste to spearmint that— AND THIS IS IMPORTANT—has been found to be highly poisonous and can be fatal if consumed, even in small amounts.)

"The crumb of a penny loaf [a loaf of bread] grated, three quarters of a pound of beef-suet, the same of currants, four eggs, a little brandy, a little thyme and pennyroyal, a handful of parsley shred; mix all well, roll them up with flower; put them into cloths: three quarters of an hour boils them."

Very tasty until it kills you.

• **A common potato pudding to be fired below roasted meat**
From *Cookery and Pastry, as Taught and Practiced by Mrs. Maciver,* 1789

(Note: Though this is a Scottish dish, the book was printed and sold in London, so we say it counts.)

"Boil and skin as many potatoes as will fill the dish, beat them; and mix in some sweet milk; put them on the fire with a good piece of butter; season them properly with salt and spices. Some choose an onion shred small, and put in it. Put it in the dish, and fire it below the meat, until it is of a fine brown on the top; cast three eggs well, and mix in with the potatoes before you put them in the dish; it makes it rise, and eat light; pour off all the fat that drops from the meat before you send it to the table: it eats very well with roasted beef or mutton."

The primary ingredient in Broiled Unicorn

• Swan pie
From John Thacker's *The Art of Cookery*, 1758

"When it is pick'd, sing'd, and drawn, bone it, take off the head and legs first, season it within with Pepper and Salt, let it lie two days, tie or sew up the vents where you took out the bones, make a kettle of water boil, put in your Swan til it is plump'd up, take out all the threads when cold, make a coffin for it . . . [and] ornament it . . . The pye is to be filled with a Goose boned and cut into pieces, season all well with pepper and salt; lay a good deal of butter on the top, lid it, and bake it three hours; when baked fill it with clarified butter. This is a proper standing pye for Christmas."

• To broil a unicorn
From (most likely) the mid-14th-century cookbook of Geoffrey Fule, chef to the Queen

The recipe instructs the chef to "taketh one unicorne" before marinating it with cloves and garlic, and then roasting in a griddle.

·Sites Associated With the Life of Princess Diana·

It's been more than 30 years since Charles, Prince of Wales, introduced the wider world to Diana Spencer. And while the story of their marriage turned less than fairy tale, there was still something about the woman that fascinates people around the world, despite (or perhaps in part because of) her early death in August 1997. Here are several sites you can visit with links to the late princess.

The Diana Memorial Fountain *(royalparks .org.uk)*
Located just west of the Serpentine in Hyde Park, this circular, flowing memorial fountain, opened by the Queen in 2004, attempts to reflect both the turbulent and calm of the princess's life.

The Diana Memorial Playground *(royalparks .org.uk)*
The Royal Parks Foundation has been operating this park, a few hundred yards north of Kensington Palace, since 2000, in honor of Diana's charitable work on behalf of children worldwide. The playground is usually restricted to children and their parents (adults without accompanying

Diana, Princess of Wales

children can visit the park from 9:30 to 10 a.m. daily).

Harrods *(harrods.com)*
There are two memorials located in Harrods, which was formerly owned by Mohamed Al-Fayed, father of Diana's companion, Dodi Fayed. On the lower ground floor is a candlelit shrine to Dodi and Diana, while at Door 3, a second remembrance includes a life-size bronze statue of Diana and Dodi dancing, titled "Innocent Victims."

Kensington Palace *(hrp.org.uk)*
The former home of Diana and Charles showcases her dresses alongside other mementos of her life. For days following her death, Londoners laid thousands upon thousands of flowers outside the gates of the palace. It was said the flowers' bouquet wafted in the air for hundreds of yards in all directions.

Spencer House *(spencer house.co.uk)*
Built in the 18th century by John, First Earl of Spencer, an ancestor of Diana, this St. James's house has recently been restored to its original grandeur (see Aristocratic Houses, p. 24).

·From a Century of National Geographic Reporting·

Empire Stadium, known today as Wembley Stadium, hosting the 1936 F. A. Cup Final

National Geographic has been dispatching firsthand reports from London since early in its 125-year history. Some atmospheric and/or transporting snippets of note:

• "We will come thereby to Trafalgar Square, the official center, the tourist heart of London, and perhaps glimpse the beautiful cross in Charing Cross Station yard— that is, if taxis, motors, hansoms, paper "boys" and flower "girls" of all ages will let you think and see."
—*"London," Florence Craig Albrecht,* National Geographic *magazine, September 1915*

• "In the early years of this century, it was quite vogue to go down to Westminster Bridge, the Embankment, and London Bridge, and purchase twopenny bags of sprats from itinerant venders ... The birds exhibited remarkable aptitude in catching the small fish in midair, and also evinced amazing audacity. I have seen a man catch one of the gulls by the legs as it hovered, ready to take a sprat held in the fingers."
—*"Black-Headed Gulls in London," A. H. Hall,* National Geographic *magazine, June 1925*

• "The British taxi driver has a bad reputation, but after driving through the streets of Paris among French taxicabs, I came to the conclusion that he was worthy of a halo."
—*"From England to India by Automobile," F.A.C.*

Forbes-Leith, National Geographic *magazine, August 1925*

• "From a bus top one looks down, part and parcel of all he sees, understanding and being thrilled by a thousand activities. It is true that one sees the centuries without order or sequence; but that is as it should be in London, where to-day, tomorrow and 1,800 years elbow each other companionably."
—*"London From a Bus Top," Herbert Corey,* National Geographic *magazine, May 1926*

• "During the last century it was the fashion to consider Buckingham [Palace] an extremely ugly structure. A beautiful new facade added in 1913 has changed the appearance of the palace completely and given it a dignity worthy of the Empire."
—Geographic News Bulletin, *December 31, 1928*

• "The Temple Bar Griffin, perched on his plinth, is not an object to be disregarded. Everybody knows that he marks the spot where the Strand suddenly changes into Fleet Street and where Westminster ends and the City Proper begins . . . and that the King never goes east of him officially without the invitation of the Lord Mayor."
—*"Some Forgotten Corners of London," Harold Donaldson Eberlein,* National Geographic *magazine, February 1932*

• "About midnight I stepped out into the almost empty streets of Bloomsbury, strode down to Hyde Park Corner, and joined a lively crowd at a coffee-stall—one of those red-painted shops on wheels that attract with their cheerful hospitality all classes in London."
—*"Vagabonding in England . . ." John McWilliams,* National Geographic *magazine, March 1934*

• "When the Empire [Wembley] Stadium is filled for England's great annual soccer game—the Cup Final—the onlooker is treated to a thrilling sight. The King and the Prince of Wales present cups and medals to the players, bands play stirring tunes, thousands of voices join in community singing . . . and England becomes as wildly excited as the United States does for the World Series."
—Geographic News Bulletin, *March 25, 1935*

• "Before the Mansion House a soldier

FAST FACT

The first edition of *National Geographic* was published in October 1888, when the Society consisted of only 209 members. The magazine's readership is now more than 60 million monthly.

demonstrates an antiaircraft gun, while another pleads for recruits. Beneath its routine hurly-burly, all London is uneasy. Thoughts of war and bombs are with it always . . ."
—*"As London Toils and Spins," Frederick Simpich,* National Geographic *magazine, January 1937*

• "In the [Covent Garden] flower market, the sun streams through the glass roof onto colorful, fragrant masses of blooms . . . Chirping of sparrows in the rafters overhead adds a note of outdoor gaiety . . . 'Lavender, lady, lavender?' and 'Yes, my dear, anything you want?' cry the jolly market women."
—Geographic News Bulletin, *December 13, 1937*

• "The thing that impresses me most about wartime England is the attitude of the people. Their morale is magnificent . . . I think

there was a brief period, at the very beginning of the Blitzkrieg, when the people might have cracked . . . Surely, we thought, human beings cannot stand such punishment. The people stood fast . . . It may well be that the fortitude of the ordinary people of London . . . will mean the difference between defeat and victory for the British Empire."
—*"Everyday Life in Wartime England," Harvey Klemmer,* National Geographic *magazine, April 1941*

• "To soften the worst scars of the battle

The Temple Bar Griffin

for London, Nature intervened with one of those small miracles that human beings find strangely touching in the harsh environment in which they must live. A profusion of wild flowers sprang up in the ragged cavities left by the blitz and the havoc created by the robot bombs."
—*"London Wins the Battle," Marquis W. Childs,* National Geographic *magazine, August 1945*

• "Women looked happy, and Bond Street was elegant again. Every other motorcar wore a little Union Jack on its bonnet . . . From hundreds of billboards, from thousands of shop windows, one face gazed gravely at the crowds. It was the face of a beautiful young woman who wore a diamond tiara and a shimmering evening gown . . . So the Queen looked out on her London."
—*"In the London of the New Queen," H. V. Morton,* National

Petticoat Lane (Middlesex Street) has been a commercial hub since the 17th century.

Geographic magazine, September 1953

• "Street markets have a long tradition in London, and Petticoat Lane (Middlesex Street) is one of the oldest. According to legend, the lane got its nickname because the pitchmen are such clever sleight-of-hand artists that they can divest a housewife of her petticoat and sell it back to her as a new garment."
—*"The City'—London's Storied Square Mile," Allan C. Fisher, Jr.,* National Geographic *magazine, June 1961*

• "It's ultrafashionable in today's London to live in a mews, or area of horse stables. Of course the horses have long since moved out, and the coach rooms and lofts have been thoroughly—and expensively—renovated. London abounds in these mews, tucked away behind the Victorian edifices they once served."
—*"One Man's London," Allan C. Fisher, Jr.,* National Geographic *magazine, June 1966*

• "Ten minutes from London's whirling Piccadilly Circus, by the Tube . . . lies a 'village'

so unlike the rest of London that even other Londoners tour it. Chelsea, though now a part of London, has always remained a place apart . . . an enclave where Britannia waives the rules . . . Today the flamboyantly beautiful 'dolly birds' who stroll the King's Road . . . *un*-clad in superminis or flimsy hot pants, embody an obvious, fleeting aspect of Chelsean rebelliousness."
—*"Chelsea, London's Haven of Individualists," James Cerruti,* National Geographic *magazine, January 1972*

Daily life during the Blitz

• "On a winter's day in London you slip into a pub as you would into a hot bath—gratefully . . . The pub seems blessedly old-fashioned in a hurry-up world. Here are the open fire, the aged oak paneling, the frosted windows, the steak-and-kidney pies, the landlord with a waiting pint of bitter—and, of course, the regulars, throwing darts or chatting about the day's news or gossiping."
—*"Warm World of the London Pub," Jerry Camarillo Dunn, Jr.,* National Geographic Traveler *magazine, January/February 1989*

• "East of the Tower of London, another London begins . . . the docks. Scarcely four miles from Buckingham Palace, it has echoed through the ages with the greatest names of maritime and commercial history, from Nelson to Cook to Captain Kidd, the *Mayflower* crew, Frobisher, and Drake. It has always been a world apart, and happy—no, proud—to remain so. But with a tidal wave of money and promises, all that is changing."
—*"Docklands—London's New Frontier," Erla Zwingle,* National Geographic *magazine, July 1991*

• "Inspired by the millennium and fueled in part by the National Lottery, London is in the middle of a building frenzy. The farther east we flew, the more I began to catch sight of the new buildings that are redefining its skyline . . . Invention and integration, the synthesis of old and new, sum up the work of Norman Foster, who is changing the face of London more than any architect since Sir Christopher Wren."
—*"London on a Roll," Simon Worrall,* National Geographic *magazine, June 2000*

Nine Record Auction Sales at Sotheby's

Below are the recent record prices from some of the departments at Sotheby's London auction house—sales in other cities may have set higher prices.

Old Master paintings

£49,506,650 ($79,210,540) in 2002 for Rubens's "Massacre of the Innocents."

Jewelry

£4,521,250 ($7,234,000) in 2010 for a 1952 onyx and diamond bracelet by Cartier.

Books and manuscripts

£7,321,250 ($11,714,000) in 2010 for *The Birds of America* (four volumes, first edition, 1827) by John James Audubon.

Wine

£82,800 ($132,500) in 2011 for 12 bottles of Romanée-Conti 1990 Domaine de la Romanée-Conti.

Silver

£2,505,250 ($4,008,000) in 2010 for the Great Silver Wine Cistern of Thomas Wentworth (1705-1706), attributed to John Rollos.

Rugs and carpets

£2,729,250 ($4,366,800) in 2009 for a late 16th-century Safavid silk, wool, and metal-thread prayer rug from Isfahan, central Persia.

Prints

£1,609,250 ($2,575,000) in 2012 for a complete set of ten color screenprints of "Mao" (1972) by Andy Warhol.

19th-century European paintings

£3,065,250 ($4,904,000) in 2010 for "Young Fisherman, Valencia" (1904) by Joaquín Sorolla.

Islamic and Middle Eastern art

£7,433,250 ($11,893,000) in 2011 for "Faridun in the Guise of a Dragon Tests His Sons" (ca 1525), an illustrated folio in ink, opaque watercolor, and gold on paper.

·Twenty-Three London Firsts·

Throughout the years, Londoners have come up with a lot of ideas. So there is the first problem—the sheer number of the capital's inventions and innovations. The second is the fact that when someone claims to have invented something, someone somewhere else will claim to have come up with it beforehand ... only they didn't get around to telling anyone, applying for a patent, or having it produced. As a result, this list contains only a small selection of London's firsts, and it is as much about claims and conjecture as it is a collection of documented inventions.

The Daily Courant (est. 1702) was London's first daily newspaper.

• 1633 Banana
The first banana seen in Britain was sold in London on April 10 of this year.

• 1662 Sparkling wine
Scientist and physician Christopher Merret was the first to document the practice of adding sugar and molasses to create secondary fermentation in wine and thus a "sparkling wine," a term he was the first to use. He presented an eight-page paper on the subject, based on experiments by the cider-makers of his native Gloucestershire, to the Royal Society in London—a full 35 years before Dom Pierre Pérignon, a French Benedictine monk and cellar-master, stumbled by accident upon his own particular sparkling wine.

• 1702 Daily newspaper
Elizabeth Mallet published the first British newspaper, *The Daily Courant*, on March 11, 1702, from premises above the White Hart "against the Ditch at Fleet Bridge." A single sheet with advertisements on the back, it ran until 1735.

• 1731 Magazine
The first periodical to use the term "magazine"—from the French for "storehouse"—was the monthly *Gentleman's*

Magazine, published by Edward Cave in his home in St John's Gate. It remained in circulation until 1922.

• **1760 Roller skates**
John Joseph Merlin (1735-1803), a Belgian-born mechanical instrument-maker, first showed off his patented wheeled boots at a party at Carlisle House in Soho Square. Unfortunately, he had not mastered the ability to turn or brake. He also overreached by attempting to play a violin at the same time that he demonstrated his invention. He careened through his host's ballroom before crashing into a mirror, severely wounding himself in the process.

• **1766 Jigsaw puzzle**
John Spilsbury (1739-1769), an apprentice to the Royal Geographer, is credited with creating the first commercial jigsaw puzzle—a map—in his studio in Russell Court off Drury Lane. It was created as a geographical aid for children, designed to help them learn how countries fit together as they pieced together the puzzles. All commercial jigsaws for the next 20 years would come in the form of Spilsbury's "dissected maps."

• **1768 Circus**
Philip Astley (1742-1814) retired from the army and became an equestrian trick rider before opening a riding school in 1768 near Westminster Bridge. He offered lessons in the morning, tricks in the afternoon; he found the best size of ring for the latter was 42 feet (13 m) in diameter—the size of today's standard circus ring. He eventually added dancing dogs, jugglers, acrobats, tightrope walkers, and clowns to his performances.

• **1809 Indian restaurant**
Dean Mahomet (later Sake Dean Mahomed) opened the first Indian-owned London curry house, the Hindostanee Coffee House, at 34 George Street, near Portman Square. It also offered an early version of food to go: "Such ladies and gentlemen as may be desirous of having India Dinners dressed and sent to their own houses will be punctually attended to by giving previous notice."

• **1843 Christmas card**
The first commercially produced seasonal card was designed by London

A salmon was caught in the Thames on November 12, 1974—not the first time it had happened, but the first time, because of the river's previously foul waters, for over 125 years.

artist John Callcott Horsley—known as "Clothes Horsley" for his aversion to nude models—and was not without controversy: It depicted a child glugging a glass of wine.

• **1855 Underground municipal lavatories**
Public lavatories were nothing new—the ancient Romans had them, for a start—but London was the first to put them underground, courtesy of William Haywood, a City of London Corporation engineer. For more than a century, the charge to use one would remain one pence, hence the euphemistic British phrase "to spend a penny."

• **1856 Plastic**
Alexander Parkes patented Parkesine, the world's first plastic, in 1856, and formed a company in Hackney Wick, east London, to mass-produce the cellulose-based substance ten years later. Within two years the firm was out of business, sunk by the low-quality product created by Parkes's determination to keep down costs.

• **1860 Dog food**
James Spratt was born in Ohio to English parents. In later life, he invented a new type of lightning conductor and, on landing in London to promote it, his interest was piqued by the packs of starving dogs at the docks hoping to be fed on the sailors' hard-tack biscuits. In response he patented his own "Meat-Fibrine Dog Cakes," shaped like a bone and made of wheat, vegetables, and cows' blood. He then set up the first dog-food factory in High Holborn in 1860.

• **1864 Traffic island**
It was privately built on St. James's Street near Piccadilly by Colonel Pierpoint to make it easier for him to reach his club—to no avail, for he was knocked down by a horse-drawn cab upon stepping off his island.

• **1865 Tuxedo**
A celestial blue evening coat was created by tailors Henry Poole & Co. of 15 Savile Row (still in existence) as informal dinner wear for "Bertie," then the Prince of Wales and future Edward VII. William Waldorf Astor, Robert Goelet, Ogden Mills, and Pierre Lorillard, founding fathers of the Tuxedo Club in Tuxedo Park, New York, were Henry Poole customers in the 1860s and probably asked for copies of Bertie's first prototype dinner jacket.

• 1868 Traffic light

A railway engineer, John Peake Knight (1828–1886), devised the first traffic lights—gas-powered, manually operated, and installed initially at the junction of Bridge Street and Great George Street outside the House of Commons. The lights were abandoned after they exploded, killing a policeman and causing the horses of a passing cavalry troop to bolt. The first modern three-color lights were installed in London at Piccadilly on August 3, 1926.

• 1876 Ice rink

The world's first indoor "skating-rink," the Glaciarium, opened in Covent Garden before moving to Grafton Street, near Tottenham Court Road, in 1844. Unfortunately, at the time, ice couldn't be manufactured and kept frozen in sufficient quantities to create a proper rink. The appalling smell of the substitute, a mixture of pig fat and salts, would be the project's undoing.

By January 1876, however, refrigeration technology was such that John Gamgee was able to open the world's first mechanically frozen rink in a tent just off King's Road. Gamgee had stumbled across his patented freezing method in 1870 while trying to devise ways to freeze meat for import into Britain from Australia and New Zealand.

• 1880 Telephone directory

What was probably the world's first telephone

THE FLOATING

GLACIARIUM,

FOOT OF NORTHUMBERLAND AVENUE,

CHARING CROSS.

By special permission of the Metropolitan Board of Works, the Floating Swimming Bath, Charing Cross, has been turned into a Glaciarium, on Mr. John Gamgee's system.

REAL ICE SKATING

Can be enjoyed continuously during the Present Winter.

THE HOURS OF ADMISSION ARE:—

9 a.m. to 11 a.m. for Ladies and Gentlemen.
12 noon to 2 p.m. „ „
3 p.m. to 5 p.m.* „ „
7 p.m. to 10 p.m. for Gentlemen only.

Ladies not admitted after 5 p.m., except on specially reserved occasions to be duly announced.

ADMISSION TWO SHILLINGS.

Tuesday and Thursday from 3 p.m. to 5 p.m., 5s.

SKATES SIXPENCE.

Skaters having Approved Skates not charged Skate Money.

Skating Manager and Instructor,

MR. ROBERT G. AUSTIN, CHAMPION SKATER OF AMERICA.

F. E. BREWER, Lessee.

Promoting the world's first ice-rink, the Glaciarium

directory was issued in January 1880 and ran to six pages. It listed the names and addresses—but not the actual phone numbers—of just 255 people.

• 1884 Machine gun

It was invented by Hiram Maxim (1840-1916) in Hatton Garden at its junction with Clerkenwell Road and first manufactured on the same site. The world's earliest known multi-shot weapon, James Puckle's "Puckle Gun," was also patented in London, on May 15, 1718.

• 1896 Motorized traffic fatality

A Rogers-Benz driven by Arthur Edsell ran over Bridget Driscoll, a 44-year-old mother of two, on August 17, 1896, at Crystal Palace. Poor Bridget froze in the road when she saw the car bearing down on her at a staggering 4 miles an hour. At her inquest, the coroner said he hoped "such a thing would never happen again."

• 1898 Escalator

A smooth slope, not a moving staircase, made from 224 pieces of leather joined together was installed in Harrods in 1898. Shop assistants were on hand to dispense brandy and smelling salts, to men and women respectively, who became giddy during their first ride.

• 1920 Airport

It's only an airport if you have to pass through customs, and the first of these opened on March 29, 1920, in Croydon, centered on an aerodrome built in 1915 to help defend London from German Zeppelins in World War I. Croydon also opened the world's first purpose-built airport terminal and hotel in 1928.

• 1926 Television

Today it's a room above the celebrated Bar Italia on Frith Street in Soho, but on January 26, 1926, it was where John Logie Baird made the world's first demonstration of what would become known as television. Selfridge's department store sold the world's first TV set in 1928.

• 1928 Penicillin

Sir Alexander Fleming made one of the greatest accidental discoveries of all time—*Penicillium rubens*—at St. Mary's Hospital, Paddington. The hospital was the scene of another first some years earlier in 1874: the creation of diacetylmorphine, better known as heroin.

> **FAST FACT**
> **A sample of Alexander Fleming's original penicillin mold is on display at the Science Museum in South Kensington (see Museum District, p. 216).**

·London Lasts·

Times change, and in London much has fallen by history's wayside. Here is a miscellany of some of the things that have disappeared forever—or dwindled to a single example or two.

Beefeaters: beards now optional

• **Bank** Only one independent bank, C. Hoare and Co., survives. It has been owned and run by members of the Hoare family since its founding in 1672. In 1690, the business moved to Fleet Street, where it remains to this day at #37. Its customers have included Jane Austen, Lord Byron, and Samuel Pepys.

• **Beefeater beards** The last time Beefeaters in the Tower of London were required to have beards as a condition of employment was 1936.

• **Coin** The Royal Mint has operated for more than 1,000 years: It was based in the Tower of London from the late 13th century until 1810, and then moved to Tower Hill. It was there that the last coin to be minted in London, a gold sovereign, was struck on November 10, 1975, though the Royal Mint itself had by then been moved to Wales.

• **Court dwarf** George III's mother, Princess Augusta of Saxe-Gotha-Altenburg (1719-1772), kept England's last official court dwarf.

• **Curtsy** Queen Elizabeth II curtsied to the coffin of her late father, George VI, in 1952, and again, for the last time, in 1953 to the coffin of her late grandmother Queen Mary.

• **Galleried coaching inn** Recorded in the 1540s but rebuilt in the 17th century, The George, or George Inn (*77 Borough High Street, SE1*), is the last of London's once numerous inns with wooden galleries, or balconies (many were lost in the Blitz). The George is a national monument owned by the National Trust.

• **German bomb of World War II** A V2 flying bomb fell on Hughes Mansions, Vallance Road, Stepney, on March 27, 1945, killing 130 people.

• **Royal last rites** The last rites of British monarchs were traditionally held after dark. William IV was the last monarch buried at night, in 1837. The funeral of Queen Victoria in 1901 was the first to take place by day.

• **Tollgate** Until the 1860s, London had more than 100 tollgates (turnpikes). Only one survives, on College Road, Dulwich, SE21, and dates from 1789.

·London Lasts—Crime and Punishment·

A counterfeiter is burned at the stake in 1789, a year before the punishment was banned.

Though the United Kingdom doesn't execute convicted criminals any more, as recently as the beginning of the 19th century, there were more than 200 capital offenses, most of mind-boggling triviality (see 1800, p. 118).

• **Briton in the Tower**
Norman Baillie-Stewart—known as "The Officer in the Tower"—was the last Briton to serve a sentence in the Tower of London (rather than merely awaiting transfer).

He was convicted in 1933 of selling military secrets to Germany and sentenced to 140 years but released in 1937.

• **Burning at the stake**
The traditional punishment for a woman accused of treason, though executioners generally strangled the accused first; abolished in 1790.

• **Last drink** Convicts being led to execution by wagon from Newgate Gaol to Tyburn (near present-day Marble Arch) could step down and enjoy a last (free) drink at The Mason's Arms, a tavern that survives to this day in Upper Berkeley Street, W1. The expressions "on the wagon" and "off the wagon" derive from this tradition.

• **Execution at the Tower**
Josef Jakobs was a German spy, injured and captured after parachuting into England in 1941. As a combatant, he was shot rather than hanged on

August 15, 1941. Sixteen other spies were executed during World War II, and 11 in World War I.

• **Flogging** Outlawed for women in 1820, though courts could call for it as late as 1948 for men; ten prisoners were flogged as recently as 1954.

• **Gallows** The death penalty remained on the statute books for high treason and piracy with violence long after it had been abolished for other crimes. London's last official gallows remained in readiness at Wandsworth Prison until 1994. The law was changed in 1998.

• **Hanging** Henryk Niemasz was hanged for murder at Wandsworth Prison on September 8, 1961.

• **Hanging in chains** Particularly wicked criminals were executed and then hanged in chains, near the scene of their crime, as a deterrent: The practice was abolished in 1834.

• **Hulks** "Hulks," as prison ships on the Thames were known, were notorious for their appalling conditions. The last, the *Defence*, was abandoned in 1857.

• **Pentonville execution** Pentonville prison (1842) became the principal place of execution in London following the closure of the infamous Newgate Gaol in 1902. More people died there in the 20th century than in any other British jail, among them 112 murderers, six spies, and two traitors. The last was the 21-year-old murderer Edwin Bush, on July 6, 1961.

• **Public beheading** In 1820, the Cato Street Conspirators—who plotted to kill the prime minister, Lord Liverpool, along with his entire cabinet—were hanged first and then lost their heads.

• **Public hanging** Irish nationalist Michael Barrett was hanged outside Newgate Gaol on May 26, 1868.

• **Stake through the heart** The punishment for suicide was once to be buried at a crossroads with a stake through the heart. John Williams was the last to suffer this fate, in 1811, at New Road and Cannon Street, E1.

• **Woman to be hanged** The 28-year-old Ruth Ellis, at Holloway on July 13, 1955, for murdering her lover.

FAST FACT

London's principal gallows stood in the corner of what is now Connaught Square (W2) and could hang 24 people at a time. Executions proceeded in order: highwaymen first, then common thieves, then those convicted of treason.

•Eyewitness Accounts of London's Victorian-Era Slums•

Although poverty wasn't new to London, the Industrial Revolution of the late 18th and 19th centuries helped create a dramatically divided society of haves and have-nots. Cramped in squalid slums, London's poor didn't escape the notice of contemporary writers, some of whom worked hard to expose the degradation.

Jacob's Island on the now buried Neckinger River

• Brick Lane

"Black and noisome, the road sticky with slime, and palsied houses, rotten from chimney to cellar, leaning together, apparently by the mere coherence of their ingrained corruption. Dark, silent, uneasy shadows passing and crossing—human vermin in this reeking sink, like goblin exhalations from all that is noxious around. Women with sunken, black-rimmed eyes, whose pallid faces appear and vanish by the light of an occasional gas lamp, and look so like ill-covered skulls that we start at their stare."
—*Arthur Morrison,* *"Whitechapel,"* The Palace Journal, *April 24, 1889*

• Clerkenwell

"At another cottage a young woman was standing, waiting for her mother to return . . .

While we were talking to the young woman, the mother came back, with her bonnet in her hand, and her apron all in tatters. She had been roughly treated in the crowd at the soup-kitchen, as all the really poor, weak, and helpless always are; and while greasy tramps, low thieves and their girls, and other unworthy objects got in, the decent . . . wife came empty away. She burst into tears as she told her daughter this, and was some time before she could be comforted. They were not beggars, not tramps, and were clean and honest."
—*John Hollingshead,* Ragged London in 1861

• **A Den of Thieves**
"Not far from this place was a house occupied solely by thieves; . . . at one end [was] a large fire-place, round which were gathered five or six thieves cooking their evening meal . . . It is often said, that villainy is stamped upon the countenance; if so, the men before us were favourable specimens, for certainly they were not particularly ill-favored; perhaps there was something of the low narrow forehead about some of them, which phrenologists are fond of assuming to be types of this class; but this was far from being universal. Their manner was courteous and civil."
—*Thomas Beames,* The Rookeries of London: Past, Present, and Prospective, *1852*

• **Jacob's Island**
"The striking peculiarity of Jacob's Island consists in the wooden galleries and sleeping rooms at the back of the houses, which overhang the dark flood, and are built on piles, so that the place has positively the air of a Flemish street flanking a sewer instead of a canal; while the ricketty bridges that span the ditches . . . give it the appearance of the Venice of drains."
—The Morning Chronicle, *1849*

• **Saffron Hill**
"Oliver . . . could not help bestowing a few hasty glances on either side . . . A dirtier or more wretched place he had never seen. The street was very narrow and muddy, and the air was impregnated with filthy odours. There were a good many small shops; but the only stock in trade appeared to be heaps of children, who . . . were crawling in and out at the doors, or screaming from the inside . . . Covered ways

---

FAST FACT

Thomas Beames alludes above to phrenology, a now discredited pseudoscience of the mid-19th century that attributed behavior and mental capabilities to the size and shape of the human skull.

The rookery of St. Giles, back in the day

houses, and not a large one, [the author] hath numbered fifty-eight persons of both sexes, the stench of which was so intolerable, that it compelled him, in a short time, to quit the place."
—*Henry Fielding, "Causes of the Late Increase of Robbers," 1749*

and yards . . . disclosed little knots of houses, where drunken men and women were positively wallowing in filth."
—*Charles Dickens,* Oliver Twist, *1838*

• Soho

"There is a mouldy, smoky, dilapidated air about the whole; . . . You are struck by the curious appearance of some of the lower windows in these houses—old bonnets, veils, articles of dress, faded indeed . . . are exposed as if to tempt those who pass by; these are unlicensed pawn shops, where women deposit their wearing apparel, and

with the money they obtain gratify their passion for drinking at the next public house."
—*Thomas Beames,* The Rookeries of London: Past, Present, and Prospective, *1852*

• St. Giles

"In . . . St. Giles there are a great number of houses set apart for the reception of rogues and vagabonds . . . all properly accommodated with miserable beds, from the cellar to the garrett; . . . in these beds, several of which are in the same room, men and women, often strangers to each other, lie promiscuously, . . . In one of these

• Whitechapel

"The most approved way of passing the evening, among the Jew boys, is to play at draughts, dominoes, or cribbage, and to bet on the play . . . The dwellings of boys such as these are among the worst in London, as regards ventilation, comfort or cleanliness. They reside in the courts and recesses about Whitechapel and Petticoat-lane . . . I am told that the care of a mother is almost indispensable to a poor Jew boy, and having that care he seldom becomes an outcast."
—*Henry Mayhew,* London Labour and the London Poor, *1851*

St. Paul's Cathedral

 ome monumental numbers on one of London's most recognized monuments, a building that in its various incarnations has been an important feature of the city for more than 1,400 years.

Cost £747,661 ($1,196,000)

Sir Christopher Wren's annual salary £100 ($160)

Height 365 feet (111.3 m)

Estimated height of the "old" St. Paul's 493 feet (150.2 m)

Horses stabled in the old nave when it was used as a barracks during the English Civil War 800

Outer height of dome 278 feet (85 m)

Steps to the dome 528

Daily visitors 2,000

Distance a whisper can be heard in the "Whispering Gallery" 112 feet (34 m)

Annual grant from Parliament Around £50,000 ($80,000)

Largest monument on the cathedral floor
Duke of Wellington (1912)

Time to complete the monument 56 years

Time to complete St. Paul's 36 years

Annual number of new burials 0; no burials now take place at St. Paul's

St. Paul's Cathedral by Year

St. Paul's figures large in London's history. It is the seat of the Bishop of London and the cathedral church of London. For centuries it was the capital's loftiest building (see Tallest Structures, p. 129), and its dome, Sir Christopher Wren's masterpiece, has long been a dominant feature of the city skyline.

A.D. 604 St. Mellitus (d. 624), a monk with St. Augustine's mission from Rome to Britain, is made the first Saxon Bishop of London and founds the first St. Paul's.

1087 Following the loss of early churches on the site to fire and Viking raids, the post-Conquest Normans found the medieval St. Paul's, which will stand for almost six centuries.

1561 Lightning causes a fire that destroys the cathedral's roofs and steeple. Falling timbers cause structural damage from which the medieval building never recovers.

1606 Four of the Gunpowder Plotters, who in 1605 had planned to blow up the House of Lords during the State opening of Parliament, are executed in St. Paul's churchyard.

1633 The architect Inigo Jones (1573-1652) begins restoration work, but the project is interrupted by the outbreak of the English Civil War (1642-1651).

1660 After numerous disputes, a restoration plan by Christopher Wren (1632-1723) involving the addition of a dome is accepted. Six days later the cathedral is destroyed in the Great Fire of London.

1675 Work on Wren's cathedral begins after a decade of planning.

1697 The first service is held in the unfinished cathedral, a Thanksgiving for peace between England and France after the Nine Years' War.

1708 Two sons named after their fathers formally lay the cathedral's "last" stone:

FAST FACT

Ludgate Hill, where St. Paul's Cathedral stands, is the City of London's highest point.

Christopher Wren, Junior, and Edward Strong, the son of the building's master mason. Building work, however, will continue for several years.

1924 Fears about the cathedral's integrity arose as early as 1710, and on Christmas Eve the dean is served legal notice of structural dangers. The cathedral remains closed for repairs for five years.

1940 St. Paul's somehow survives one of the worst nights of the Blitz, on December 29, when 29,000 bombs and 100,000 incendiary devices destroy virtually everything in the cathedral's vicinity and beyond. Its survival will become a symbol of London's own survival and spirit during the Blitz.

1958 St. Paul's dedicates the American Memorial Chapel, commemorating more than 28,000 U.S. service personnel based in Britain who died during World War II. Their names are recorded in a 500-page roll of honor presented by General Eisenhower in 1951. A page of the book is turned every day.

1964 Dr. Martin Luther King (1929-1968) speaks from the cathedral's west steps en route to collect the Nobel Peace Prize. In 1969, his widow, Coretta Scott King (1927-2006), becomes the first woman to preach in St. Paul's.

1981 HRH the Prince of Wales marries Lady Diana Spencer. In contrast, in 2011, their son William will marry Kate Middleton in Westminster Abbey.

Wren Churches

In addition to St. Paul's, Sir Christopher Wren and his office built or rebuilt 51 churches in London. Of these only 12 survive intact.

- St. Benet, Paul's Wharf, EC4
- St. Clement, Eastcheap, EC4
- St. Edmund, King and Martyr, Lombard Street, EC3
- St. James Garlickhythe, Garlick Hill, EC4
- St. Margaret Lothbury, Coleman Street, EC2

- St. Margaret Pattens, Eastcheap, EC3
- St. Martin, Ludgate Hill, EC4
- St. Mary Abchurch, Abchurch Lane, EC4
- St. Mary Aldermary, Bow Lane, EC4
- St. Michael, Cornhill, EC3
- St. Peter, Cornhill, EC2
- St. Stephen, Walbrook, EC4

Quotations in Favor of London . . .

Indifference is rarely an option in London, but over the years locals and visitors alike have often been moved to opposing views of the city, from the praise lavished in the comments below to the less complimentary views expressed to the right.

"Paris strikes the vulgar part of us infinitely the most, but to a thinking mind London is incomparably the most delightful subject for contemplation."
—Samuel Rogers, *Italian Journal*, 1814

"The man who has stood upon the Acropolis/And looked down over Attica, or he/Who has sailed where picturesque Constantinople is,/Or seen Timbuctoo . . . May not think much of London's first appearance–/But ask him what he thinks of it a year hence?"
—Lord Byron, *Don Juan*, 1819-1824

"I like the spirit of this great London which I feel around me. Who but a coward would pass his whole life in hamlets; and for ever abandon his faculties to the eating rust of obscurity?"
—Charlotte Brontë, *Villette*, 1853

"London, a nation not a city."
—Benjamin Disraeli, *Lothair*, 1870

"Nowhere else is so much human life gathered together . . ."
—Henry James, *An English Easter*, 1877

"It was summer time, and London is so beautiful in summer. It lay beneath my window a fairy city veiled in golden mist . . . an Aladdin's cave of jewels."
—Jerome K. Jerome, Preface to the second edition of *Three Men in a Boat*, 1909

"London is the most interesting, beautiful and wonderful city in the world to me, delicate in her incidental and multitudinous littleness . . ."
—H. G. Wells, *The New Machiavelli*, 1911

"London is a bad habit one hates to lose."
—William Sansom, *Blue Skies, Brown Studies*, 1961

. . . and Quotations Against

"May my enemies live here in summer!"
—Jonathan Swift, *Journal to Stella,* May 1711

"As early as I knew/This town, I had the sense to hate it too."
—Alexander Pope, *The Second Satire of Dr. John Donne,* 1713

"That tiresome dull place! Where all people under thirty find
so much amusement."
—Thomas Gray, Letter, 1764

"Nothing is certain in London but expense."
—William Shenstone, quoted in *Curiosities of Literature* by Isaac D'Israeli, 1791

"The single spot whereupon were crowded together more wealth, more splen-
dour, more ingenuity, more world wisdom, and, alas! More worldly blindness,
poverty, depravity, dishonesty and wretchedness, than upon any other spot in
the whole habitable earth."
—Robert Southey, *Letters From England,* 1807

"Hell is a city much like London."
—Percy Bysshe Shelley, *Peter Bell the Third,* 1819

"All I can say is that standing at Charing Cross and looking east west north and
south I can see nothing but dullness."
—John Keats, Letter, 1820

"London is a splendid place for those that can get out of it."
—George John Gordon Bruce, Seventh Lord Balfour, *Observer,* 1944

"When it's three o'clock in New York, it's still 1938 in London."
—Bette Midler, *The Times,* 1978

"Do you realise that people die of boredom in London suburbs?
It's the second biggest cause of death amongst the English in general.
Sheer boredom . . ."
—Alexander McCall Smith, *Friends, Lovers, Chocolate,* 2005

Most Popular Baby Names

Of particular note on the boys' list is the fact that after a century of Johns, Davids, and Pauls, the most popular baby name in London in 2013 was Mohammed (if we include all the variant spellings).

Boys

Rank	1904	1954	1974	2013
1	William	David	Paul	Mohammed
2	John	John	Mark	Harry
3	George	Stephen	David	Oliver
4	Thomas	Michael	Andrew	Jack
5	Arthur	Peter	Richard	Charlie
6	James	Robert	Christopher	Jacob
7	Charles	Paul	James	Thomas
8	Frederick	Alan	Simon	Alfie
9	Albert	Christopher	Michael	Riley
10	Ernest	Richard	Matthew	William

Girls

Rank	1904	1954	1974	2013
1	Mary	Susan	Sarah	Amelia
2	Florence	Linda	Claire	Olivia
3	Doris	Christine	Nicola	Jessica
4	Edith	Margaret	Emma	Emily
5	Dorothy	Janet	Lisa	Lily
6	Annie	Patricia	Joanne	Ava
7	Margaret	Carol	Michelle	Mia
8	Alice	Elizabeth	Helen	Isla
9	Elizabeth	Mary	Samantha	Sophie
10	Elsie	Anne	Karen	Isabella

FAST FACT

The three most popular baby names for boys in the United States in 2013 were Noah, Liam, and Jacob. For girls, they were Sophia, Emma, and Olivia.

·Worst Days Ever to Be a London Moneyer·

There's only one day on this list.

In medieval England, coins were still produced individually by "moneyers," whose main output was handmade silver pennies. In 1124, King Henry I—who was in Normandy putting down a rebellion—requested that coins be shipped to the continent from England to pay his soldiers. When the coins arrived, it quickly became apparent that they had been "debased"—meaning, the coins were made more out of tin than silver, with unscrupulous moneyers pocketing the excess precious metal.

Henry thus ordered his chief minister, Roger of Salisbury, to summon all the moneyers of the realm to Winchester on Christmas 1124. There, Roger had them all castrated and their right hands chopped off. Yikes.

Of about 150 moneyers working in England at the time, 94 were so mutilated (some appeared to have bought their way out of punishment). So on our list of the worst days ever to be a London moneyer, that day in 1124 wins, hands down.

·A Buckingham Palace Miscellany·

Buckingham Palace is the monarch's official London residence— St. James's Palace is the ceremonial royal residence. It takes its name from John Sheffield, who was created Duke of Buckingham in 1703 and built what was then Buckingham House as his London home.

• George III bought Buckingham House in 1761 for £21,000 (£2.8 million/$4 million today)

Buckingham Palace

for his wife, Queen Charlotte. She bore 14 of her 15 children there.

• In 1826, George IV requested £500,000 ($800,000) to remodel the house as a palace, £350,000 ($560,000)

more than the "utmost sum" Parliament said it would grant. The eventual cost was more than £700,000 ($1.12 milion).

• No monarch lived in the palace until Queen Victoria moved there in July 1837, three weeks after her accession. But Victoria found the palace too small and all but uninhabitable: faulty drains, no sinks, unventilated lavatories, servants' bells that didn't ring, doors that wouldn't close, and windows that wouldn't open.

The solution was to move Marble Arch, then located at the Palace entrance, and build a brand new wing. The cost, £106,000 ($170,000), was largely met by selling George IV's Royal Pavilion in Brighton.

• The Palace suffered nine direct bomb hits during World War II.

• The Palace has 775 rooms, including 19 staterooms, 52 royal and guest bedrooms, 78 bathrooms, 92 offices, and 188 staff bedrooms. The largest room is the Ballroom, where Investitures and State banquets take place. It is 120 feet (36.6 m) long, 59 feet (18 m) wide, and 44 feet (13.5 m) high.

• The Palace has its own chapel, post office, swimming pool, staff cafeteria, doctor's surgery, and cinema.

• It has 1,514 doors, 760 windows—which are cleaned every six weeks—and 40,000 lightbulbs.

• The 800 employees include a fendersmith (someone who mends and looks after metal fireplaces, and in the past would also have lit fires), a flagman, and two full-time "horological conservators" to attend to the 350 clocks and watches (see Jobs, p. 97).

• The 40 acres of grounds include a helicopter pad, a lake, and a tennis court. It is home to 30 different species of birds and more than 350 different kinds of wildflowers.

• The gravel on the palace forecourt (created in 1911) is "dragged"—cleaned and combed—first thing every day, even on Christmas Day. Two inspections take place later in the day.

• The monarch lives in a suite of 12 rooms on the Palace's north side.

• A flag always flies above the Palace: the Royal Standard when the monarch is in residence; the Union Flag at other times.

• Fifty thousand guests step inside the palace annually—30,000 for garden parties; the other guests are invited to the State banquets or the 25 Investitures held to award medals, Orders, and decorations.

• Garden parties typically involve around 400 staff, 20,000 sandwiches, 20,000 slices of cake, and 27,000 cups of tea.

❝ Notwithstanding the expense which has been incurred in building the palace, no sovereign in Europe, perhaps no private gentleman, is so ill lodged as the king of this country. ❞

~**Duke of Wellington,** *Speech to the House of Lords, 1828*

·Actual Jobs You Can Apply for in the Royal Household·

Has it been your lifelong dream to bring the morning newspaper to someone you need to address as "Your Royal Highness"? Here are actual (edited) descriptions of royal jobs that were available in 2013 and 2014. Some even include lodging at Buckingham Palace itself, conjuring up images of casually running into the Queen (don't forget a polite neck bow) as you go out for your morning constitutional. Check out the latest jobs on offer at *royal.gov.uk*.

A royal cook at work

• Chauffeur
Location: Buckingham Palace
Salary: £23,000 ($36,800)
Job description:
The Royal Mews supplies all coaches and cars for State, official, and unofficial occasions. It also cares for and trains Her Majesty's carriage horses.
Partial list of responsibilities:
• Driving members of the Royal Family, household officials, guests, and official visitors as directed by the Head Chauffeur.

• Cook in the Duke & Duchess of Gloucester's Household
[NOTE: The current Duke of Gloucester is Prince Richard, cousin of Queen Elizabeth II.]
Location: Kensington Palace
Salary: £22,000 ($35,200)
Job description:
You will be responsible for the provision of all meals for TRH [Their Royal Highnesses] The Duke and Duchess of Gloucester and guests on both official and private occasions.
Partial list of responsibilities:
• To plan menus and prepare and cook a range of meals for TRH.
• To prepare and cook for TRH's family and guests when required.
• To be responsible for the purchasing of all food within budget.
• To be responsible for the preparation and cooking of official and private lunch and dinner parties, receptions, and other entertainment events as required.
• To ensure that food preparation is of the highest standards at all times.

• Director of Music
Location: St. James's Palace
Salary: £21,500 ($34,400)
Job description:
Joining the Ecclesiastical

Butlers belong to the Master of the Household's department.

• **Footman/Trainee Butler**
Location: Buckingham Palace
Salary: £15,000 ($24,000) Accommodation is available
Job description:
We are recruiting a Footman to provide the highest standards in the service of wine, food, valeting, messenger duties, and reception in a friendly and efficient manner. Internally the post holder will have contact with Members of the Royal Family, guests, and all levels of Royal Household staff.
Partial list of responsibilities:
• To assist in the setting, clearing, and serving of Royal and Household meals whether Official or Private at all residences, and occasionally abroad.
• To be responsible for the valeting of guests and Members of the Royal Household invited to stay with the Royal Family, ensuring that clothes and uniforms are cared for to the highest standards.
• To see guests in and

Team within The Queen's Household, you will be responsible for the recruitment, performance, training, and welfare of the Chapel Royal Choir, which consists of ten Choristers, up to three probationers, and six men.
Partial list of responsibilities:
• To prepare and deliver music for Sunday Services at the Chapel Royal between 1 October and 31 July.
• To be responsible for the preparation and delivery of the music for Epiphany Service, Ash Wednesday, Maundy Thursday, Ascension Day, Joint Hampton Court Evensong, Remembrance Sunday, Carol Services, Christmas Day, and Royal and other occasions as required, e.g. Weddings, Funerals, and Memorial Services.
• To ensure that the standards of the Chapel Royal Choir are maintained and enhanced and that the boys are well behaved, smartly turned out, and punctual.
• To decide when Choristers should retire (during the term of their 14th birthday or when their voice changes, whichever is earlier).
• To engage with the parents of the Choristers to update them and explain the challenges ahead, pressure points, and also inform them of any social events.

out of residences both on private and official occasions, and to serve drinks for receptions and other large functions in a polite and welcoming manner.

• To collect and deliver tea/coffee trays, breakfast trays, and newspapers for Royal and Household purposes in an efficient manner.

• **Gardener**
Location: Buckingham Palace
Salary: £14,950 ($23,900)
Job description:
The Gardener is responsible for the maintenance and on-going development of the gardens and grounds whilst always looking to improve practices with regard to environmental consideration and efficiency issues.
Partial list of responsibilities:
• To maintain lawn areas to the highest standards required.

• To carry out green waste recycling duties including transporting the Royal Mews skips [waste containers] to allotment sites.

• **Horological Conservator**
Location: Buckingham Palace
Salary: £31,200 ($49,900)
Job description:
The Horological Conservator works with a team of three based out of workshops in Buckingham Palace and Windsor Castle, maintaining in excess of 1,000 clocks, including many items of great historical importance and rarity, whilst also repairing a range of horological items and Turret clocks.
Partial list of responsibilities:
• Winding clocks on a weekly basis, including setting all clocks and Turret clocks in line with BST and GMT.

• To ensure that all clocks in the Royal Apartments are in perfect working order at all times when The Queen and the Royal Family are in residence and that any repairs are undertaken immediately.

• To take responsibility for the clockmaker's workshop and store, ensuring that all areas are kept clean and tidy and that a safe working environment is maintained.

• Occasionally to give lectures, presentations, and tours about the clocks in the Palace to interested groups and to staff.

• **Liveried Helper**
Location: Buckingham Palace
Starting salary: £17,600 ($28,200) Accommodation is available
Job description:
The Royal Mews cares for and trains Her Majesty's

FAST FACT

The Royal Household, charged with supporting the day-to-day functions of the Queen and the Royal Family, employs 1,200 people in official residences throughout Britain.

carriage horses. As a liveried helper, you will join the team responsible for all aspects of horse care and for cleaning and maintaining harness and liveries. The job holder will have contact with members of the Royal Family and guests, all levels of Royal Household employees, and members of the public.
Partial list of responsibilities:
• To exercise horses on a daily basis, which may be in the Riding School or in the local area to Victoria. This may be ridden or driven, singles or pairs.
• To assist the Coachman in the training of young horses.
• To assist, ride, and drive on State and ceremonial occasions.

• HM Marshal of the Diplomatic Corps
Location: St. James's Palace
Salary: Unstated
Job Description:
The Marshal of the Diplomatic Corps is The Queen's Representative at the Court of St. James's, where Heads of Foreign Diplomatic Missions are accredited.
Partial list of responsibilities:
• To represent The Queen on appropriate occasions, including the paying of Farewell and other calls on Heads of Mission on Her Majesty's behalf.
• To organise the participation of Heads of Foreign and Commonwealth Missions in London at State and other official occasions, including the presentation of their Credentials to The Queen, attendance at Garden Parties, the State Opening of Parliament, Trooping of the Colour and at The Queen's Evening Reception for the Diplomatic Corps.
• To act as a source of non-official, non-political advice to Heads of Mission and to retain their confidence as a top level interlocutor.

• Trainee Butcher
Location: Windsor Farm Shop
Salary: £14,600 ($23,400)
Job description:
As a Trainee Butcher … you will learn how to cut and de-bone meat and prepare sausages for the counter at the Farm Shop.
Partial list of responsibilities:
• Working as part of the butchery team, you will also provide excellent customer service, promote new products, and ensure counters are fully stocked each day.
• With an understanding of food hygiene and a meticulous approach to cleanliness, you will ensure fridges are cleaned and stock is appropriately rotated.

FIRST PERSON

❝All employees are expected to attain and demonstrate the high standards expected of an organisation which serves The Queen.❞
~From **royal.gov.uk,** *the British Monarchy website*

London's Urban Myths

Hoax and urban myth often intertwine in London. Here are some of the best known myths—and why they aren't true:

In 1935, Phyllis Pearsall couldn't find her way to a party and decided to make a new map of London, getting up at 5 a.m. daily and walking 3,000 miles along all London's 23,000 streets. The result was the A-Z, London's first street atlas.
An oft-repeated claim, but no, says the Map Library department at the British Library. She adapted and collated sources dating back to at least 1623, though she may have directly researched newer districts. English Heritage has refused her a Blue Plaque for the same reason.

The Queen is at Buckingham Palace when the Union flag is flying.
It's the other way around: She's not there when the Union flag flies. Look out for the Royal Standard—that's when she's home.

The statue at the center of Piccadilly is Eros.
No, it's his twin brother, Anteros, son of Ares and Aphrodite in Greek mythology (see Statues, p. 199).

Nylon is a contraction of the abbreviations for New York and London.
Manufacturer DuPont considered more than 350 names for the fabric, including No-Run, Nuron, and Nilon, before choosing Nylon. "Ny" is meaningless and "lon" just sounded right.

Pregnant women are allowed to urinate in a London policeman's helmet.
Best not to try this. Although it is illegal for anyone to urinate in public, exceptions may be made for pregnant women if no facilities are available. This somehow got turned into the idea they could urinate *anywhere* in public.

You're never more than six feet from a rat in London.
More like 164 feet (50 m), according to research reported by the BBC.

England will fall if there are fewer than six ravens in the Tower of London.
Victorians invented the notion to spice up stories about the Tower.

·Six London Hoaxes·

Scams, hoaxes, rip-offs, practical jokes on a vast scale: London has seen more than its fair share over the centuries. Here are some of the best known:

• April Fool

The year 1972 marked the 100th anniversary of a round-the-world trip organized by Thomas Cook, one of the world's first travel tour operators. To celebrate, *The Times* of London ran an article on April 1—April Fools' Day—saying that Thomas Cook would offer a similar tour at 1872 prices to the first 1,000 people to contact Thomas Cook or apply in writing to a "Miss Avril Foley." The company's phone lines and travel agents' offices were swamped. The paper was forced to apologize, and the journalist responsible was fired but later reinstated.

The New Theatre Haymarket during a hoax-free performance

• The Berners Street Hoax

In 1810, Theodore Hook bet a friend he could turn any address into the most talked-about house in London. After he sent out hundreds of letters and invitations, 54 Berners Street [now a hotel] was duly besieged. Twelve chimneysweeps arrived, followed by grocers, fishmongers, and shoemakers. Massive deliveries of coal then arrived, along with bakers bearing wedding cakes and 2,500 raspberry tarts. "Six stout men" delivered an organ; a dozen pianos followed. Doctors, lawyers, vicars, and priests arrived to minister to someone "dying in the house"; dignitaries paying a house call included the Duke of York, the Lord Mayor, and the Archbishop of Canterbury. Fights broke out, and by nightfall a large part of London had been brought to a standstill.

• **Dickens Met Dostoevsky in London**
No, he didn't. Scholarly error begat scholarly error as a purported meeting between the two writers in London in 1862 threatened to become fact. An article published in 2002 in the *Dickensian,* the organ of the Dickens Fellowship, was the first to allude to it in English. The notion was picked up by several respected Dickens biographies and discussed in the *New York Times.* It was a hoax, the work of mysterious London-based writer Arnold Harvey. Supporting evidence included, among other things, a "letter from Dostoevsky" written 16 years after the supposed meeting, and research by Soviet scholar "K. K. Shaiakhmetov," published in the (fictitious) "Vedomosti Akademii Nauk Kazakskoi SSR: Institut Istorii, Filologii i Filosofii vol. 45 (Alma Ata 1987), pp. 49-55 at 53-54."

• **The Great Bottle Hoax**
In 1749, the New Theatre Haymarket was packed to the rafters after the Duke of Portland bet the Earl of Chesterfield that if he advertised an impossible feat would be performed—a man jumping into a bottle—they would "find fools enough in London to fill a playhouse and pay handsomely for the privilege." After the time for the performance came and went, a lighted candle was thrown onstage, prompting a riot as disgruntled spectators both sought to escape in panic and ripped anything they could from the theater and burned it on the street outside. The Duke had proved the public's gullibility, but thieves stole his box-office takings in the melee.

• **The Platypus Play**
A suspected hoax: George Shaw, Keeper of the Department of Natural History at the British Museum, received from Australia in 1799 the first duck-billed platypus to be seen in Britain. The animal was so strange—venomous, egg-laying, duck-billed, beaver-tailed,

FAST FACT

In 2008, more than 100 scientists deciphered the DNA of the duck-billed platypus. Its genes are a strange amalgam derived from the worlds of reptiles, birds, and mammals.

otter-footed—that he found it "impossible not to entertain some doubts as to the genuine nature of the animal, and to surmise that there might have been practised some arts of deception in its structure." Many suspected Chinese sailors, notorious for their skill in stitching together "mermaids" and other "creatures" and for the "monstrous impostures they had so frequently practised on European adventurers."

• **Washing the Lions**
Sending unsuspecting visitors to see the annual "washing" of the (nonexistent) lions at the Tower of London was popular in the 18th and 19th centuries, and it is one of the earliest recorded London April Fools' Day pranks:

The April 2 edition of *Dawks's News-Letter* from 1698, for example, reported that "Yesterday being the first of April, several persons were sent to the Tower Ditch to see the Lions washed." Early dupes were told the washing would take place in the Tower's moat; later victims were told to report to the Tower's (nonexistent) "White Gate."

Londons in the U.S.A.

- **London**, Alabama
- **London**, Arkansas
- **London**, California
- **New London**, Connecticut
- **London Mills**, Illinois
- **London**, Indiana
- **New London**, Indiana
- **London**, Kentucky
- **London Township**, Michigan
- **London**, Minnesota
- **New London**, Minnesota
- **New London**, Missouri
- **New London**, New Hampshire
- **Little London**, Ohio
- **London**, Ohio
- **New London**, Ohio
- **London Springs**, Oregon
- **New London**, Pennsylvania
- **London**, Tennessee
- **London**, Texas
- **New London**, Texas
- **London**, West Virginia
- **London**, Wisconsin
- **New London**, Wisconsin

·The 15 Oldest Stores·

One of the joys of shopping in London today comes from discovering any number of traditional stores that have remained little changed since they were founded hundreds of years ago. These are some of the oldest:

• 1676

Lock & Co. Hatters (*6 St. James's St., SW1, tel 020 7930 8874, lockhatters .co.uk*) is both the world's oldest hat store and one of the oldest family businesses still in existence. Sir Winston Churchill, Charles Chaplin, and Admiral Lord Nelson, among other luminaries, have donned Lock headwear. Let's not forget Firmin & Sons, which doesn't retain an old store but survives as probably the third oldest business in London after the Whitechapel Bell Foundry (1570, see Small Museums, p. 192) and the *London Gazette* (1665). It made belts, buttons, uniforms, and insignia; the company supplied buttons to every British monarch, officially, since 1796.

• 1689

Ede & Ravenscroft (*93 Chancery Lane, WC2, tel 020 7405 3906, edeand ravenscroft.co.uk*). The oldest tailor, wig-, and robe-maker in London (and probably the world) began in the Aldwych area of the city. It was soon supplying robes to William and Mary and has continued to serve the monarchy, as well

Lock & Co., hatters to the rich and famous

❝London is a kind of Emporium for the whole Earth.❞

~Joseph Addison, The Spectator #69, May 19, 1711

as the legal, clerical, municipal, and academic professions.

• 1698

The "Widow Bourne" established London's oldest wine business, **Berry Brothers & Rudd** *(3 St. James's St., SW1, tel 0800 280 2440, bbr.com),* more than three centuries ago. Eight generations later, it's still in the same family, at the same address. During its long history, it first supplied the royal family in 1830 as well as the wine for the *Titanic* (see also Smallest, Shortest, Narrowest, p. 113).

• 1706

In 1706, Thomas Twining bought Tom's Coffee House at 216 Strand. The location, between the City and Westminster, was ideal for picking up business from wealthy Londoners displaced west by the Great Fire. **Twinings & Co** *(tel 020 7353 3511, twinings.co.uk)* still sells tea and coffee from the same address.

• 1707

William Fortnum was a footman at the court of Queen Anne and had a sideline selling partly burned candles from the royal candelabra. Using the money he amassed, he set up a grocery store with his landlord, Hugh Mason. The fine food emporium **Fortnum & Mason** *(181 Piccadilly, London, W1, tel 0845 300 1707, fortnumandmason .com)* remains on the same site to this day.

• 1730

Does any store smell better than **Floris** *(89 Jermyn St., SW1, tel 020 7747 3600, florislondon.com),* a perfumer still at the site on which it was founded in 1730 by Spaniard Juan Famenias Floris? Much of the store's beautiful interior dates from 1851, when the counter and wooden display cases were brought from the Great Exhibition of that year.

• 1750

Swaine Adeney Brigg *(7 Piccadilly Arcade, St. James's, SW1, tel 020 7409 7277, swaineadeney .co.uk)* still makes the exquisite leather goods for which it first became famous, along with hats and umbrellas.

• 1760

Hamleys *(188-196 Regent St., W1, tel 0871 704 1977, hamleys.com)* is the world's oldest toy store, but it has moved several times since its first incarnation—a store known as Noah's Ark founded in 1760 by William Hamley at 231 High Holborn, WC1, which was destroyed by fire in 1901.

• 1787

James J. Fox, or Robert Lewis as it then was *(19*

St. James's St., SW1, tel 020 7930 3787, jjfox.co.uk), provided possibly the most famous cigars in the world—those smoked by Sir Winston Churchill—and is the world's oldest cigar merchant. It has a museum *(closed Sun., free)*, with cigar memorabilia dating back to the firm's foundation.

• 1790
D. R. Harris & Co. *(29 St. James's St., W1, tel 020 7930 3915, drharris .co.uk)* began as Harris's Apothecary, established by surgeon Henry Harris to sell lavender water, cologne, and English flower perfumes to the fashionable set of St. James's. It is still there, a few doors down from the original address, and still sells shaving products, aftershaves, colognes, and skincare items from beautiful old premises.

• 1797
Hatchard's *(187 Piccadilly, W1, tel 020 7439 9921, hatchards.co.uk)* is the United Kingdom's oldest bookstore and still trades from Piccadilly, where the company was founded. Most of the great British authors of the recent and distant past have visited the store, which often has an extensive collection of signed copies for sale.

• 1797
Paxton & Whitfield *(93 Jermyn St., London, SW1, 020 7930 0259, paxton andwhitfield.co.uk)* smells almost as good as its nearby neighbor, Floris, but in a different way, for this is a purveyor of fine cheeses. The company has its roots in the county of Suffolk and operated a market stall at Aldwych before moving to this site in 1797.

• 1806
Henry Poole & Co. *(15 Savile Row, W1, 020 7734 5985, henrypoole.com)* is acknowledged as both the first tailor shop to set up on Savile Row (in 1846) and as the place where the dinner jacket, or tuxedo, was invented (see London Firsts, p. 78).

• 1830
There can be only one place for umbrellas, canes, and walking sticks in London: the historic premises of **James Smith & Sons** *(53 New Oxford St., WC1, tel 020 7836 4731, james-smith.co.uk)*, which have remained almost unaltered for more than 140 years—though the business is older still.

Fortnum & Mason has been a Piccadilly institution since 1707.

Heathrow Airport

Love it or hate it, odds are you've passed through Heathrow Airport at some point in your travels. For us, it's love—on arrival, at least, as that means we're back in London.

Year first opened to commercial flights 1946

Number of passengers arriving and departing, 2012 70 million (an average of more than 190,000 daily)

If those 70 million people started their own country, the world ranking in population for that country 21st

Number of flights, 2012 471,341

Average number of daily flights, 2012 1,288

Number of airlines served 84

Percentage of travelers who flew on British Air, 2012 45%

Number of destinations served 184 in 80 countries

Top five most popular destinations New York, Dubai, Dublin, Frankfurt, and Amsterdam

Number of aircraft gates 174

Busiest day ever recorded at Heathrow July 31, 2011, with 234,000 passengers

Number of terminals 5

Largest terminal Terminal 5, at 422,200 square yards (353,000 sq m)

Rank among world airports for total international passengers 1st

Old London Bridge, now spanning the waters of Lake Havasu City, Arizona

·London on the Move·

Time, war, and architectural vandalism have taken their toll on London, but a handful of treasures that might otherwise have been lost have found new homes, often far from their original sites.

• **All Hallows Tower**
London's authorities weren't to know in 1938 that the Blitz would rob the city of so many Wren masterpieces, so you can forgive them—just—for demolishing the church of All Hallows (1686) on Lombard Street, EC3, after it was deemed unsafe. Not all was lost, however, for the tower was rebuilt as part of All Hallows Church in Twickenham, which also inherited its predecessor's furniture and many of its monuments.

• **The Baltic Exchange**
The Baltic Exchange is a market for maritime derivatives whose headquarters (built for the Exchange 1903-1909) at St. Mary Axe, EC3, were damaged by an IRA bomb in 1992. After the building was razed in 1998, stained glass from the memorial to Exchange employees killed in the world wars went to the National Maritime Museum, Greenwich. The granites, marbles, plaster interiors, and more were stored until 2003, when they were bought by a salvage dealer. He sold many of the remnants

online to two Estonian businessmen for £800,000 ($1.28 million), shipping them in 49 containers to Tallinn, Estonia, in 2007, where their fate remains undecided.

• **Charles II statue**
This statue of Charles II trampling over Oliver Cromwell was commissioned by the Polish ambassador to London to show King John Sobieski of Poland riding over a defeated Turk. When the ambassador was unable to pay for the work, it was bought in 1672 by a royal admirer, Sir Robert Vyner. Sobieski acquired a new head, but "Cromwell" retained his turban. The statue was moved in 1738-1739 to make way for a new Mansion House and resided in a builder's yard until 1779, when a Vyner descendant took it to Gautby Park, Lincolnshire, the family's country home. In 1883 it moved again, this time to the grounds of Newby Hall in North Yorkshire.

St. Antholin's Spire, ca 1850

• **London Bridge**
London Bridge (opened in 1973) replaced a five-arched stone bridge that had spanned the river since 1831. It was sold in 1968 to a Missourian oil and chainsaw entrepreneur, Robert P. McCulloch, for $2,460,000 (£1,538,000). McCulloch topped off his original $2.4 million bid with another $60,000—$1,000 for each year of his age at the time he believed the bridge would be rebuilt in the United States. Around 10,000 tons of the bridge's

stones were numbered, shipped from London, and reassembled over three years in Lake Havasu City, Arizona. After it opened in 1971, ghostly figures in Victorian dress were reportedly seen walking through the surrounding scrub.

• Old London Bridge

The penultimate London Bridge (1831-1967) went to Arizona, but parts of the bridge before that—the much repaired medieval one that had stood since 1176 or 1210—remained closer to home. Two alcoves were moved to Victoria Park, Hackney, E9; a third to a courtyard in Guy's Hospital; and a fourth to Courtlands, a 1930s apartment building in East Sheen. St. Botolph's churchyard at Bishopsgate has some of the iron railings, and stones from one of the arches are incorporated into Adelaide House on King William Street, EC4.

• St. Antholin's Spire

St. Antholin (1678-1684) was one of Wren's finest churches, though this didn't stop it from being demolished in 1875 during the construction of Queen Victoria Street. However, part survives: In 1829, the spire's upper section was replaced and the original fragment sold for five pounds (eight dollars) to Robert Harrild, who eventually added it to his home, Round Hill House in Sydenham, where it remains to this day.

• St. Mary the Virgin Aldermanbury

Today, the site where St. Mary stood, at Love Lane in the City of London, is a garden noted for its statue of Shakespeare, who probably visited the church (built ca 1181) before it was destroyed in the Great Fire of 1666. The Wren church (1672-1677) that succeeded it also succumbed to fire during the Blitz, on the night of December 29, 1940. The gutted building languished for 25 years before some 7,000 of its stones were shipped to the United States and rebuilt (1965-1969) as a memorial to Sir Winston Churchill at Westminster College in Fulton, Missouri. Churchill made his famous speech describing the "iron curtain" that had descended on Europe at the college on March 5, 1946.

• Temple Bar

Temple Bar was the most important of several "bars" erected to regulate trade in and out

---

of London. It existed on Fleet Street in some form since at least 1293; in its last incarnation it was an arched Wren masterpiece from 1672. By 1878, the City of London Corporation, wishing to widen the street, dismantled it and stored its 2,700 stones. Henry Meux, a brewer, bought the 400 tons of arch with the encouragement of his wife, a former banjo-playing barmaid, and used them to build a gateway to his home, Theobalds House, in Hertfordshire. There it remained in a state of decay until purchased for £1 ($1.60) and rebuilt in 2004 in Paternoster Square alongside St. Paul's Cathedral.

• Seven Dials Obelisk

Seven Dials is a junction of seven streets in

Today's Seven Dials Obelisk

Covent Garden that, from about the 1690s, was marked by an obelisk containing six sundials (the junction then had only six streets). The area became a notorious slum, and in 1773, as part of an effort to prevent "undesirables" from congregating, the obelisk was removed (urban myth says it was torn down by the mob who believed treasure was hidden at

its base). An architect, James Paine, bought and kept the obelisk at his home in Addlestone, Surrey, before it was bought by public subscription in 1820 and moved to The Green in Weybridge, Surrey. The current obelisk at Seven Dials is a copy of the original design and was installed in 1989.

• Wellington statue

A 40-ton statue of the Duke of Wellington atop his horse, Copenhagen, made largely from cannon bronze captured at the Battle of Waterloo, was raised in 1846 on a triumphal arch at Hyde Park Corner. Road improvements in 1883 saw it toppled, and it lay in Green Park for a year before being moved to Round Hill, Aldershot, where it remains to this day.

FIRST PERSON

❝Perhaps the biggest jigsaw puzzle in the history of architecture. ❞

~The Times, 1969, on the reassembly of St. Mary the Virgin Aldermanbury in Fulton, Missouri

Ghoulish London South of the Thames

The South Bank (near Westminster Bridge) and Southwark (near London Bridge) are dueling it out for the honor of being proclaimed London's primary theme park for the macabre. Go. Sample. Scream. Enjoy.

The South Bank

The London Dungeon
(Riverside Building, County Hall, Westminster Bridge Rd., SE1, thedungeons.com)
Rides and realistic depictions of medieval torture, disease, poverty, and despair . . . perfect for a family holiday.

London's Death Trap
(Riverside Building, County Hall, Westminster Bridge Rd., SE1, londonsdeathtrap.com)
If you enjoy being chased and grabbed in dark rooms by live actors pretending to be disease-ridden ghouls . . . this is the place for you.

Southwark

The Clink Prison Museum
(1 Clink St., SE1, clink.co.uk)
On the site of the famous old jail, this is less a scare show than a real educational museum—though it nonetheless uses live actors and a creepy atmosphere to grab attention.

The London Bridge Experience
(2-4 Tooley St., SE1, thelondonbridgeexperience.com)
A time-traveling depiction of the worst of London Bridge's rich history throughout the centuries.

London Tombs (part of the London Bridge Experience)
(2-4 Tooley Street, SE1, thelondonbridgeexperience.com)
Ghosts, snakes, blood-dripped walls, ghouls, claustrophobic spaces, the various undead . . . and built on an actual plague pit to boot!

The Old Operating Theatre and Herb Garret
(9a St. Thomas St., SE1, thegarret.org.uk)
For some real-life terror, this 19th-century operating theater and its medical museum depict the nature of surgery in the days before anesthesia or proper hygiene.

·Smallest, Shortest, Narrowest·

Big cities tend to generate big statistics. But instead of biggest, highest, and longest, how about smallest, shortest, and narrowest?

• Smallest bar

The Dove Pub in Hammersmith, W6, has the smallest area of any London bar, at 4 feet 2 inches by 7 feet 10 inches (1.27 m by 2.39 m), though the Rake in Borough Market, SE1, has claims to the capital's smallest single pub. However, there are other claimants to this latter title, including the Cask and Glass at 39-41 Palace Street, SW1.

• Smallest church

The smallest church in the City of London is St. Ethelburga-the-Virgin in

10 Hyde Park Place

Bishopsgate, EC2, which dates from at least the 13th century. It measures 56 feet by 30 feet (17 m by 9.1 m).

• Smallest statue

Two tiny mice fighting over a piece of cheese have adorned the cornice at the left side of the building on the corner of Philpot Lane at

Eastcheap, EC3, since 1862. They're said to be a memorial to two men working on the Monument nearby who fell to their deaths during a scuffle when one accused the other of eating his lunchtime cheese sandwich. Mice were subsequently discovered to have been the culprits.

• Smallest police station

This circular stone former police post stands in a corner of Trafalgar Square and dates from 1926. It had space for one policeman.

• Smallest house

Historically this title has gone to 10 Hyde Park Place, W2, which dates from 1805 and measures around three

---

---

feet (95 cm) across. It is now part of Tyburn Convent, but may have been built originally to seal an alley and deprive would-be grave robbers access to the nearby St. George's churchyard.

• Smallest borough
Kensington & Chelsea is London's smallest borough by area, at 4.7 square miles (12.2 sq km).

• Smallest square
London's smallest open public space is Pickering Place, off St. James's Street, SW1—and alongside Berry Brothers and Rudd wine merchants, established by the Widow Bourne in 1698. The widow's son-in-law, James Pickering, created Pickering Court, which would later become notorious for bear-baiting; as the site of the last duel fought with swords in London; and, in a fact recorded on a plaque, the home of the legation, or embassy, "for the ministers from the Republic of Texas to the Court of St. James 1842-1845."

• Shortest street
Until it was restricted to pedestrians only in 2010, Clennam Street, SE1 (85 feet/26 m long), was often described as London's shortest "genuine" street—that is, one that has buildings on it, is separately named, and links somewhere to somewhere else. After 2010, Candover Street, W1, north of Oxford Street (135 feet/41 m), took the title.

• Smallest listed building
London's most modest "listed" (protected) building is the Ostler's Hut at Lincoln's Inn, WC2. It was built in 1860 to house the inn's ostler, a man who took care of the

Brydges Place

horses of students and other arriving guests.

• Shortest thoroughfare
Take away one of the above definitions of a street, and London's shortest thoroughfares include Leigh Hunt Street, SE1 (36 feet/ 11 m), or rather its remnant (just a street plate remains), as it was cut short by the creation of a park. Kirk Street, WC1 (50 feet/15 m), is London's shortest "street" with an address (the Dickens, a former pub), but it is a paved pedestrian-only thoroughfare.

• Shortest street name
Hide, E6. Not Hide Street or Hide Lane, just Hide. At 150 feet (45 m) in length, the street itself is not terribly long either.

• Narrowest alley
Among several challengers, Brydges Place, WC2, connecting St. Martin's Lane and Bedfordbury in Covent Garden, has a good claim to the title, narrowing to just 15 inches (38 cm).

•Antiquated Laws of Years Past•

Practicing archery was required by law in late medieval London.

England has been around for quite a while, and during the centuries has accumulated all sorts of laws that to us may seem quaint at best, gruesome at worst. To wit:

• **Under Norman law,** a slanderer was forced to stand in the town market, hold his nose between his fingers, and publicly declare himself a liar. And also pay damages.

• **Richard I issued a law in the late 12th century** spelling out the punishment for sailors caught stealing en route to the Holy Land during the Third Crusade: "Whosoever is convicted of theft shall have his head shaved, melted pitch poured upon it, and the feathers from a pillow be shaken over it . . . and shall be put on shore on the first land that the ship touches."

• **The 1275 Statute of Westminster** directed that people who refused to enter a plea of guilty or not guilty to the courts be starved into submission. The problem appears to have persisted: In 1405, a new law required those who refused to enter pleas to be chained to the ground with weights piled on top of them until they either made a plea . . . or were crushed to death.

• Under Edward I, in about 1281, it was commanded that, "no woman of the City shall from henceforth go . . . out of her house, with a hood furred with other than lambskin or rabbitskin, on pain of losing her hood to the Sherrifs . . . And this, because . . . nurses, and other servants, and women of loose life, bedizen themselves, and wear hoods furred with gros vair [costly pelts] . . . in guise of good ladies." Similar laws, aimed at keeping the social classes distinguishable, were later enacted.

• The Royal Prerogative of 1324 decrees that any whale or sturgeon caught or washed up on the British coast is a "royal fish" and belongs to the monarch.

• Edward III passed the Sumptuary Act in 1336, making it illegal for any man to have more than two courses at any meal. And don't try to claim to the judge that the soup you were eating was a sauce and not a complete course; the law directly addressed this clever maneuver.

• In 1346, under Edward III, a royal mandate banished lepers from London. The law notes that, "many people . . . being smitten with the blemish of leprosy, do publicly dwell among the other citizens and sound persons, and there continually abide; . . . and that some of them, endeavoring to contaminate others with that abominable blemish, (so that, to their own wretched solace, they may have more

fellows in suffering) . . . do so taint persons who are sound."

• In the late 14th century, under Richard II, an ordinance for pastelers (piebakers) required that, "no one of the said trade shall bake rabbit in pastries for sale . . . Also, that no one shall bake beef in a pastry for sale, and sell it as venison." This because "the pastelers have heretofore baked in pastries rabbits, geese, and garbage (incl giblets), not befitting, and sometimes stinking, in deceit of the people."

• In 1419, a regulation was made that "Serjeants and other officers of the Mayor, Sheriffs, or City, shall not beg for Christmas gifts." It seems these folks "have begged many sums

---

FAST FACT

Medieval bakers were so fearful of being accused of short-selling (punishment for which ranged from public humiliation to destruction of their ovens), they threw in a 13th loaf for every dozen sold—hence, the baker's dozen.

Faux Guy Fawkeses keep up the spirit of the now repealed Observance of 5th November Act.

of money of brewers, bakers, cooks, and other victuallers; and in some instances have more than once threatened wrongfully to do them an injury if they should refuse to give them something." Punk 15th-century serjeants.

• **A law enacted by Edward VI in the 16th century** mandated that anybody found breaking a boiled egg at the narrower end be sentenced to 24 hours in the stocks. To which we say: Let's bring that law back, just for fun.

• **The Unlawful Games Act of 1541** made a variety of games illegal, mainly because it was distracting Englishmen from their archery. The Act required that every able-bodied male between the ages of 17 and 60 keep a long-bow and arrows in his house and practice his shooting; it also mandated that any "man-child" between the ages of 7 and 17 be taught archery.

• **After the failed Gunpowder Plot of Guy Fawkes in 1605,** the Observance of 5th November Act was passed that same year; it mandated that every Englishman celebrate "with unfeigned thankfullness . . . the joyful day of deliverance . . . for all

FAST FACT

Most laws passed during the interregnum were simply ignored once Charles II reclaimed the throne in 1660.

ages to come." Well, it worked—although the law was repealed in 1859, Guy Fawkes Day is still a major annual event.

• **James I passed a law in 1623** that sentenced anyone going bankrupt to two hours in the pillory. And having his ear nailed to the pillory. Oh, and then having his ear cut off after the two hours. More incentive to balance your checkbook.

• **Henry VIII passed a law** mandating that shoes be no more than six inches in width at the toe. At the time, prominent square-toed shoes were the fashion rage.

• **Elizabeth I banned** any woman from duping a man into marriage by using any duplicitous devices such as false hair, makeup, or high-heeled shoes. And she wasn't kidding: Offenders were punished as if they were witches.

• **Ever the zealots, the Puritans passed a law in 1648** making it a capital offense to deny the Trinity or to doubt that the Old Testament books of Habakkuk, Zephaniah, Haggai, Zecharia, and Malachai were the word of God.

• **For a while, it was illegal to be the king of England.** In 1649, during the interregnum of Oliver Cromwell, Parliament passed a law declaring that it was high treason to adopt the "name, style, dignity, power, prerogative or authority of king of England."

• **Cromwell also mandated that mince pies not be eaten at Christmas** (as it was believed the custom had pagan origins).

• **George I passed a law in the early 18th century** that made it an offense for the animal of a commoner "to have carnal knowledge of a pet of the Royal House."

Interesting Old Laws About Parliament:

• A law passed in 1313 by Edward II and still in force makes it illegal to enter the Houses of Parliament in a suit of armor or to be otherwise armed.

• In 1351, Edward III declared that "it is forbidden, on pain of imprisonment, that any child . . . shall play in any place in the Palace of Westminster, during the Parliament . . . such as taking off the hoods of people, or laying hands upon them . . . or in other ways causing hindrance." Punk 14th-century kids.

• It is forbidden to die in the Houses of Parliament. Or, at least, the body must be removed before a death certificate is issued (to prevent having every dying MP become eligible for a state funeral, which is the practice for anyone expiring in a Royal Palace such as the Palace of Westminster).

Crimes for Which You Could Be Executed in 1800

Starting in the late 17th century, the number of capital offenses on the books in England began to increase dramatically (from about 50 in 1660 to 288 by 1815). The general prosperity of the realm combined with the burgeoning industrial revolution created a wealthy and powerful middle class intent on maintaining its property and interests. This inspired Parliament to enact a series of harsh laws that was later termed the "bloody code." The following were all capital offenses in the early 19th century:

- arson (including setting fire to haystacks)
- assaulting or obstructing a revenue officer
- beastiality
- being seen in the company of gypsies
- burglary
- carnally abusing girls under the age of ten
- cutting down a young tree in gardens or on avenues
- false coining
- damaging Westminster or Fulham Bridge
- deer hunting, stealing, or killing
- embezzling (by servants of the Bank of England)
- extortion
- forging a birth certificate or baptism/marriage record
- forging a cheque
- highway robbery
- horse/cattle/sheep-stealing
- house-breaking

- impersonating a Chelsea Pensioner
- manslaughter
- murder
- pilfering from a Navy Dockyard
- piracy
- rape
- rioting
- robbing the mails
- sacrilege
- shoplifting
- showing false signals to cause shipwreck
- stealing in a dwelling house
- stealing from a shipwreck
- stealing on board a barge or or ship
- suicide (including failed suicide attempts)
- taking false oaths to receive a seaman's wages
- treason
- unlawful shooting at a person (even if the shot missed)

With so many laws, there were inevitable inconsistencies. It was only a misdemeanor to attempt to kill one of your parents, for example, but to pick a pocket of more than a shilling was punishable by death.

FAST FACT

The age of criminal responsibility in England in 1800 was seven. It was a sad matter of course for children under the age of ten to be charged with crimes and executed.

Noteworthy Executions Around Town

Ah, executions—unfortunately, we'd need a whole book to cover this list adequately. Here's a list of some of the more noteworthy executions in London's happy history:

William Fitz Osbert (leader of an early peasant rebellion and the first man executed at Tyburn)—Hanged, 1196

William Wallace (Scottish nationalist leader)—Hanged, drawn, and quartered at Smithfield, 1305

Roger Mortimer (lover of Edward II's wife, Queen Isabella, and rumored murderer of the king)—Hanged at Tyburn, 1330

William, Lord Hastings (Lord Chancellor of Edward IV)—Beheaded on Tower Green, 1483

Perkin Warbeck (Frenchman who proclaimed himself to be one of the lost Princes in the Tower and pretender to the throne)—Hanged at Tyburn, 1499

James Tyrrell (possible/confessed murderer of the Princes in the Tower)—Beheaded on Tower Hill, 1502

Cromwell's posthumous execution of 1661

Thomas More (philosopher/Councillor to Henry VIII)—Beheaded on Tower Hill, 1535

Queen Anne Boleyn (second wife of Henry VIII)—Beheaded on Tower Green, 1536

Thomas Cromwell (Councillor to Henry VIII)—Beheaded on Tower Hill, 1540

Queen Catherine Howard (fifth wife of Henry VIII)—Beheaded on Tower Green, 1542

Lady Jane Grey (proclaimed queen for nine days in 1553)—Beheaded on Tower Green, 1554

Guy Fawkes (and the three other conspirators of the Gunpowder Plot to blow up Parliament)—Hanged, drawn, and quartered, Old Palace Yard, Westminster, 1606

Sir Walter Raleigh (explorer and nobleman)—Beheaded, Old Palace Yard, Westminster, 1618

Oliver Cromwell (Lord Protector of the Commonwealth)—Hanged posthumously at Tyburn, 1661

Captain Kidd (Scottish pirate)—Hanged at Execution Dock, Wapping, 1701 (The rope broke on the first try, but he died on the second attempt.)

Jack Sheppard (popular English highwayman thief and jailbreaker)—Hanged at Tyburn, 1724

George Davis and William Watts (sailors convicted of murdering a ship captain, and the last men hanged at Execution Dock)—1830

Josef Jakobs (German spy and the last man executed at the Tower)—Shot in the Tower's rifle range, 1941

FAST FACT

Bodies of pirates were left hanging at Execution Dock on the shore of the Thames until three tides had washed over them.

Fun London Laws Still on the Books

The Metropolitan Police Act of 1839 (which has never been repealed) is a treasure trove to entertaining laws. It's illegal in London, or at least a civic offense . . .

to roll "any cask, tub, hoop, or wheel . . . on any footway, except for the purpose of loading or unloading any cart or carriage."

to fly a kite on a public thoroughfare, slide on ice or snow, build bonfires, set off fireworks, ring doorbells (without a lawful excuse, mind you), or "willfully extinguish the light of any lamp." What killjoys.

to be found drunk in a pub. More accurately, it's illegal for a pub owner to allow you to get drunk in a pub. But still.

to fire a cannon ("or other firearm of greater calibre than a common fowling-piece") within 300 yards (274 m) of a dwelling house. (And, in case you wondered, it's also not okay to point your cannon AT a dwelling house from within 300 yards.)

to "beat or shake any carpet, rug or mat in any street" . . . but it is permitted to shake a doormat, as long as you do it before 8:00 a.m.

to keep a pigsty in front of your house unless duly hidden.

to sing any "profane, indecent, or obscene song or ballad or write or draw any indecent or obscene word, figure, or representation."

for any servant to stand on the sill of any window to clean or paint it.

to clean your privy between the hours of 6:00 a.m. and midnight.

to blow any horn (or "use any other noisy instrument") unless you're a guardsman or a postman.

and (our personal favorite) for anyone who "lives within a mile of any arsenal or store for explosives" to own a pack of playing cards.

·Infamous Murders and Their Locations·

The 1888 murders in Whitechapel were ascribed to the still unidentified Jack the Ripper.

Amsterdam has the highest murder rate in Western Europe with 4.4 murders per 100,000 people, followed by Glasgow (3.3), and Brussels (3). New York's rate is 5.6; London's 1.6 (2012). Although London's historical rate is also low, some of the murders in the city over the years, and their locations, have become among the world's most notorious.

• **Whitechapel, E1**
Five Whitechapel locations and five or more murders may or may not be linked to Jack the Ripper. In 1888, the locations were known as Buck's Row (now Durward Street); Hanbury Street; Dutfield's Yard on Berner Street (now Henriques Street); Mitre Square; and Miller's Court, Dorset Street. The murders began in 1888 and ended abruptly the same year. The murderer

or murderers have never been identified.

• **16 Batty Street, E1**
The murder here in 1887 of lodger Miriam Angel—six months pregnant, killed by having nitric acid forced down her throat—was attributed to Israel Lipski. Lipski—who was found under Angel's bed with burns in his mouth—pleaded his innocence and blamed two fellow umbrella salesmen for the

crime. His controversial trial raised accusations of anti-Semitism, but he was convicted and hanged in Newgate Prison.

• 39 Hilldrop Crescent, N7

In 1905, this address in north London was home to Michigan-born "Dr." Hawley Harvey Crippen, who poisoned his wife and then fled to Canada with his mistress. His crime was discovered, and he was arrested on his arrival in Quebec. He was hanged in 1910.

• 79 Gloucester Road, SW7

John Haigh—the "Acid Bath Murderer"—killed the first of his six (he would claim nine) victims in the basement here, placed the body in sulphuric acid, and two days later disposed of the resultant sludge down a manhole. Haigh killed his victims for their money and used acid to dispose of all the bodies. He mistakenly believed if no body could be found then no murder could be proved. He was undone by superb forensic work and hanged at Wandsworth Prison in 1949.

• The Blind Beggar, Whitechapel Road, E1

This East End pub is notorious as the place where Ronnie Kray, one of the Kray Twins—London's most infamous post-war gangsters—killed rival gang member George Cornell by shooting him through the eye in 1966. In 1904, a petty villain known as "Bulldog" Wallis stabbed a man to death in the same pub by driving an umbrella into his eye.

• 10 Rillington Place, W11

John Christie killed at least eight people here between 1940 (or possibly 1943) and 1953. Bodies were left buried in the garden and hidden in the house—an innocent man, Timothy John Evans, was hanged for one of the murders after police failed to search the property properly. The house and street have since been obliterated, and Bartle Road—not Ruston Mews, as is often claimed—is the nearest street to the scene of the crimes.

• 195 Melrose Avenue, NW2

Dennis Nilson lured 12 lovers back to this address between 1978 and 1983 and murdered them in their sleep or when they tried to leave. He killed three other victims after moving to 23 Cranley Gardens in Muswell Hill. The crimes were discovered when workmen summoned to unblock drains found them choked with human flesh. Upon arriving at the house, police found a human head in a cooking pot on the stove.

FAST FACT

A World War II bomb destroyed Dr. Crippen's former home. Margaret Bondfield House now stands on the site.

London's Bobbies

lthough the word "bobby" usually refers to a London police-man on the beat, we'll use it to encompass the entire London police force.

Person for whom the word "bobby" was coined Sir Robert Peel, who formed the Metropolitan Police Service in 1829

Current officers on the Metropolitan Police Force 32,400

Officers on the Metropolitan Police Force in 1952 16,400

Number of horses employed by the Metropolitan Police Force 120

Year in which the first (horse-drawn) police vans were introduced 1858

Number of police officers dismissed in 1863 for drunkenness 215

Minimum height requirement for police officers in 1870 5 feet 8 inches (173 cm)

Most famous unsolved crime Jack the Ripper's rampage, 1888

Reasons for which most candidates for the force were rejected under new rules issued in 1895 flat feet, stiffness of joints, narrow chests, and deformities of the face

Number of police cameras currently in use throughout London 7,431

Number of police cameras currently in use throughout Paris 326

·Great Riots and Disturbances·

The Gordon Riots—a late 18th century anti-Catholic rampage

Historically, London should have been a recipe for violent disorder: huge numbers of people, most of them poor; cramped and miserable living conditions; and a small or virtually nonexistent police force until comparatively recently. The city was also the seat of power, and thus a natural focus for discontent. But in truth, while medieval and later London was often a dangerous and unpleasant place, it should probably have seen more, and worse, civic unrest over the centuries. That said, when things got out of hand, they often did so to spectacular effect. Here are some of the most infamous examples:

• 1517, Evil May Day
On May 1, after a rabble-rousing call for "Englishmen to cherish and defend themselves, and to hurt and drive out aliens," John Lincoln led a mob through the city killing and destroying the property of foreign merchants and artisans accused of taking Londoners' jobs and livelihoods. Troops restored order, and only Lincoln and 12 others were executed.

• 1668, The Bawdy House Riots
London apprentices had long made ritualized attacks on brothels, or "bawdy houses," on

Shrove Tuesday. High spirits were usual, but things got more out of hand than usual in 1668, possibly because of resentment at the extravagance of Charles II's recently restored royal court. Thousands rioted throughout five days. At least four ringleaders were found guilty of high treason and hanged, drawn, and quartered.

The inflammatory Sir Oswald Mosley

next 64 days continued to rebel, albeit more good-naturedly, bringing whistles, rattles, trumpets, and even farmyard animals to make their point as noisily as possible. The pre-fire prices were eventually restored.

• 1780, The Gordon Riots

This string of riots, rooted in anti-Catholic sentiment, was sparked during a march by the Protestant Association and led by Lord George Gordon on the House of Commons. During the days of violent chaos that followed, numerous Catholic and other buildings, including the Bank of England and Newgate Prison, were looted, attacked, and burned. At least 565, and perhaps as many as 850, people were killed, and 25 of the 160 rioters arrested were executed—though not Gordon.

• 1809, Old Price Riots

In 1808 Covent Garden Theatre burned down. When it reopened ticket prices were raised. Theatergoers at the first performance (*Macbeth*) were outraged, shouting "Old price, old price!" They then ran amok. Audiences during the

• 1855, Hyde Park Riots

Karl Marx, then working in London, had high hopes for this riot, writing the following: "We do not think we are exaggerating in saying that the English Revolution began yesterday in Hyde Park." The disturbances were sparked by a proposal to abolish Sunday trading. As Sunday was the only day most working people had off, this would have prevented many from buying food and other goods. Running battles with soldiers broke out

FIRST PERSON

❝. . . the guards and militia of the town have been in armes all this night . . . and the 'prentices have made fools of them, sometimes by running from them and flinging stones at them. Some blood hath been spilt . . .❞

~Samuel Pepys's diary entry *Wednesday, March 25, 1668*

among the crowd that had assembled in the park to protest. The riot was quickly put down and the proposals quietly abandoned.

• 1936, The Battle of Cable Street

On October 4, a crowd variously estimated from 100,000 to 250,000 gathered to prevent a march led by Sir Oswald Mosley, leader of the British Union of Fascists, through areas of the East End with large Jewish populations. Barricades on Cable Street led to a confrontation between protesters, marchers (possibly as many as 5,000), and 6,000 police. Mosley agreed to end the march after 175 people, including women and children, were injured.

• 1958, Notting Hill Riots

A series of incidents during the summer of 1958 in Notting Hill, home to many immigrants from the Caribbean, flared into riots on the holiday weekend at the end of August as gangs of white youths burned buildings and attacked locals. By September 5, police had arrested 140 rioters; 108 were charged and nine defendants were given "exemplary" sentences of five years' imprisonment. The Notting Hill Carnival was founded a year later in St. Pancras Town Hall as a response to the riots, and still takes place in the Notting Hill area during the last weekend in August.

• 1990, Poll Tax Riots

The "poll tax"—officially the Community Charge—was a per-person levy designed to replace the tiered property taxes ("rates") used to finance council (City Hall) spending. A demonstration in Trafalgar Square on March 31, 1990, against its introduction erupted into rioting that spread throughout the West End. Shops were looted, and more than 100 people were injured and 334 were arrested. Widespread noncompliance and nonpayment of the tax eventually led to its demise.

The Notting Hill race riots raged for a week in 1958.

·A Thousand Years of London's Tallest Structures·

Here's how the highest point in London has changed during the course of almost 1,000 years. Dates and heights are necessarily approximate for early structures: Elsewhere dates are given for completion or "topping out," and heights include spires and masts.

• 1098-ca 1310
White Tower
90 feet/27.4 m

The White Tower survives to this day. The tower and central keep of the Tower of London was begun between 1075 and 1078. It may have replaced a wooden palisade, William the Conqueror's earliest fortification on the site after the Norman Conquest.

• ca 1310-1666
Old St. Paul's Cathedral

St. Paul's Cathedral

493 feet/150.2 m
(estimate)

London and the Western world's tallest building when it was completed, but only briefly: Lincoln Cathedral in eastern England, probably completed in 1311, was taller. But when Lincoln's spire fell in 1549, St. Paul's regained its worldwide preeminence. Lightning toppled St. Paul's own spire in 1561, but the surviving part of the cathedral remained London's and the world's tallest structure.

• 1666-1677
Southwark Cathedral
163 feet/49.7 m

When Old St. Paul's was damaged in the Great Fire of London in 1666 and subsequently demolished, the title of London's tallest structure passed to this church on the south bank of the Thames. While the building itself probably dates back to the 12th century or earlier, the central tower that made it the capital's tallest point was completed in 1520.

• 1677-1680
The Monument
202 feet/61.6 m

This column (1671-1677) commemorates the 1666 Great Fire. Its height—202 feet (61.6 m)—is also its precise distance from the site of the Pudding Lane bakery where the fire started.

FIRST PERSON

❝I don't know what London's coming to—the higher the buildings, the lower the morals.**❞**

~**Noël Coward,** *"Law and Order,"* Collected Sketches and Lyrics, *1931*

**St. Mary-le-Bow features in the famous "church" nursery rhyme
"Oranges and Lemons": "I do not know/Says the great bell of Bow."**

• 1680-1710
**St. Mary-le-Bow
224 feet/68.3 m**
St. Mary-le-Bow has at
least 11th-century origins
and has long been con-
sidered the most import-
ant church in the City of
London after St. Paul's.
Tradition has it that you
must be born within ear-
shot of its bell to be a real
Cockney. After architect
Christopher Wren rebuilt
the church (1671-1673),
its new spire, completed
after 1677, became Lon-
don's highest point.

• 1710-1962
**St. Paul's Cathedral
365 feet/111.3 m**
In 1661, five years before
the Great Fire, Wren was
consulted about renovat-
ing the old St. Paul's; he
proposed replacing the
dilapidated tower with
a dome. Work began on
the new St. Paul's in 1675
and the cathedral, com-
plete with Wren's dome,
was finished in 1710. The
structure would remain

London's highest point
for more than 250 years.

It's worth noting two
rival claims. Some main-
tain that Battersea Power
Station, completed in
1935, just pipped St. Paul's
at 370 feet (112.8 m),
depending upon where
you measured; others say
that its towers fell short
at 338 feet (103 m). Then
came the Crystal Palace
TV transmitter in the
1950s. It reaches 720 feet
(219 m), but is discounted
by many who are unim-
pressed by its freestand-
ing metal lattice tower
and claim (falsely) that
it's not really in London.

• 1962-1990
**BT Tower
614 feet/188 m**
The Post Office Tower, as it
was originally known, over-
took St. Paul's Cathedral as
London's tallest structure
during its construction in
1962. However, it was briefly
superseded by the 1963
Vickers Tower (now Mill-
bank) at 387 feet/118 m; the

Post Office Tower regained
its crown as it neared
completion. Without its
masts, the tower would
have been superseded
in 1981 by the NatWest
Tower (now Tower 42) at
600 feet (183 m).

• 1990-2012
**One Canada Square
800 feet/243.8 m**
Most Londoners know
this 50-story Docklands
office building, errone-
ously, as Canary Wharf.

• 2012-present
**The Shard
1,016 feet/309.6 m**
This 87-story skyscraper
near London Bridge
takes its name from
its distinctive shape.
Although it is the
highest freestanding
structure in London, the
Arqiva Tower in West
Yorkshire, better known
as the Emley Moor
Transmitting Station, is
the highest freestanding
structure in Britain, at
1,084 feet (330.4 m).

·Where Famous Londoners Lived·

If you've ever walked the streets of London, you've no doubt come across the famous blue plaques that are mounted outside select buildings, announcing which person of merit once lived inside. The program to erect plaques began in the 1860s as a way to help preserve the buildings themselves.

The Blue Plaque outside Charles Dickens's house on Doughty Street

There are nearly 900 plaques in London now. A panel of experts meets three times a year to decide who warrants one. If you're hoping your house will be so honored, you may want to know that, to be eligible, you must be dead for at least 20 years or have been born at least 100 years earlier.

• **J. M. Barrie (1860-1937)**
100 Bayswater Rd., W2
The novelist and playwright wrote *Peter Pan* at this home.

• **Thomas Becket (ca 1118-1170)**
86 Cheapside, EC2
The future Archbishop of Canterbury, martyr, and saint was born in a house near this marker in about 1118.

• **Vice Admiral Bligh (1754-1817)**
100 Lambeth Rd., SE1
The famous commander of the *Bounty* lived for a short time here in his post-mutiny days. (Bligh survived the 1789 mutiny and saw three of the mutineers hanged.)

• **Simón Bolívar (1783-1830)**
4 Duke St., W1
The Venezuelan political and military leader/liberator/revolutionary lodged briefly in this Marylebone residence in 1810.

• **Elizabeth Barrett Browning (1806-1861)**
50 Wimpole St., W1 (as in *The Barretts of Wimpole Street*)
The poet's romance with playwright and fellow poet Robert Browning began here.

• **Richard Burton (1925-1984)**
6 Lyndhurst Rd., NW3
One of the acting world's leading men in the 1960s, Burton lived in this Hampstead home from 1949 to 1956.

• Sir Winston Churchill (1874-1965)
28 Hyde Park Gate, SW7
Britain's prime minister lived and died here.

• Charles Dickens (1812-1870)
48 Doughty St., WC1
Dickens wrote *Oliver Twist* during the two years (1837-1839) he lived at this house in Bloomsbury. It's the author's only surviving London residence.

• Benjamin Franklin (1706-1790)
36 Craven St., WC2
Franklin arrived in London in 1757 as agent to the General Assembly of Pennsylvania. He lived in this house just south of the Strand for 16 of the next 18 years before leaving England for good in 1775.

• Sigmund Freud (1856-1939)
20 Maresfield Gardens, NW3
The father of psychoanalysis called this Hampstead address home during the year before his death in 1939.

• Mahatma Gandhi (1869-1948)
Kingsley Hall, Powis Rd., E3
Gandhi stayed in this East London settlement house during his London visit in 1931. Gandhi has a second plaque at 20 Baron's Court Road, W14, where he lived as a law student.

• Sir Alfred Hitchcock (1899-1980)
153 Cromwell Rd., SW5
The master-of-suspense film director and producer lived in this South Kensington house from 1926 to 1939.

• Dr. Samuel Johnson (1709-1784)

17 Gough Square, EC4
Johnson's house was very close to the Ye Olde Cheshire Cheese pub (still going strong), which was the favorite haunt of the lexiconer and his friends, including his biographer James Boswell, Oliver Goldsmith, Sir Joshua Reynolds, and others.

• John Keats (1795-1821)
Wentworth Place, Keats Grove, NW3
The Romantic poet developed his ultimately fatal case of consumption at this house in northwest London. Keats has a second plaque at 85 Moorgate, EC2, to mark the spot of his birth in 1795.

• Vivien Leigh (1913-1967)
54 Eaton Square, SW1
This Belgravia home was the residence of two-time Academy Award–winning British actress Vivien Leigh.

FAST FACT

The first blue plaque was erected in 1867 on Holles Street (W1), near Oxford Circus, at the site of Lord Byron's birthplace. The plaque no longer exists, as the building was razed 22 years later.

• **John Lennon (1940-1980)**
34 Montagu Square, W1
The musician and songwriter lived in this Marylebone home in 1968.

• **Guglielmo Marconi (1874-1937)**
71 Hereford Rd., W2
This was the inventor of wireless radio technology's home for a few months in 1896. It was here that he first demonstrated the new technology.

• **Sir Thomas More (1478-1535)**
20 Milk St., EC2
The Renaissance-man counselor to Henry VIII (and later Catholic saint) was born near the site of this plaque in February 1478.

• **Wolfgang Amadeus Mozart (1756-1791)**
180 Ebury St., SW1
Mozart has one plaque on Ebury Street, where he composed his first symphony at age eight in 1764. He also has another plaque at 20 Frith Street in Soho, where he lived

Oscar Wilde's plaque in Chelsea

as a boarder with his father and sister and entertained as a musical prodigy in 1765.

• **Horatio Nelson (1758-1805)**
103 New Bond St., W1
The hero of the Battle of Trafalgar lived in this Westminster house in 1798.

• **Napoleon III (1808-1873)**
1c King St., SW1
Listed, appropriately, right after Lord Nelson (who defeated his uncle Napoleon Bonaparte at Trafalgar), the emperor of France lived in exile in St. James's in 1848.

• **Florence Nightingale (1820-1910)**
10 South St., W1
Famed for her

compassion tending to wounded soldiers during the Crimean War, the nurse lived in a house on this site in Westminster.

• **Alfred, Lord Tennyson (1809-1892)**
9 Upper Belgrave St., SW1
The poet who would rather have loved and lost than never have loved at all called this house in Belgravia home from 1880 to 1881.

• **Oscar Wilde (1854-1900)**
34 Tite St., SW3
The Irish dramatist and his wife moved into this Chelsea house in 1884 and remained until his arrest for "gross indecency" in 1895.

• **Virginia Woolf (1882-1941)**
29 Fitzroy Square, W1
This writer and founding figure of the Bloomsbury Group lived here (yes, in Bloomsbury) from 1907 to 1911. The house was once the home of playwright George Bernard Shaw as well.

·Romantic London·

Your intrepid authors are (we like to think) two rugged guys who would just as soon be playing a hard-tackling soccer match in Regent's Park or rhythm guitar in a gritty Brixton club as trying to determine if it's a daisy or peony bouquet that most effectively says "I love you very much" ... so we admit we may not be the best ones to select London's most romantic places and activities. But we checked with some of our friends and are feeling good about the results.

• Browse the flowers and shop on Columbia Road *(columbiaroad.info)* Open on Sundays only, the Columbia Road Flower Market in East London is the perfect spot to test out those daisy and peony bouquets. You can wander the colorful flower stalls before shopping for antiques or art at one of the street's many boutiques and galleries. Then share some cakes at Lily Vanilli *(lilyvanilli .com)* in a little courtyard off Ezra Street (see Best Markets, p. 203).

• Ice-skate at Somerset House *(November to early January, somersethouse.org .uk/ice-rink)* Spend a lovely winter evening ice-skating with your best gal or guy in front of Somerset House's 18th-century facade. Warm up afterward with mulled wine or hot chocolate at Tom's Skate Lounge overlooking the rink.

• Picnic on Hampstead Heath Boasting some of the city's finest views, Hampstead Heath—with nearly 800 acres (324 ha) of space to spread your blanket—is a great spot for a quiet picnic. Although the name doesn't evoke cuddling, the Hampstead Butcher (56 Rosslyn Hill, NW3, *hampsteadbutcher.com*) in Hampstead village has all the wine, bread, and cheese you need for your lunch out on the hillside.

• Row on Hyde Park's Serpentine *(Easter to*

Rowing among the swans on the Serpentine

October, royalparks.org .uk)

Pick a warm summer day, hire a pedal boat or rowboat for two, and glide among the swans on the Serpentine's 40 acres (16 ha) of calm waters. Don't miss the 150-year-old Italian Gardens at the northern edge of the lake.

• Share a flute (two straws, please) at the Champagne Bar

(Upper Concourse, St. Pancras International Station, N1, searcys.co.uk)
Champagne = romance, so a fine option (especially if you're en route to Paris for even *more* romance) is the Searcys St. Pancras Champagne Bar at St. Pancras station. The impressive 322-foot-long (98 m) bar features 17 varieties of bubbly by the glass. While you're in the area, take a gander at the recently renovated St. Pancras Renaissance London Hotel (see Railway Hotels, p. 36), which

proclaims itself the city's "most romantic building."

• Trot through Hyde Park

(hydeparkstables.com)
Take the reins and lope through Hyde Park, including the famous

Riding in Hyde Park

Rotten Row bridle path. Hyde Park Stables offers year-round horseback riding. Be sure to wave to your fellow romantics in the boats as you amble past the Serpentine.

• Sample chocolate for two

(William Curley, 198

Ebury St., SW1, william curley.com)
With the chocolate-lover lover in your life, stop at the flagship store of William Curley in Belgravia and partake of all the sweet trimmings your heart could desire (including a weekend-only Dessert Bar). From there, it's not too long a walk (you just ate a pound of chocolate; the exercise will do you good) to the Victoria & Albert Museum on Cromwell Road, which has been voted Britain's most romantic museum.

• Walk in Little Venice

This stretch of the Grand Canal in northwest London is a surprising and quiet haven just off the busy Edgware Road. Colorful houseboats moored on the charming and tranquil waterways make the area a delight to stroll (hand in hand, of course). Best spots are Blomfield Road and Brownings Pool.

Best Views From Bars and Restaurants

London has many bars and restaurants that serve up outstanding views.
These are some of the best:

Coq d'Argent

(No.1 Poultry, EC2, tel 020 7395 5000, coqdargent.co.uk)
A popular City of London restaurant, with a panoramic rooftop garden.

Madison Restaurant, Tapas & Cocktail Bar

(1 New Change, EC4, tel 020 8305 3088, madisonlondon.net)
There's nowhere better for a close-up view of St. Paul's Cathedral.

OXO Tower Bar and Brasserie

(OXO Tower Wharf, Barge House St., SE1, tel 020 7803 3888, harveynichols.com)
One of London's most iconic river views—the Houses of Parliament.

Paramount Restaurant, Centre Point

(101-103 New Oxford St., WC1, tel 020 7420 2900, paramount.uk.net)
Boasts 360-degree views and claims to offer the city's "highest afternoon tea."

Radio Rooftop Bar, ME Hotel

(336-337 The Strand, WC2, tel 0808 234 1953, melia.com)
This glamorous bar offers a view that extends to almost every major and famous
element of the city's skyline.

Tate Modern Restaurant

(Bankside, SE1, tel 020 7887 8888, tate.org.uk)
Gaze out the vast windows and admire the City of London skyline.

Vertigo 42

(Tower 42, 25 Old Broad St., EC2, tel 020 7877 7842, vertigo42.co.uk)
Majestic views from this sleek Champagne bar on the 42nd floor of a
City of London skyscraper.

Vista Bar, Trafalgar Hotel

(2 Spring Gardens, SW1, tel 020 7870 2900, thetrafalgar.com)
Get some idea of the view Nelson is enjoying at this bar high above Trafalgar Square.

·Some Intriguing Items in the British Museum·

We were thinking of trying to list either the oldest, the most important, or the oddest items among the millions and millions of artifacts in the British Museum. But we ended up settling on some of the most interesting.

• Flood tablet

This seventh-century B.C. Mesopotamian tablet relates a portion of *The Epic of Gilgamesh,* considered to be the world's oldest written work of literature. This part of the epic relates the Noah-esque story of Utnapishtim, who learns of the gods' plans to flood the world. Utnapishtim constructs a boat to save skilled craftsmen, his possessions and family, and animals of all sorts.

• The H.M.S. *Beagle's* chronometer

Chronometers were timekeepers for ships at sea, and this specimen was used onboard the H.M.S. *Beagle,* the vessel that took Charles Darwin around the world from 1831 to 1836 while he considered the origin of species.

• Jomon pot

Created about 7,000 years ago by the Jomon hunter-gatherers in Japan, this ancient relic is among the world's earliest known cooking pots. The Jomon's food-rich environment allowed them the relative luxury of settling in one spot for several years at a time. These very early settled communities produced pots—something that would await the invention of agriculture in other parts of the world.

• **The Lewis chessmen**
Created around 1175, probably in Norway, these detailed and charming ivory chess pieces—the expressions on their little chess-piece faces are full of personality—were discovered off the west coast of Scotland in 1831.

• **A mechanical galleon**
This 16th-century "automaton" used the mechanisms of a clock to animate a gilded mini-ship. Built in what is now Germany, it would have rolled down a wealthy dining-room table, playing music, striking the hours, with the crew moving and

The British Museum's impressive "mechanical galleon"

miniature cannons firing.

• **The Parthenon sculptures**
Sometimes called the Elgin Marbles, these sculptures were created in the fifth century B.C., during ancient Greece's golden age, to decorate Athens' greatest building: the Parthenon, Temple of Athena. In the early 19th century, Lord

The Lewis chessmen are so called because they were discovered (in a sand dune) on the Outer Hebrides island of Lewis.

Examples of the medieval Lewis Chessmen

Elgin, Britain's ambassador to the Ottoman rulers of Greece, brought many of the surviving sculptures to London.

• **The Rosetta Stone**
Can't miss this one. Carved in 196 B.C. and discovered in 1799, the Rosetta Stone was the key that unlocked the secrets of ancient Egyptian hieroglyphics. It was written in three scripts, but scholars used the familiar Greek words to decipher the two other sets of writing: the hieroglyphic and demotic characters of the Egyptians.

• **A stone chopping tool**
This unassuming lump of gray rock from Olduvai Gorge in Tanzania is one of the oldest pieces in the museum's entire collection. Two million years old, it's an example of one of the very first tools intentionally created by humans. It was used for chopping, cutting, and scraping.

• **Statue of Tara**
An eighth-century Sri Lankan gilded bronze statue of the Buddhist goddess Tara, this willowy figurine is considered one of the most beautiful human images in the museum.

• **The Sutton Hoo Treasure**
A sixth- or seventh-century royal burial ship, unearthed and excavated at Sutton Hoo in East Anglia in 1939, contained the greatest riches of Anglo-Saxon jewelry, weapons, armor, drinking horns and cups, gold, coins, clothes (etc.) ever found in Britain.

❝The Parthenon sculptures were conceived and created as an integral part of the temple [of Athena]. Having kept them apart from the rest of the monument for nearly two centuries is long enough and should no longer be tolerated.❞

~**Theodoros Pangalos,** *Greek Minister of Culture, 2000*

Eleven Benchmark Years for Taxis

If you are sitting in a black London taxi, you might think taxis were a relatively recent phenomenon. Not so: Londoners have been taking cabs in one form or another for more than 400 years.

1605
The first documented hackney coach service appears. "Hackney" does not refer to the district in east London, but derives from the French *haquenée*, meaning an ambling horse.

1630s
Thames watermen, worried by the arrival of horse-drawn hackney coaches and sedan chairs, have them banned from London unless their journeys end a certain distance from the river.

1634
The first taxi stand appears, on the Strand outside the Maypole Inn. Five years later the Corporation of Coachmen obtains the first license to operate and ply for hire on City of London streets.

1654
Oliver Cromwell authorizes the Fellowship of Hackney Coachmen—then disbands it three years later because it became too powerful.

1823
The first 12 *cabriolets de place,* hence "cabs"—two-wheeled, one-horse carriages from Paris—are introduced at a stand on Portland Street.

1843
A metal badge showing a cab's license number is made compulsory. A taxi driver's license is issued for three years.

1897
The first horseless taxi—the two-ton Bersey electric-powered vehicle—appears courtesy of the London Electric Cab Company. The weight of the onboard batteries makes them slower than horse-drawn cabs, and within five years only 19 survive, compared with more than 10,000 horse-drawn vehicles.

1903

The first taxi with an internal combustion engine appears. London's police had refused to allow such vehicles on the streets before that.

1907

Taxi meters, invented in Germany in 1891, become compulsory. Their metal flags, pulled down when the cab is hired, survived until 1959, when they were replaced by illuminated orange signs on the taxi roofs.

1947

London's last horse-drawn cab license expires, and the last horse-drawn cab, which had worked from Victoria Station, calls it a day.

2014

Taxi drivers block central London streets to protest the arrival of Internet car-booking app Uber.

FAST FACT

Why are London cabs black? Mostly because in the 1950s the Austin Motor Company charged more for other colors so drivers plumped for black, the cheapest option.

Taxi Drivers' Slang

Cabbies' language was among the foulest heard in London in the 18th century, and part of the reason that Queen Anne laid down a fine of 5 shillings (25 pence/42 cents) for swearing. Here are some of the more polite slang terms used by drivers:

- **Bilker** A customer who refuses to pay
- **Brooming off** Passing on a bad hire to the next cab on the rank
- **Brushing** Refusing a fare
- **Butter boy** A new cabbie (as in "but a boy")
- **Butterfly** A cabbie who only works in summer
- **Cock and hen** Male and female passengers
- **Copperbottom** A cabbie who drives too many hours

- **Flyer** A trip to an airport
- **Hanging up** Waiting outside a hotel, light off, for a porter to offer a lucrative job
- **Kipper season** Slack time of the year
- **Legal** The precise fare, without a tip
- **Mush** or **musher** Owner-driver
- **Roader** A long journey
- **Single pin** One passenger

London's Taxis

Londoners have increasingly grumbled during the past decade about the one figure that matters on a taxi journey: rising fares. But there are other, less alarming numbers connected with the city's cabs.

Licensed London taxi drivers more than 221,500

Horse-drawn cabs in 1903 10,380

Daily journeys about 200,000

Passengers carried daily about 300,000

Average distance per journey 3.2 miles (5.12 km)

Official London taxi stands, or "ranks" 450

Percentage of London taxis that are wheelchair accessible 100

Streets in the "Knowledge"—the test cabbies must pass—within six miles (9.7 km) of Charing Cross 25,000

Number of routes or "runs" 320

Number of landmarks 20,000

Average time to prepare for the Knowledge 3 years

Number of traffic light sets in London 6,000

Largest amount of cash found in the back of a taxi £20,000 ($32,000)

Turning radius of a London black cab 25 feet (7.6 m)

·Fourteen Odd London Locations·

Things aren't all staid, prim, and proper in the city of London—here's a potpourri of fun and quirky sights (and sites) around our entertaining English capital.

• Jeremy Bentham's skeleton

In the South Cloisters of the main building of London's University College stands a cabinet containing the clothed skeleton of philosopher and reformer Jeremy Bentham (1748-1832). (The head you see is actually Bentham's wax-covered skull.) The cabinet used to contain Bentham's entire mummified body, but his corpse didn't cooperate and he decayed. By the way, Bentham, one of the inspirations for the founding of University College, specifically requested that his body be dissected after death and then preserved in this fashion.

• Burlington Arcade's Beadles

Burlington Arcade, since 1818 the posh passageway of shops coming off of Piccadilly, actually has its own legal jurisdiction. Instead of security guards, "Beadles" in Edwardian dress will politely ask you to leave if you run, whistle, hum, open an umbrella, or otherwise flaunt your scofflaw nature.

• The Duke of Wellington's horse block

On the east side of St. James's Waterloo Place, SW1, a small white block

Jeremy Bentham's clothed skeleton

stands curbside. It's a horse block laid by the Duke of Wellington in 1830 as a means to help gentlemen of a certain age (or diminished height) mount their rides. A fine 19th-century relic.

• The Eisenhower Centre/Goodge Street deep level shelter

Protective deep level air-raid shelters—complete with bunks, bathrooms, kitchens, and medical facilities for 8,000 people—were built at eight strategic tube stops during World War II. The one across Tottenham Court Road from the Goodge Street tube stop (WC1) is particularly noteworthy, as it doubled as General Dwight Eisenhower's command base during D-Day. One of the shelter entrances—on Chenies Street, close to the junction of North Crescent—is still visible and has been renamed the Eisenhower Centre in the president's honor.

• The Bells of St. Sepulchre

The church bells of St. Sepulchre-without-Newgate, near the Old Bailey, have a long history of announcing and/or portending doom. For centuries, the large bell in the church tower was rung to mark executions at nearby Newgate Prison. In addition, from the 17th to the 19th centuries, the clerk of St. Sepulchre's was responsible for ringing a small handbell outside the death row cells of Newgate prisoners—at midnight on the day of their execution—to help the condemned prepare to meet their maker. This Execution Bell is kept in a glass case in the church's nave.

• Ferryman's seat

On the south side of

A Beadle at Burlington Arcade

the Thames, on Bear Gardens, Bankside, SE1, not far from the Globe Theatre, is a stone chair carved into a building wall. This was a ferryman's seat, the taxi stand of the Middle Ages, where watermen would wait for fares to cross the Thames. This pint-size alcove is said to be London's last remaining example.

• Leinster Terrace's fake housefronts

The neighborhood around Leinster Terrace, W2, just north of Bayswater Road, was already a populated and upscale area when the first tube line was built through the area in the 1860s. These early underground trains needed periodic venting for their engines to cast off steam and smoke, so the fake town house facades at 23-24 Leinster Terrace were cleverly built to hide the tracks and belching fumes behind.

• Macklin Memorial

Charles Macklin, one of London's most famous 18th-century actors, once killed a fellow actor during a backstage argument by stabbing him in

The York Watergate in the days when it functioned as a working Thames-side watergate.

the eye. Although found guilty of manslaughter, Macklin never went to prison. He immortalized the shame of his deed on his own memorial plaque—in the churchyard of St. Paul's Church in Covent Garden—which depicts a knife plunging through the eye of a theatrical mask.

• The Roof Gardens

High atop the hustle/bustle of Kensington High Street, W8, is an incongruous 1.5-acre (0.6 ha) man-made oasis of rosebushes, fruit trees, evergreen shrubs, oaks, lavender, and more. The Roof Garden—free and open to the public—consists of three themed gardens, complete with wandering flamingos and a fish-stocked stream.

• Sewer lamp

On Carting Lane, WC2, just off the Strand, stands the noble sewer lamp. Story goes that this lamp runs on methane fumes provided (slightly indirectly) from the, ahem, by-products of the Savoy hotel's guests next door. Such lamps were indeed built in England to help diffuse methane from sewers, and Carting Lane's is often cited as London's last—but all evidence points to the fact that the original sewer lamp was damaged in a traffic accident and replaced by the replica you see today.

• **John Snow's water pump**

You can still see the original water pump that helped spark the terrible cholera outbreak of 1854. On Broadwick Street, W1, on the western edge of Soho, stands what's become known as John Snow's water pump. Dr. Snow traced the area's many cholera deaths to contaminated water from this source, marking one of the first instances of evidence-based sleuthing to try to control an epidemic. Until then it was thought the illness was a result of a general miasma in the air and/or the base moral makeup of the poorer classes who were often hit hardest by disease.

• **The stone nose of Admiralty Arch**

Admiralty Arch's northernmost arch (the one on the left as you look toward Trafalgar Square) is home to a mysterious life-size stone nose that protrudes about halfway up the wall. Urban legends about the nose (and several others spotted around the city) circulated until it came to light in 1997 that an artist named Rick Buckley had placed these objects to protest the growth of London's expansive (and "nosy") anti-crime closed-circuit television (CCTV) cameras.

• **London's first water fountain**

On the corner of Holborn Viaduct and Giltspur Street, EC1, carved into the side of St. Sepulchre-without-Newgate church, you'll find the handiwork of 19th-century philanthropists who worked to improve Londoners' access to clean drinking water. This public fountain, the first of 85 built around the city from 1859 to 1865, drew water from springs unconnected to the putrid Thames.

• **York Watergate**

Before the Victoria Embankment was built in the 1860s, the great houses on the Strand had pride of place, with gardens that fronted the Thames. Among them was York House, the home of the first Duke of Buckingham, built in 1237. The mansion's Thames watergate, from 1626, is all that remains; the house itself was razed in 1675. The watergate can now be found within Embankment Gardens, 150 yards (137 m) inland from the riverbank.

❝The researches of Dr. [John] Snow are among the most fruitful in modern medicine. He traced the history of cholera.❞
~The Lancet, 1866

Remaining Visible Damage From WWII

On September 7, 1940, Germany began the World War II bombing campaign of England known as the Blitz. For eight months, through May 10, 1941, London was besieged by hundreds of Luftwaffe raids. (Later in the war, the Germans unleashed V1 and V2 rockets, wreaking more havoc on the city.) While most of the damage has long since been cleared and buildings repaired, there are still a few visible reminders of these dark days in London's history.

Deep pockmarks remain on the west facade of the **Victoria & Albert Museum,** SW7, about 100 yards up Exhibition Road from Cromwell Road. A memorial plaque at the spot reads, "The damage to these walls is the result of enemy bombing during the Blitz of the Second World War 1939-1945 and is left as a memorial to the enduring values of this great museum in a time of conflict."

St. Clement Danes (Strand, WC2). Visible damage remains on the outside walls of the church, which was gutted by bombs in May 1941.

The **Officers Mess Hall** on the grounds of the Tower of London (near the ravens, between the White Tower and Wakefield Tower) was destroyed by wartime bombing. The rubble still remains; visitors tend to think it's the ruin of some historic medieval site.

St. Dunstan-in-the-East (St. Dunstan's Hill, EC3). This Sir Christopher Wren–designed church was mostly destroyed by German bombs, though the old tower and steeple remain intact. The ruin was converted into a quiet public garden in the 1970s and remains so today.

On **Portugal Street,** WC2, a sign at the old W. H. Smith headquarters shows damage suffered in 1940.

FIRST PERSON

❝The German air force has unleashed a wave of heavy bombing raids on London ... The Ministry of Home Security said the scale of the attacks was the largest the Germans had yet attempted.**❞**

~BBC coverage, *September 7, 1940*

The **Guard's Memorial,** across Horse Guards Road from Horse Guard's Parade, SW1, at the east end of St. James's Park, still shows pockmark bomb damage.

Tate Britain museum, SW1, suffered multiple hits during the war. The building's exterior absorbed numerous bomb splinters; look for marks on the west side of the building and along Atterbury Street.

On **Mansell Street,** E1, at the corner of Prescot Street, a few hundred yards north-east of the Tower Hill Tube stop, the exterior brickwork displays dramatic pockmarks from a nearby bomb blast.

St. Bartholomew's Hospital, EC1, still shows splinter damage. Look on the exterior wall, next to William Wallace's memorial facing Smithfield market.

Southwark Cathedral, SE1. Damage sustained in the bombing raids of February 1941 is still visible on the outer wall of the cathedral.

A World War II bomb bent the sword in **the equestrian statue (1856) of Richard the Lionheart** outside the Houses of Parliament.

London in Any Language

- **Londres** (French)
- **Londres** (Spanish)
- **Londra** (Italian)
- **Londen** (Dutch)
- **Llundain** (Welsh)
- **Lunnainn** (Scots Gaelic)
- **Lontoo** (Finnish)
- **Lundúnir** (Icelandic)
- **Londona** (Latvian)
- **Londýn** (Czech)

·Irreplaceable Buildings Lost in WWII·

Holland House was mostly destroyed in 1940 by German bombs.

The toll of World War II's bombing campaigns on London and Londoners is hard to understate. Along with 30,000 people who lost their lives, 50,000 seriously injured, and countless more made homeless, the physical landscape of the city was forever changed. More than 3.5 million buildings suffered damage of some sort—the East End and the City were particularly hard hit, with a majority of the latter's buildings damaged or completely destroyed. While many structures were rebuilt, many were not and are now lost forever.

• **Brooke House (Hackney)**
This fascinating Tudor house, built in the 15th century, had a succession of prominent owners, including Henry VIII and Thomas Cromwell. A private mental hospital from 1759 to 1940, the house at the corner of Lower Clapton and Kenninghall Roads was gutted during the war and finally razed in 1955.

• **Church of St. John the Evangelist (Red Lion Square, Holborn)**
The fine redbrick Victorian church, completed in 1878, that sat on Red Lion Square (said to be the final burial place of Oliver Cromwell and other regicides) was first damaged in 1941. The church ruins weren't cleared until 1960, when the construction

of Proctor Street wiped away the western side of the square.

• **The Great Synagogue of London (Duke's Place, Aldgate)**
The 1690 Great Synagogue was the first London Ashkenazi synagogue built after the 17th-century return of Jews to England. The temple destroyed by bombs in 1941 was actually the third synagogue on the site. It was built in 1790 to accommodate the Jewish community's rapid growth.

• **Holford House (Regent's Park)**
Holford House, a Palladian villa in the northwest corner of Regent's Park, was built in the 1830s by James Holford, a wealthy wine merchant. The largest of all the extravagant villas in the park, the house became Regent's Park College's home for 70 years after Holford's death in 1854. It was never rebuilt after being damaged in the war.

• **Holland House (Holland Park, Kensington)**
At the time of the English Civil War, Holland House was the country home of the Hollands, a family of Royalists (the losing side). After the Earl of Holland lost his head at the Tower of London, his home (then called Cope Castle) went into the hands of Cromwell and the Puritans, who used it as an army headquarters. Badly damaged in 1940, the 1607 house today incorporates a youth hostel and restaurant within its once-aristocratic walls.

• **The Inner Temple Library (Fleet Street)**
The history of the Inner Temple's law library goes back to at least the 16th century. In 1827, the library moved to an elaborate Gothic building on Fleet Street. After several expansions the following century, the library was leveled by German bombs in a series of attacks from 1941 to 1942.

• **The Louse Church (Bermondsey)**
Officially called St. John's Horsleydown, the 1732 Louse Church just south of Tower Bridge was instantly recognizable by the unusual gilded weather vane in the shape of a comet atop its tall spire . . . but which looked to creative Londoners like a louse (the singular of "lice"). The church was hit in 1940 and pulled down in 1948.

• **Montagu Place (22 Portman Square, Marylebone)**
Elizabeth Montagu, an 18th-century high society

woman of letters, is best known for hosting "bluestocking" parties at Montagu Place, her London home and the Algonquin Hotel Round Table of its day. Literary figures and the social elite would gather to discuss philosophy, literature, and other worldly topics. The large 1780 town house was damaged in 1941 and razed after the war.

• St. Alban's (Wood Street)

A Wren church, St. Alban's is dedicated to the first British Christian martyr and dates from the 1680s. It was mostly ruined by bombs in 1940; the remaining church tower stands alone on an island in the middle of Wood Street.

• St. Anne's Church (Wardour Street, Soho)

This post–Great Fire church was originally built by William Talman, a student of Sir Christopher Wren. All that remains is the 1803 steeple; most of the church was destroyed in 1940. A new church, built around the surviving steeple, was rededicated in 1991.

• St. Mary the Virgin Aldermanbury (Aldermanbury)

Near St. Alban's, St. Mary the Virgin on Aldermanbury was another Wren-designed church that didn't survive the war. The ruins were taken apart and shipped to Westminster College in Fulton, Missouri (the location of Churchill's famous "iron curtain" speech), where the 7,000 pieces were reassembled in the late 1960s to Wren's original plan.

• St. Mildred's (Bread Street)

St. Mildred's was, until its destruction in 1941, the only Wren interior to have survived unaltered since the 17th century. It was at St. Mildred's that the poet Percy Shelley married Mary Wollstonecraft Godwin, the future *Frankenstein* author, in 1816.

• St. Nicholas Cole Abbey (Queen Victoria Street)

St. Nicholas was the first City church designed by Christopher Wren after the Great Fire. Long associated with the city's fishmongers, it was destroyed in 1941 along with nearly everything else along Queen Victoria Street. Restored in 1962 to Wren's original design, the deconsecrated church is today used for conferences and events.

FIRST PERSON

❝Bombs came shrieking down at the rate of one a minute. A good share of the City . . . was wiped out. The crash of bombs and the glow of the fires gave us the feeling of . . . some sort of medieval nightmare.❞

~**Harvey Klemmer,** National Geographic *magazine, April 1941*

·Up and Down the Thames·

The Thames provides unique vantage points for landmarks such as Hampton Court Palace.

After years in the doldrums, the Thames has once again begun to play a larger part in the life of the city. Commuter transit services on the river have appeared, and several private operators run boats that allow you to travel from Hampton Court in the west as far as the Thames Barrier in the east. Between these two points, the river offers a window on some 2,000 years of history and many of the capital's principal attractions. Here is a summary of key sights on or near the river from west to east, with an indication of whether they are on the north (N) or south (S) banks:

• **Hampton Court Palace and Gardens** (N) Create a superb day out by taking a train from Waterloo (*nationalrail.co.uk*) to visit one of Europe's greatest palace and garden complexes (*hrp.org .uk*), before taking a boat (*wpsa.co.uk, closed Nov. to mid-April*) back to Richmond or beyond.

• **Richmond** (S) It's a lovely town of old streets, waterfront pubs, and green spaces (*visit richmond.co.uk*), with a Tube and Overground rail station (*tfl.gov.uk*) if you want to combine a boat trip (*wpsa.co.uk, closed Nov. to mid-April*) with a quicker return journey to the city center.

• **Kew Gardens** (N) Like Richmond, Kew (*kew .org;* see Gardens, p. 18) has a Tube station (450 yards from the gardens' Victoria Gate entrance) and railroad services to Waterloo, allowing you to combine a boat trip to

London's finest gardens with faster transit links.

• **Tate Britain** (S) This was the original Tate Gallery *(tate.org.uk)* before part of the collection was hived off into the now more prominent Tate Modern; this gallery contains some of Britain's most famous older works of art.

• **Houses of Parliament** (N) Take in one of the most familiar sights on this or any other river. If you're embarking or disembarking here, don't forget nearby Westminster Abbey.

• **London Eye** (S) Originally intended as a temporary attraction, the Eye is now a fixture of both the river and London's skyline *(londoneye.com)*.

• **Southbank Centre** (S)

The Globe Theatre

The auditoria and open spaces were created primarily for the 1951 Festival of Britain; now the Centre ranks as the world's largest unified arts complex *(southbankcentre.co.uk)* in a constantly evolving riverfront district that offers summer beaches, outdoor entertainment, and many eating and drinking options.

• **Tate Modern** (S) The conversion of a monolithic former power-generating plant into a space for modern art *(tate.org.uk)* has been a

resounding success: The gallery attracts more than five million visitors a year.

• **St. Paul's Cathedral** (N) Visit Tate Modern and then St. Paul's on the opposite bank by using the London Millennium Footbridge, which opened in 2000.

• **Shakespeare's Globe** (S) This replica offers a delightful dramatic and architectural experience in a theater *(shakespearesglobe .com)* opened in 1997 near the site of the original wooden Globe, an Elizabethan playhouse completed in 1599.

• **The Monument** (N) This column commemorates one of the most calamitous events in London's history: the Great Fire of London, which began on Sunday, September 2, 1666 *(themonument.info).*

• **London Bridge** Today, sadly, it's an unexceptional bridge, but for centuries it provided London's only river crossing. In previous incarnations, notably when it was laden with shops, London Bridge would have been one of the city's most remarkable sights (see London on the Move, p. 108).

• **Southwark Cathedral** (S) Close to the site of the old Roman crossing of the Thames, and opposite the City of London, it ranks among the capital's most important and historic places of worship. Its origins are obscure, but its roots date back 1,000 years, probably more.

• **The Shard** (S) London's highest building (see Tallest Structures, p. 129) takes its name from its distinctive shape. It is loved by some, reviled by others.

Whatever you think, there's no ignoring it, either from the river or from much of the rest of the city.

• **HMS *Belfast*** (S) It's hard to miss the bristling guns and battleship gray of this nine-deck former Royal Navy cruiser (launched in 1938), moored close to Tower Bridge and now run in conjunction with the Imperial War Museum as a museum ship *(iwm.org.uk).*

• **Tower of London** (N) Proud and unmistakable, London's principal fortress for around 1,000 years is one of the city's must-see attractions *(hrp.org.uk).*

• **Tower Bridge** Like the Tower, the eponymous bridge (see Tower Bridge, p. 226), although of much more recent vintage, is every bit as much an iconic symbol of London *(towerbridge.org.uk).*

• **Canary Wharf** (N) This area is at the heart of a nearly four-decade redevelopment project aimed at regenerating London's vast docklands. The name has become synonymous with One Canada Square, the first of several skyscrapers that helped create a successful new business and residential district in the

Iconic Tower Bridge at the eastern end of central London

eastern reaches of the city (see Tallest Structures, p. 129).

• **Greenwich** (S) There's the famous clipper ship *Cutty Sark (rmg.co.uk/cuttysark)* right on the riverbank, and beyond it the major sights of this key historic and maritime area of the city: Greenwich Park, the National Maritime Museum, and the Royal Observatory *(rmg.co.uk/royal-observatory)*.

• **The O2** (S) Cost and an uncertain eventual purpose gave this vast domed arena a shaky start as one of the United Kingdom's signature projects to mark the millennium. But since being relaunched as the O2 *(theo2.co.uk)*, it has become one of the capital's most successful large performance and entertainment spaces.

• **Emirates Air Line** A cable car *(emiratesairline .co.uk)* across the Thames, aimed at both visitors and commuters, it offers breathtaking views of the river and the rest of east London.

• **The Thames Barrier** A piece of engineering that combines beauty and purpose, its rotating bastions (operational since 1982) are designed to stop upstream storm and tide surges engulfing floodplain areas of the capital *(environment -agency.gov.uk)*.

Thames River Rides: The Options

• **River Bus** Use pay-as-you-go Oyster cards or single fares to ride scheduled, round-trip transit routes (mainly in Central and East London) *(tfl.gov.uk/river)*.

• **Bateaux Cruises** Bateaux features river tours combined with afternoon tea, lunch, or dinner *(bateauxlondon.com)*.

• **City Cruises** The river's largest cruise operator offers open-top boats with multilingual commentary between Westminster and Greenwich every 35 minutes *(citycruises.com)*.

• **Crown River Cruises** A flexible hop-on, hop-off circular service, with round-trip rides: Westminster–Embankment–Festival Hall–Bankside–St. Katharine's *(crownriver cruise.co.uk)*.

• **London Eye River Cruise** Departing roughly hourly, these circular 40-minute sightseeing cruises from the London Eye Pier take in Tower Bridge, the Houses of Parliament, and points in between *(londoneye.com)*.

• **Thames Rib Experience** Exhilarating trips in small, fast RIBs (rigid inflatable boats), with a general 50-minute sightseeing option, depart from Embankment Pier *(thamesrib experience.com)*. **London Rib Voyages** operates similar trips *(londonribvoyages.com)*.

• **Thames River Services** This company offers longer trips than many other operators. Daily, roughly every 40 minutes from Westminster to the Thames Barrier *(thamesriverservices.co.uk)*.

• **Westminster Passenger Service Association** This is the only company that operates regular service west along the river, following a route from Westminster Pier to Hampton Court taken by monarchs since Henry VIII *(wpsa.co.uk)*.

·Functions of the Tower of London·

The Tower—a former citadel, prison, royal mint, execution site, and more

The Tower of London has taken on a variety of eclectic and critical roles since it was first established more than 900 years ago by William the Conqueror.

• Citadel/Fortress

The Tower's primary use was as a citadel when it was first created—a Norman fortress clearly meant to remind the English who was now in charge. The White Tower, built in 1098, is 90 feet (27.5 m) high and would have dwarfed the one- and two-story buildings for miles around it (see Tallest Structures, p. 128).

• Residence and refuge

Although not intended to be a main royal residence, the Tower housed many kings, especially in times of conflict: King John, Henry III, Edward II, and Richard II all sought refuge there.

• Prison

The Tower's best known function was that of royal prison (see Prisoners, p. 157).

• Execution site

Medieval justice was cruel, and those who fell afoul of the monarch (or just lost out in the power politics of the era) met the executioner's block. Although its reputation as an execution site isn't unfounded, it was actually the site of

The Menagerie was a must-see of Tower visits for hundreds of years.

only seven beheadings, although there were military executions there during the two world wars (see Noteworthy Executions, p. 120).

• Royal Mint

From about 1250 to 1810, the bulk of the kingdom's coins were minted on the Tower's premises. Machinery was installed in the 1600s for mass production; until then, coins were forged by hand as they had been for thousands of years. In 1810, the mint was moved to just outside the Tower walls.

• Military base

Oliver Cromwell installed the Tower's first permanent garrison in the 1650s. Later, kings and queens realized that was a pretty good idea, and the Tower was used as an armory and military base to stem any troubles that might pop up in the capital.

• Home of the Crown Jewels

The Tower of London has been home to Britain's glittering Crown Jewels since 1660. Many of the crowns, scepters, and

FAST FACT

The keepers of the Tower's Menagerie would sometimes feed the polar bears by sending them out to fish on the Thames with chains around their necks.

tiaras were made new that year for the coronation of Charles II. Cromwell had had the previous set melted down, along with the monarchy, during the interregnum of 1649-1660 (see Crown Jewels, p. 159).

• **Menagerie**
The Tower's Royal Menagerie housed London's exotic animals, many sent by well-wishing foreign dignitaries, for more than 600 years. The first animals recorded were lions sent to King John in 1210. Other Menagerie residents throughout the centuries included polar bears, monkeys, hyenas, alligators, ocelots, and elephants. The Menagerie was a popular tourist draw from Elizabethan times until it closed in the 1830s (and moved to Regent's Park as the new London Zoo). And why did it close? Besides the general trouble imposed on Tower staff to tend to all those living creatures, the animals had the pesky tendency to escape their confines and attack and kill their handlers, tourists, and each other.

• **Tourist attraction**
The Tower's rich history has made it a popular tourist attraction since it opened fully to the public in the mid-19th century (though certain sections were open for visits centuries before that). More than 2.5 million people now visit annually.

Prisoners at the Tower

The first state prisoner was brought to the Tower at the turn of the 12th century; the last in the 1940s. Among the notables who served time at the Tower throughout the centuries:

Ranulf Flambard, Bishop of Durham. He became the Tower's first prisoner in 1100. He was also the first to escape, using a rope that had been smuggled into his cell in a cask of wine.

King Richard II. Held at the Tower after he was deposed in 1399 (and before he was likely murdered at Pontefract Castle in Yorkshire the following year).

King Henry VI. Imprisoned and later killed in the Tower after his capture by King Edward IV's forces in 1471.

The Princes in the Tower. Twelve-year-old King Edward V and his nine-year-old brother, Richard, were held and no doubt murdered in the Tower on the order of their uncle, Richard III, in 1483.

Queen Anne Boleyn, second wife of Henry VIII. Anne was held in the Tower on charges of treason, adultery, and incest for two weeks before being beheaded in 1536.

Thomas More, philosopher and councillor to Henry VIII. Held for more than a year before being executed in 1635.

Thomas Cromwell. Another adviser to Henry VIII (it was a high-risk job), he was imprisoned and executed in 1540.

Sir Walter Raleigh. The explorer, courtier, and nobleman was imprisoned for 13 years (1603-1616), though he lived in relative luxury with his wife and two children. Raleigh was eventually released . . . but later executed.

Guy Fawkes. The Catholic explosives expert tried to blow up the Houses of Parliament (with the king and nobility of England inside) in the Gunpowder Plot of 1605. Fawkes was held and interrogated at the Tower, but executed in the Old Palace Yard at Westminster in 1606.

William Penn. The future founder of Pennsylvania was sent to the Tower in 1668 for seven months for the crime of pamphleteering.

Sir Robert Walpole. Imprisoned for several months in 1712 for corruption, he later became the prime minister.

Rudolph Hess, Deputy Führer of Nazi Germany. Held at the Tower for four days in May 1941, after he parachuted into Scotland with an unauthorized peace proposal to end hostilities between Germany and England. Hess was the last official state prisoner held at the Tower.

FAST FACT

Sir William de la Pole—the longest serving Tower prisoner—was incarcerated for 37 years (1502-1539) for allegedly plotting against King Henry VII.

•Most Prized Crown Jewels•

After the execution of Charles I in 1649, the Parliament ordered the sale or destruction of all things "royal," including the finest Crown Jewels—the regalia and ornaments of the sovereigns of England, some of which dated back at least to the days of Edward the Confessor (1003-1066). Some of the newer Jewels, however, made since about 1661, contain remnants of these destroyed items or incorporate much older precious stones from elsewhere that had already been cut.

• The Imperial State Crown

The big one—literally: It contains 2,868 diamonds, 17 sapphires, 11 emeralds, 5 rubies, and 269 pearls. The principal diamond is the Second, or Lesser Star of Africa (or Cullinan II), the world's second largest top quality cut diamond at 317.4

Glittering St. Edward's Crown

carats. Among the other jewels is one known as the Black Prince's Ruby—actually a different gemstone, spinel, rather than a ruby—and possibly one of the gems Henry V wore on his helmet in the defeat of the French at the Battle of Agincourt in 1415.

• The Sovereign's Sceptre With Cross

Contains the First Star of Africa, the world's largest flawless, colorless cut diamond, at 530.2 carats. It was cut, along with the Lesser Star (in the Imperial State Crown), from the Cullinan Diamond

(3,025 carats uncut) and presented to King Edward VII in 1907 by the government of the Transvaal (South Africa). In 1910, it was added to the Sceptre, which had to be reinforced, so great was the weight of the diamond. The feature holding the diamond is hinged so that the stone can be removed and worn separately.

• The Crown of Queen Elizabeth the Queen Mother

This sports a mere 2,800 diamonds, including the most famous stone of all, the Indian Koh-i-Nûr, or Mountain of Light. Its fame rests not so much on its size—a relatively modest 105.6 carats—as on its mysterious origins. It arrived from India in 1850, one of the spoils of empire. Before that, ownership can be traced through Indian and Afghan kings and emperors to at least 1526, though it is probably older.

The ancient spoon used in the coronation service to anoint the new monarch

• **St. Edward's Crown**
This is the solid-gold crown with which the new monarch is actually crowned, though it is so heavy (5 pounds/2.23 kg) that few kings or queens wear it for long. It's also the crown depicted in coats-of-arms, badges, and insignia to suggest the authority of the reigning monarch. It may have been made from gold recovered from the royal regalia destroyed after 1649, and it is set with 444 stones that include sapphires, tourmalines, amethysts, topazes, and citrines.

• **The Anointing Spoon**
This isn't a "royal" ornament, which is probably why it survived destruction in 1649, and it is not a contender in terms of jewels and obvious splendor. But its value is one of age, for at more than 800 years old it is the most venerable item in the collection. It is used during a solemn moment of the coronation service, when holy oil is poured into the spoon and applied to the new sovereign's head, hands, and chest.

FAST FACT

The Koh-i-Nûr diamond is said to bring bad luck to any male owner and so only women can wear the crown in which it is set.

The Underground

Dozens of stations, hundreds of trains, thousands of passengers: The London Underground, or Tube, is a number cruncher's dream. Here is a selection of some of the most intriguing.

Total length of the network 249 miles (401 km)

Passenger journeys annually 1.17 billion (2011-2012)

Estimated number of mice 500,000

Distance covered annually by each Tube train 114,500 miles (184,269 km)

Annual distance covered by all trains 45 million miles (72.4 million km)

Average train speed, including stops 20.5 miles an hour (33 kph)

Escalators 426

Elevators 167

Longest escalator 197 feet (60 m), rising 90 vertical feet (27.4 m), at Angel station

Stations 270

Busiest station Waterloo (82 million exits and entries annually)

Station with most platforms Baker Street (10)

Line with most stations The District (60)

Record time for visiting all stations 16 hours, 29 minutes, and 13 seconds

Shortest distance between stations 984 feet (300 m), from Leicester Square to Covent Garden

Longest distance between stations 3.89 miles (6.3 km), from Chesham to Chalfont & Latimer

Journeys of less than a minute between stations 14

Longest possible journey without transferring 34.1 miles (54.9 km), on the Central Line from West Ruislip to Epping

·Ghost Tube Stations·

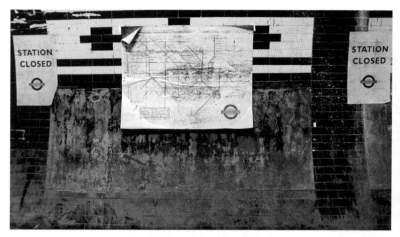

The Aldwych Tube stop closed for service in 1994.

More than 40 Tube stations have been closed, resited, planned but never opened —or existed only in the realm of urban myth. The first was the short-lived King William Street, which opened in 1890 and closed in 1900. Others have been demolished, partially closed, or bricked up.

• Aldwych

It was open from 1907 to 1994 and is now one of the few ghost stations you can visit, but only rarely *(ltmuseum.co.uk)*. In World War II it was used as both an air-raid shelter and to store artifacts from the British Museum. The station entrance, a protected historic structure, is visible at Surrey Street with its original 1907 name, Strand Station.

• BBC Central

A persistent rumor relating to abandoned stations and secret tunnels suggests the existence of a special platform, possibly part of a World War II "Stronghold" basement area, on the Bakerloo Line that served BBC Broadcasting House, then located in the heart of London. Not true, says Transport for London, which claims to have no records of any such platform.

• British Museum

Opened in 1900 and closed in 1933 after the merging of two rival railroad companies, this station can be seen while traveling on the Central Line between Holborn and Tottenham Court Road. The ghost of a mummy from the nearby British Museum is said to haunt the area. A new building at 133 High Holborn replaced the station's entrance.

• Brompton Road

Opened in 1906 on the Piccadilly Line between Knightsbridge and South Kensington, this station closed in 1934 because its proximity to other stations rendered it underused. During World War II, it was the headquarters for London antiaircraft operations, and much of the complex remained the property of the Ministry of Defence until it was sold—to a Ukrainian billionaire in 2013 and then to an anonymous buyer in 2014. Part of the old frontage is visible on Cottage Place, near Brompton Square.

• Down Street Station

This Piccadilly Line station between Green Park and Hyde Park Corner (1907-1932) closed before it could be included on Harry Beck's famous Tube map of 1933. During World War II, it was a shelter and occasional war room for Winston Churchill and his War Cabinet. Churchill sometimes slept there, in what he called "The Burrow." The station's oxblood brick–tiled facade and large underground areas survive.

• North End

Also known as Bull and Bush Station, after a nearby pub, this partially built Northern Line station closed before it opened in 1907, the victim of planning and financial problems. It would have been the network's deepest station (at 221 feet/67.3 m), deeper than nearby Hampstead, the next deepest (at 192 feet/ 58.5 m). In the 1950s, when staircase access was built, the site was rumored to be the London Underground's headquarters in the event of a nuclear attack. The station can be glimpsed when traveling between Hampstead and Golders Green stations.

• Mark Lane

The present Tower Hill station stands on the site of the old Tower of London station (1882-1884), which remained open just two years before being replaced by the larger Mark Lane station some distance away. Mark Lane in turn closed in 1967, but it can be glimpsed on the District Line while traveling between Monument and Tower Hill.

FAST FACT

Aldwych appeared in the movie *Atonement* (2007) and was visited by Lara Croft in *Tomb Raider III*. It was built on the site of the Royal Strand theater and the ghost of an actress is said to haunt its platforms.

Cottage Place's former entrance to the Brompton Road Tube stop

• **South Kentish Town** The station, opened in 1907 on the Northern Line between Camden Town and Kentish Town, closed in 1924 due to low ridership; it was used during World War II as an air-raid shelter. Soon after its closure, a passenger is said to have alighted onto one of the old platforms, an incident that inspired "South Kentish Town" (1951), a short story by Sir John Betjeman. The surface building—now a store—is still visible on Kentish Town Road near Castle Road.

Ten Movies Shot in Underground Stations

- *An American Werewolf in London,* Tottenham Court Road (1981)
- *Atonement,* Aldwych (2007)
- *Bend It Like Beckham,* Piccadilly Line (2002)
- *Billy Elliot,* Westminster (2000)
- *The Bourne Ultimatum,* Charing Cross and Waterloo (2007)
- *Bridget Jones's Diary,* Piccadilly Circus (2001)
- *Bridget Jones: The Edge of Reason,* Waterloo (2004)
- *Harry Potter and the Order of the Phoenix,* Westminster (2007)
- *Love Actually,* Canary Wharf (2003)
- *Sliding Doors,* Waterloo and City Line (1997)

·Museums That Are Houses/ Houses That Are Museums·

Look around your home. One day, if you do something especially impressive, people might pay money to see your furnishings and your collections in the exact rooms where you once displayed your genius. Here's a sampling of some houses that have already made the grade.

• Carlyle's House
(24 Cheyne Row, SW3, nationaltrust.org.uk)
The personality of 19th-century philosopher and historian Thomas Carlyle pervades the Chelsea house where he lived for 47 years. Carlyle—who became famous after the publication of his account of the French Revolution—and his witty, accomplished wife would receive the likes of John Stuart Mill, Charles Dickens, Robert Browning, Charles Darwin, or William Thackeray in rooms still graced by many original furnishings.

• Dennis Severs' House
(18 Folgate St., E1, dennis severshouse.co.uk)
The house/brainchild of artist Dennis Severs (who ran the house from the 1970s until his death in 1999) is both an historic home and an art installation. Each of the ten period rooms is packed with dozens of subtle details to evoke the daily lives of the elusive (and fictitious) Jervis family, who theoretically lived in

A slept-in bed at Dennis Severs' House

the home from the 18th to the 20th centuries, and whose muffled voices and footsteps we hear faintly from the house's distant corners.

• Dr. Johnson's House
(17 Gough Square, EC4, drjohnsonshouse.org)
Dr. Johnson lived in this house in Gough Square, set amid the small lanes just north of the Strand, from 1749 to 1759. Now it is a simple, atmospheric museum with restored interiors and a period collection relating to the lexicographer, who compiled his famous dictionary there.

• Handel House
(25 Brook St., W1, handelhouse.org)
George Frideric Handel composed some of the greatest music in history—including *Messiah* and *Music for the Royal Fireworks*—at this Mayfair home, where he lived

Leighton House's glittering Arab Hall

from 1723 until his death in 1759. As a giant bonus starting in 2015, the upstairs attic rooms will display artifacts from the life of 1960s guitarist and music icon Jimi Hendrix, who coincidentally lived there intermittently in 1968-1969.

• **Eltham Palace**
(Court Yard, Eltham, SE9, elthampalace.org.uk)
In the 1930s, the famed Courtauld family built this impressive art deco house adjacent to the remains of royal Eltham Palace, boyhood home of Henry VIII. The what were then ultramodern designs and fixtures hold up to modern scrutiny (for example, a clock electronically aligned directly to the Greenwich observatory). Like any house worth its salt, it's connected to the medieval Great Hall, with its soaring timber roof, built by Edward IV in the 1470s. And don't miss the lovely and expansive gardens.

• **Hogarth's House**
(Hogarth Lane, Great West Rd., W4, hounslow.info)
William Hogarth's country cottage, built around 1700, is hidden between a noisy roundabout and elegant Chiswick House. The painter decamped with his family to this country retreat (from his main residence in central London) in 1749 and remained until his death in 1764. The house contains many of the artist's original prints and also hosts temporary art exhibitions.

• **Leighton House Museum**
(12 Holland Park Rd., W14, leightonhouse.co.uk)
Frederick Lord Leighton, a wealthy Victorian artist, built this remarkable home in the 1860s. The

❝Tom Carlyle lives in perfect dignity in a little house in Chelsea with a snuffy Scotch maid to open the door and the best company in England ringing at it. ❞
~**William Makepeace Thackeray**, *1848*

interior is a bachelor's indulgence, typified by the lack of guest rooms, while red walls, ebonized wood, and gilt decorate the main rooms downstairs. The showstopper is the beautiful Arab Hall, with its golden dome, mosaics, and glazed wall tiles. Really worth seeing.

• The Sambourne Family Home/18 Stafford Terrace
(18 Stafford Terrace, W8, rbkc.gov.uk)
The political cartoonist Linley Sambourne, born in 1844, moved into his newly built Kensington house in 1875. By his death in 1910, he had filled it to the brim with his own cartoons for *Punch* magazine, decorative porcelain, stained glass windows, and early Victorian photographs.

• Sir John Soane's Museum
(13 Lincoln's Inn Fields, WC2, soane.org)
One of London's more eccentric and atmospheric house-museums, this was where architect Sir John Soane lived from 1813 to 1837. The rambling museum displays sculptures, antique marbles, architectural models, and countless other objets d'art in its many nooks and crannies. The Picture Room is home to William Hogarth's 18th-century cautionary-tale painting series "A Rake's Progress" (see Most Important Paintings, p. 223).

Unusual Insurance Policies of Lloyd's of London

Lloyd's of London has come a long way since Edward Lloyd started selling ship and marine cargo insurance out of his London coffeehouse in the 1680s. The company has grown steadily in the ensuing 325+ years, and now insures . . . pretty much everything. Here are a few notables, in no particular order:

Forty members of an English "whiskers club" once insured their beards against fire and theft.

In 1904, Lloyd's issued its (and the world's) first motorcar insurance policy. Having only sold marine insurance for 200+ years, the company faced a slight learning curve transitioning to other forms of transport: Lloyd's defined an automobile as a "ship navigating on land."

Ben Turpin, a 1920s film star who was known for his perpetually crossed eyes, took out a policy of $25,000 (£15,600) to cover him in the dreadful event that his eyes ever uncrossed.

A 1914 homeowner's policy covered any damage caused by rampaging suffragists.

Lloyd's covered Charles Lindbergh and *The Spirit of St. Louis* for $18,000 (£11,300) on the groundbreaking 1927 nonstop flight across the Atlantic.

In the 1930s, actor Jimmy Durante insured his rather prominent nose for $140,000 (£87,500).

Marlene Dietrich insured her voice for $1 million (£630,000). Some years later, Bruce Springsteen insured his for $5.75 million (£3.6 million).

Actress Bette Davis insured her diminutive waist against weight gain for $28,000 (£17,600).

The 1940s pinup girl Betty Grable insured her legs for $1 million (£600,000). Speaking of legs, ballet dancer Rudolph Nureyev insured his gams for $34,000 (£21,400), while a similar policy was taken out by soccer's David Beckham for a whopping £100 million ($160 million) in 2006.

Carol Doda, a celebrity topless dancer at San Francisco's Condor Club, insured her silicone-enhanced breasts for $1.5 million (£900,000) in the 1960s. More recently, Dolly Parton insured her breasts for $6.25 million (£4 million).

Before the fall of the Iron Curtain, Lloyd's insured the safe delivery of dinosaur bones being transported from East Germany to Japan for $1 million (£600,000).

The hands of Keith Richards, the Rolling Stones guitarist, are insured for £1 million ($1.6 million).

The taste buds of food critic Egon Ronay have been insured for $400,000 (£250,000).

Gennaro Pelliccia, Costa Coffee's Master of Coffee, has insured his refined coffee-tasting tongue for $16 million (£10 million).

The long curly locks of American footballer Troy Polamalu have been insured for $1 million (£600,000). The policy has some strict conditions: The Pittsburgh Steeler is forbidden to take up firebreathing, plus it is verboten for him to attempt to climb Mount Everest.

·Firsthand Descriptions of Bygone Fairs·

Revelry at Bartholomew Fair

London's fairs, which had their heyday from olde times to the 19th century, were action-packed combinations of entertainment, trading, general revelry, and—usually—drunken debauchery. Luckily, quite a few contemporary accounts of the fun survive.

• "Thence away by coach to Bartholomew Fayre . . . There was a horse with hoofs like rams hornes, a goose with four feet, and a cock with three . . . We saw a poor fellow, whose legs were tied behind his back, dance upon his hands with his arse above his head, and also dance upon his crutches, . . . which he did with that pain that I was sorry to see it, and did pity him and give him money after he had done."
—*Samuel Pepys's diary entry on visiting Bartholomew Fair, September 4, 1663*

• "Thus we have . . . a graveyard full of traders, and a place of jesting . . . where men and women caroused in the midst of the throng; . . . where the sheriff caused new laws to be published by loud proclamation . . . where the young men bowled at nine-pins, while the clerks and friars peeped at the young maids; where mounted knights and ladies curvetted and ambled; where . . . the scholars met for public wrangle, oxen lowed, horses neighed, and sheep bleated among the buyers."
—*Henry Morley's* Memoirs of Bartholomew Fair, *1858*

• "Thomas Dale . . . keepeth the Turk's Head Musick Booth . . . where is a Glass of Good Wine, Mum, Syder, Beer, Ale,

The frozen-over Thames's Frost Fair of 1683-1684

and all other Sorts of Liquors, to be Sold ... There is likewise a Young Woman that Dances with Fourteen Glasses on the Backs and Palms of her Hands, and turn round with them above an Hundred Times as fast a windmill turns."
—*A 1700 Bartholomew Fair advertisement*

• "The Ice was now become so incredibly thick, as to beare not onely whole streets of boothes in which they roasted meate, & had divers shop of wares, ... but Coaches and horses passed over."
—*John Evelyn's diary describing the Frost Fair of 1683*

• "The frost was so strong and hard by the 20 of December [1683] that people began to walke upon the Thames; ... [by] about the 8 or 9 day of January there was a whole streete called the Broad Streete ... and booths built, and many thousands of people walking sometimes together

---

FAST FACT

From the 14th to the 19th centuries, the Thames froze over more than a dozen times, allowing Londoners to set up Frost Fairs— winter festivals with sports, entertainment, food, and drink.

❝What you can buy for threepence on the shore, will cost you fourpence on the Thames, or more.❞

~London rhyme on the pricing scheme *at the Frost Fairs*

at once, and many tradesmen there . . . and several bull baitings have been there, and many other games and exercises."
—*Roger Morrice's diary describing the Frost Fair of 1683*

• "I saw at Southwark, monkeys and apes dance, and do other feats of activity, on the high rope; they were gallantly clad . . . saluted the company, bowing and pulling off their hats; . . . they turned heels over head with a basket having eggs in it, without breaking any; also, with lighted candles in their hands, and on their heads, without extinguishing them, and with vessels of water without spilling a drop."
—*John Evelyn's diary describing the 1660 St. Margaret's Fair*

• "The Gyant, or the Miracle of Nature, . . . aged nineteen years last June, 1684. Born in Ireland, of such a prodigious height and bigness, and every way proportionable, the like hath not been seen since the memory of man. He hath been several times shown at Court, and his Majesty was pleased to walk under his arm, and he is grown very much since; he now reaches ten foot and a half, fathomes near eight foot, spans fifteen inches."
—*A public announcement advertising a giant at 1685's Southwark Fair*

• "A Frenchman submitted to the curious the astonishing strength of the "strong woman," his wife. A blacksmith's anvil being procured . . . [three of the men brought it up] and placed it on the floor. The woman was short, but mostly beautifully and delicately formed, and of a most lovely countenance. She first let down her hair . . . of a length descending to her knees, which she twisted round the projecting part of the anvil, and then, with seeming ease, lifted the ponderous weight some inches from the floor."
—*John Carter, describing the May Fair of 1774*

• "Bears were taught to feign death, and to walk erect after their leader, who played some musical instrument. Horses were also taught to walk on their hind legs, and one drawing . . . shows a horse in this attitude, engaged in a mimic fight with a man armed with sword and buckler."
—*Thomas Frost, describing typical fair entertainment in* The Old Showmen and the Old London Fairs, *1875*

· Eight Waterfront Pubs ·

A pint in a pub on the river is a ritual for many Londoners, especially on a sunny Sunday at lunchtime. Historic pubs dot the length of the river (the list below runs east to west). A word of warning: Some of the oldest—perfect fragments of Dickensian London—are in the east of the city, relatively far from the center and often in unprepossessing surroundings. Others are in the west (between Wandsworth and Richmond); not necessarily quicker to get to from central London, but usually in more bucolic settings.

Greenwich's venerable Trafalgar Tavern

• The Cutty Sark, Greenwich

(4-6 Ballast Quay, SE10, tel 020 8858 3146, cutty sarktavern.co.uk)
How old? The sign outside says 1695; the front door's window glass, 1795. Old enough, anyway, and with the genuine look and feel of a smuggler's den, full of barrels, antiques, low ceilings, wood panels, and plenty of window and outdoor terrace tables to enjoy the views.

• The Trafalgar Tavern, Greenwich

(Park Row, SE10, tel 020 8858 2909, trafalgar tavern.co.uk)
Convenient for the sights of Greenwich and a short walk upstream from The Cutty Sark. It was built in 1837, the year Queen Victoria came to the throne, and until around 1915 was one of several river pubs Londoners traditionally visited by boat for "Whitebait Suppers"; even the Cabinet (government minsters) came once a year. A whitebait specialty is still on the menu.

• The Grapes, Limehouse

(76 Narrow St., E14, tel 020 7987 4396, thegrapes.co.uk)
This great historic "local," dating from 1583, appears, thinly disguised, in Dickens's *Our Mutual Friend:* "A tavern of dropsical appearance ... long settled down into a state of hale infirmity. It had outlasted many a sprucer public house ..." Downstairs in the narrow bar all is wood and walls painted in warm burgundy; upstairs is a romantic dining room of white linens and candlelight.

• **The Prospect of Whitby, Wapping**
(57 Wapping Wall, E1, tel 020 7481 1095, taylor-walker.co.uk)
Founded around 1520 and claiming to be London's oldest riverside pub, it certainly looks the part, with its original flagstone floors and fine old pewter bar. Like many docklands inns, it was a notorious haunt of smugglers and pirates.

• **The Mayflower, Rotherhithe**
(117 Rotherhithe St., SE16, tel 020 7237 4088, themayflowerrotherhithe.com)
Why the name? Because the Pilgrims set sail from a mooring here in 1620, and though the current building—all beams and paneling—dates from the 18th century, there has been an inn on this site since around 1550. Timbers from the broken-up *Mayflower* were used in the pub, and the walls contain wills and other memorabilia from the original crew and passengers.

• **The Anchor, Southwark**
(34 Park St., Southwark, SE1, tel 020 7407 1577, taylor-walker.co.uk)
The present pub is from 1822, but there has been an inn on the site for around 800 years. And no wonder, for this is one of the oldest and most historic parts of the city's waterfront. The Anchor has been a brothel, a brewery, a ships' chandler. It was also the spot ("a little alehouse on bankside") from which the diarist Samuel Pepys watched the Great Fire of London grow in 1666.

• **The Dove, Hammersmith**
(19 Upper Mall, W6, tel 020 8748 9474, dove hammersmith.co.uk)
The Dove enjoys a beautiful spot on a bend of the river and is laden with history. There's been a pub on the site since the 17th century and the present brewers, Fuller's, have owned the inn since 1796. Graham Greene and Ernest Hemingway were both patrons; the poet James Thomson composed "Rule, Britannia" in one of the rooms; and Charles II romanced and dined his mistress Nell Gwyn here.

• **The White Cross, Richmond**
(Riverside, TW9, tel 020 8940 6844, thewhitecross richmond.com)
Dating from 1748, the pub was rebuilt in 1838 on the site of a Franciscan friary dissolved by Henry VIII in 1534; parts of the friary may survive in the inn's cellars. Excellent food accompanies the superb river views.

FAST FACT

One of the bars at The Dove in Hammersmith ranks in the Guinness World Records as the smallest bar room in the world (see Smallest, Shortest, Narrowest, p. 112).

Seven Great Victorian Gin Palaces

Gin was all the rage in 19th-century London. Extravagant gin palaces were built by the hundreds, with beautiful frosted and etched glass and mirrors, ornate furnishings, rich wood paneling, and interesting features such as snugs (small, semi-private bar-parlors designed for the ladies). Some worthy survivors:

Argyll Arms

(18 Argyll St., W1, tel 020 7734 6117, nicholsonspubs.co.uk)
Established in 1742 and conveniently located just off Oxford Circus.

The Dog and Duck

(18 Bateman St., W1, tel 020 7494 0697, nicholsonspubs.co.uk)
Soho's Dog and Duck boasts thousands of glazed tiles in its 1897 interior.

The Lamb

(94 Lambs Conduit St., WC1, tel 020 7405 0713, youngs.co.uk)
Snob screens and other Victorian gin palace features adorn this atmospheric Bloomsbury drinkery.

The Prince Alfred

(5a Formosa St., W9, tel 020 7286 3287, theprincealfred.com)
In Little Venice, the Prince Alfred has tiny doors to stoop under as you venture from snug to snug.

Princess Louise

(208 High Holborn, WC1, tel 020 7405 8816, princesslouisepub.co.uk)
It's often cited as a prime example of the gin palace genre; from 1872, in Holborn.

The Salisbury

(90 St. Martins Lane, WC2, tel 020 7836 5863, taylor-walker.co.uk)
In the western reaches of Covent Garden, the Salisbury was refurbished in the 1890s with all the Victorian bells and whistles and is still going strong.

The Viaduct Tavern

(126 Newgate St., EC1, tel 020 7600 1863, viaducttavern.co.uk)
This beautiful old pub in Smithfield near St. Paul's was built on the site of a former jail.

·Ten Classic Historic Pubs·

Here's a sampling of some of London's most historic pubs, many of which have been serving a thirsty clientele for centuries on end.

The George Inn and its rare gallery (balcony)

• French House
(49 Dean St., W1, frenchhousesoho.com)
French expatriates during World War II gathered at this bohemian Soho enclave—Charles de Gaulle is said to have planned Resistance strategies in the upstairs bar.

• George Inn
(77 Borough St., SE1, nationaltrust.org.uk/george-inn)
South of the Thames, bougainvillea and half-timbering set the mood at the Tudor-era George Inn, London's last remaining two-storied coaching inn. The atmospheric courtyard was once used as a performance space for Elizabethan plays; the George's second-story balconies provided excellent views of the action.

• The Grenadier
(18 Wilton Row, Belgrave Square, SW1, taylor-walker .co.uk)
Located in Belgrave Square, the Grenadier was originally the mess hall for the Grenadier Guards of the Duke of Wellington . . . hence the name. This small pub is covered with military artifacts and yellowed newspapers, adding to the historical feel of the 18th-century building.

• Hand & Shears
(1 Middle St., EC1, tel 020 7600 0257)
In Smithfield's Cloth Fair, the Hand & Shears stands on the site of a 12th-century alehouse. The no-frills pub is one of several old watering holes in London that are supposed to have been the site of condemned prisoners' last drinks en route to the gallows.

• Jerusalem Tavern
(55 Britton St., EC1, stpetersbrewery.co.uk)
Named after the Priory of St. John of Jerusalem, Clerkenwell's Jerusalem Tavern has been in business since the 14th century. The current building dates from 1720 and offers traditional craft beers from Suffolk's St. Peter's Brewery.

Ye Olde Mitre is home to the remnants of a cherry tree around which Queen Elizabeth I once danced.

• **The Lamb & Flag**
(33 Rose St., WC2, lambandflagcovent garden.co.uk)
A Covent Garden local since 1772, the Lamb & Flag earned an early reputation as host for bare-knuckle fisticuffs—and the nickname "Bucket of Blood." The tucked-away Lamb & Flag is popular with locals and tourists alike (which is code for "it can get very crowded").

• **Ye Olde Cheshire Cheese**
(145 Fleet St., EC4, tel 020 7353 6170)

Ye Olde Cheshire Cheese north of Inner Temple was built in 1667, just after the Great Fire of London. Over the centuries this pub came to be a local haunt for Samuel Johnson, Oliver Goldsmith, Charles Dickens, and Arthur Conan Doyle.

• **Ye Olde Mitre**
(1 Ely Ct., EC1, yeolde mitreholburn.co.uk)
Hidden down an alleyway in Holborn, Ye Olde Mitre was mentioned by name by Shakespeare in both *Richard II* and *Richard III*. While originally

built in 1546, the current structure is from 1772.

• **The Spaniards Inn**
(Spaniards Rd., Hampstead Heath, NW3, thespaniardshampstead .co.uk)
The Spaniards, built in 1585, appears in both Bram Stoker's *Dracula* and Dickens's *The Pickwick Papers*. This popular Hampstead Heath pub is also said to have hosted the poet John Keats and to have been the birthplace of the 18th-century English highwayman, Dick Turpin.

Hampstead Heath's Spaniards Inn pub

• **White Hart**
(191 Drury Lane, WC2, whitehartdrurylane .co.uk)
Near Covent Garden, the White Hart in Holborn is the oldest licensed bar in London. Its original licensing date was 1216, only one year after the signing of the Magna Carta.

Things to Buy on the Olde Streets of London

Social reformer Henry Mayhew's seminal surveys of street vendors in the 1850s included lists of the very eclectic wares sold by costermongers and other traders on the city streets:

- baked potatoes
- bird nests
- birds
- books
- boot laces
- cat and dog meat (meaning, offal to feed to your cat or dog)
- cats
- chickweed
- clothes
- coal
- coffee
- coke and other minerals
- combs
- crockery
- dogs
- fine arts
- fish
- flowers
- fruit
- glass and glasswares
- groundsel
- leverets (young hares)
- linen
- matches
- meat pies
- nutmeg graters
- old metal
- oysters
- poultry
- rat poison
- salt
- sand
- secondhand weapons
- sheep trotters
- shells
- shoes
- snails
- spice
- squirrels
- stationery
- tortoises
- vegetables
- walking sticks
- watercress

·Thirteen Obsolete Jobs·

In a city that's been doing business for 2,000 years, there are thousands of job skills that have become less than relevant. Here are a few from the more distant past (and if you ask us, on some of them, the more distant the better):

• **Barber-surgeons:** Until the 18th century, barbers often acted as surgeons as well as hair cutters. And even after restrictions were put in place, they were still allowed to carry on their traditional roles of dentists (oh, let's just call them "tooth-pullers") and blood-letters.

• **Costermongers:** Street vendors who sold everything from flowers and vegetables to fruit and game (see above). They would often literally sing the praises of their own wares.

• **Crossing sweepers:** They would keep streets clear by brooming away garbage and horse dung for tips. Sometimes permanent gigs were offered by local banks and other businesses.

• **Dog finders:** A slightly misleading name . . . dog finders would indeed find dogs and return them to their owners for a reward, but they

There are horrific stories of toshers being killed in mass attacks by thousands of sewer rats.

were usually the ones who stole the dogs in the first place. Less a job than a racket.

• **Gong farmers:** Lucky souls who removed human excrement from the city's privies and cesspits. Laws were passed restricting their work to the night hours, when the gong farmers collected their cargo and hauled it outside the city limits for dumping.

• **Knocker-uppers:** Human alarm clocks hired to rap on the windows of the fast asleep early in the morning.

• **Mooncursers:** In the dark days before street lighting, boys would escort people to their homes at night with a light to guide the way. The name comes from their cursing at the bright moon, a light source that would (temporarily) put them out of work.

• **Mudlarks:** Predominantly young children who would rummage along the Thames shore for bits of coal, cloth, glass, rope, and nails that had

The flower lady costermonger

fallen off ships. A very real occupational hazard was the threat of stepping on the glass and nails that were the objects of their search, leading to nasty foot injuries.

• **Patterers or death hunters:** Basically newspaper reporters/sellers who boosted sales by providing vivid descriptions of recent murders or the last words of convicted felons. They did their own reconnaissance and sold their newspapers or pamphlets on the public highways.

• **Pure collectors:** They would peruse the streets of London with a pail and (sometimes) a glove for "pure"—the name used for dog dung, which was actually a valuable commodity in the tanning industry. (One wonders if the "dog finders" and "pure collectors" shouldn't have pooled their resources.)

• **Rag and bone men:** Sometimes also known as "cafflers," these men went from street to street collecting bits of trash for tips.

• **Rat catchers:** Yes, rats . . . but the Underground also required them to round up rabbits, dogs, cats, and any other interlopers that might nibble at wires or just get in the way of speeding trains.

• **Toshers:** They rummaged through London's sewer muck for anything of remote value. No thank you.

• **Whipping boys:** Whipping boys were assigned to young royalty and took the blows when their princes misbehaved. As the whipping boys were often close companions to their masters, this practice was emotionally powerful and therefore surprisingly effective.

·Surprising Archaeological Finds·

There are some things you might expect to find under the streets of London—old Roman pottery, the remains of an Anglo-Saxon house, a medieval wine cellar. But sometimes archaeologists, or more often underground workers who then call the archaeologists, discover something especially surprising . . .

• **The Cheapside Hoard**
In 1912, a team of London workmen demolishing an old jewelry shop on Cheapside unearthed the motherlode—the Cheapside Hoard, an overflowing treasure chest of 16th- and 17th-century jewelry. The find contained nearly 500 fantastically rare jewels and precious gemstones—diamonds, emeralds, rings, rubies, etc.—most from the eras of Elizabeth I and James I, but also some ancient pieces dating

back 1,500 years. The Hoard eventually made its way to the Museum of London for safekeeping; it was exhibited there in 2013-2014. Why the massive collection was buried and never reclaimed remains a mystery.

• Fuddling cups
Ever the jokesters, Londoners have long been fond of fuddling cups. Perhaps better known today as dribble glasses, these mugs were designed to pour the liquid contents down the front of the unwary drinker. With examples at the Museum of London, the V&A, and the British Museum ranging from the late 15th to the early 19th centuries, these prankish cups seem to have entertained for centuries.

• Kew Palace Kitchen
In 1789, a great kitchen

A Cheapside Hoard cameo

was built on the grounds of Kew Palace to serve the White House, the mansion of Prince Frederick. After the death of his mother, Queen Charlotte, in 1818, the house and the nearby separate kitchen fell into disuse. Although the White House was eventually razed, the kitchen was simply shuttered up. When the kitchen was finally reopened in 2012, it was found to be in almost pristine condition, a time capsule of 1818 royal daily life, with preparation rooms

where bread was baked and all the other accoutrements of the trade still extant. The kitchen can now be toured at Kew (hrp.org.uk).

• Roman bikini bottom
It's perhaps surprising to learn that the bikini was not an invention of the mod '60s. In Roman times, the young girls who worked as dancers and acrobats apparently wore them. In 1953, a pristine pair of first-century A.D. leather bikini bottoms was discovered down a Roman well on Queen Street. This best preserved of all examples from the Roman era is on display at the Museum of London (museumof london.org.uk).

• Roman-era graffiti
Among the many Roman-era relics found around the City, one of the most fascinating contains a bit

❝The joy of London archaeology for me has always been that the finds reflect the immensely eclectic nature of the city itself—you'll never know what you'll uncover in a place that has been a nexus of several worldwide empires over the millennia.❞

~**John Maloney,** *former Principal Archaeology Officer, Museum of London*

of 2,000-year-old graffiti. Etched in a clay building tile before it was kilned was this message: "Austalis has been going off by himself every day these last 13 days." This note, most likely written by a disgruntled kiln co-worker, is believed to be a heartfelt expression of how Austalis's slacking was affecting the output quota of the work team.

• **The Stepney witch-bottle**

Although not especially rare, these are cool anyway. In 1954, archaeologists digging in East London's Stepney district discovered a stone bottle, carved into the shape of a face and filled with human hair, fingernail clippings, and some iron nails and metal wire. Behold the witch-bottle, a device used often in the 16th and 17th centuries (in both Britain and North America) to trap negative energy and thereby ward off evil witchcraft spells—and sometimes also to be a bit more proactive and cause injury to others.

• **The Thames Exchange watersite finds**

A 1988-1989 dig at the Thames Exchange buildings near Southwark Bridge in the City unearthed more than 6,000 objects, among them some unusual finds: a Roman wooden spoon depicting a head with black African features (yes, the Roman Empire encompassed large areas of North Africa, but this is the only such Roman

Fuddling cups, a favorite of pranksters since medieval days

FAST FACT

The human remains found under St. Pancras during its 21st-century renovations are likely from the graveyards of the communities that occupied the site before the station was originally built in the 1860s, including Somers Town and the notorious slums of adjoining Agar Town.

representation ever found in Britain); and a small medieval Japanese handbell. Again, this is unique for Britain, and from a time when Japan was largely closed off to the West.

• **Walrus remains**
The fact that a Pacific walrus, normally found in the faraway Bering Strait, might have spent time in London isn't entirely unbelievable—after all, there is the London Zoo. But what's surprising is that these walrus remains were found among the skeletons of 1,500 people buried under St. Pancras Station. Discovered in 2003 during the station's renovation, the 13-foot (4 m) skeleton was in a coffin along with eight sets of human remains. It's believed the deceased humans, and possibly the walrus, were used for medical research in the mid-19th century.

• **Ye Olde Cheshire Cheese's bawdy tiles**
The Cheshire Cheese makes several of our lists, being one of the oldest and most famous pubs in London. But is it possible the venerable pub once also doubled as a house of ill repute? Lining the fireplace of an upstairs room was a series of painted erotic tiles depicting ... well, erotic themes. Recovered and studied in the 1970s and dating from the 1750s, the find hinted that upstairs rooms might have served more than ale—but it's also possible they were simply adornments for gentlemen-only drinking clubs.

London's Most Common Birds

This list comes from a survey by the British Trust for Ornithology (*bto.org*), with figures for the percentage of London gardens visited by each bird:

1. Blue tit	90.7	6. Magpie	65.2
2. Wood pigeon	89.7	7. Dunnock	58.6
3. Robin	88.3	8. Starling	53.3
4. Great tit	82.4	9. Collared dove	47.2
5. Blackbird	79.1	10. House sparrow	47.1

A Selection of Fictitious Londoners

Just a few—there are plenty more to choose from.

About a Boy, Nick Hornby (1998)
The main characters, Will Freeman and Marcus Brewer (the boy), strike up their friendship in Islington.

Around the World in Eighty Days, Jules Verne (1873)
Phileas Fogg's home is at 7 Savile Row in Mayfair. After 80 days, he triumphantly returns to the scene of his original bet, the still active Reform Club at 104 Pall Mall.

Brick Lane, Monica Ali (2003)
Nazneen, the protagonist, moves to London at the age of 18. The novel's events center around the East London title street, the epicenter of London's Bangladeshi community.

The Canterbury Tales, Geoffrey Chaucer (late 14th century)
The narrator stays at the (now-gone) Tabard Inn in Southwark before departing with the band of pilgrims for Canterbury.

A Christmas Carol, Charles Dickens (1843)
Bob Cratchit lives with his family (including Tiny Tim) in Camden Town. The location of Ebenezer Scrooge's home isn't mentioned.

David Copperfield, Charles Dickens (1850)
The title character lives, works, shops, dines, pays visits, and goes sightseeing in various locales all over the city.

Death of a Ghost, Margery Allingham (1934)

The unveiling of John Lafcadio's paintings, and the ensuing unpleasantness, takes place in Little Venice.

Emma, Jane Austen (1815)

Emma's sister, Isabella Knightley, lives in Brunswick Square in Bloomsbury.

Gulliver's Travels, Jonathan Swift (1726)

Lemuel Gulliver lived on Old Jewry, Fetter Lane, and in Wapping before departing on his travels.

James Bond, Ian Fleming (first appearance: 1953)

Agent 007's home is at 30 Wellington Square in Chelsea.

Little Dorrit, Charles Dickens (1855-1857)

"Little" Amy Dorrit is raised in Marshalsea debtor's prison in Southwark, as her father is an inmate there . . . as in fact was Dickens's real-life father.

Mary Poppins, P. L. Travers (first appearance: 1934)

The Banks family home is at 17 Cherry Tree Lane, an invented street.

Moll Flanders, Daniel Defoe (1722)

Moll is born in Newgate Prison (near today's Old Bailey), where her mother is incarcerated. She later lives in Hammersmith for a time.

Mrs. Dalloway, Virginia Woolf (1925)

The Dalloways' home (and site of the novel's dinner party) is at an unnamed address in Westminster.

Oliver Twist, Charles Dickens (1838)

Fagin's den of thieves is on Field Lane in Saffron Hill. Bill Sikes lives in Bethnal

FIRST PERSON

❝What an amazing place London was to me when I saw it in the distance, and how I believed all the adventures of all my favourite heroes to be constantly enacting and re-enacting there.❞

~David Copperfield, *from Charles Dickens's book of the same name (1850)*

Green before moving to (and later dying on) Jacob's Island, a notorious slum on the south side of the Thames.

Paddington Bear, Michael Bond (first appearance: 1958)
The charming bear is found at Paddington Station and lives with the Brown family at 32 Windsor Gardens, off Harrow Road near Maida Vale. (Windsor Gardens actually exists; number 32 does not.)

Peter Pan, J. M. Barrie (Peter first appears in *The White Bird,* 1902)
Wendy Darling and her family live in Bloomsbury. Peter Pan and Tinker Bell live in Neverland, well outside of London proper.

Pride and Prejudice, Jane Austen (1813)
Edward Gardiner, uncle of the Bennet sisters, and his wife live on Gracechurch Street, near St. Paul's.

The Pursuit of Love, Nancy Mitford (1945)
Fanny Logan, heroine of the tale, works in a bookstore on a "slummy little street," aka Curzon Street (as did the author herself).

Pygmalion, George Bernard Shaw, 1912
Henry Higgins lives at 27a Wimpole Street. Eliza Doolittle practices her flower-selling trade in Covent Garden.

Sherlock Holmes, Arthur Conan Doyle (first appearance: 1887)
Sherlock Holmes's home is famously located at 221b Baker Street. Dr. John Watson resides there periodically as well, as does Mrs. Hudson, the owner of the property.

Strange Case of Dr. Jekyll and Mr. Hyde, Robert Louis Stevenson (1886)
Dr. Henry Jekyll/Mr. Edward Hyde lives in Soho.

The Time Machine, H. G. Wells (1895)
The central character, called only the "Time Traveller," lives in Richmond.

Vanity Fair, William Makepeace Thackeray (1847-1848)
Amelia Sedley lives in Russell Square, London. The family later moves to Fulham Road.

Who's Buried (or Has a Memorial) at Poets' Corner in Westminster Abbey

More than 150 literary figures are either buried or commemorated in Westminster Abbey, most of them in the South Transept's fabled Poets' Corner. Here's a sampler.

Writers and poets buried in the Abbey:

- Joseph Addison (d. 1719)
- Robert Browning (d. 1889)
- William Camden (d. 1623)
- Geoffrey Chaucer (d. 1400)
- Charles Dickens (d. 1870)
- John Dryden (d. 1700)
- David Garrick (d. 1779)
- Thomas Hardy (d. 1928)
- Dr. Samuel Johnson (d. 1784)
- Ben Jonson (d. 1637)
- Rudyard Kipling (d. 1936)
- Edward Bulwer-Lytton (d. 1873)
- Thomas Macaulay (d. 1859)
- John Masefield (d. 1967)
- Sir Isaac Newton (d. 1727)
- Nicholas Rowe (d. 1718)
- Richard Sheridan (d. 1816)
- Edmund Spenser (d. 1599)
- Alfred, Lord Tennyson (d. 1892)

Writers and poets memorialized with a plaque, statue, or window in the Abbey:

- W. H. Auden (d. 1973)
- Jane Austen (d. 1817)
- Sir John Betjeman (d. 1984)
- William Blake (d. 1827)
- Anne, Charlotte, and Emily Brontë (d. 1849, 1855, and 1848, respectively)
- Rupert Brooke (d. 1915)
- Elizabeth Barrett Browning (d. 1861)
- John Bunyan (d. 1688)
- Robert Burns (d. 1796)
- Lord Byron (d. 1824)
- Lewis Carroll (Charles L. Dodgson) (d. 1898)
- Winston Churchill (d. 1965)
- Samuel Coleridge (d. 1834)
- Sir Noël Coward (d. 1973)
- Benjamin Disraeli (d. 1881)
- George Eliot (Mary Ann Evans) (d. 1880)
- T. S. Eliot (d. 1965)
- Oliver Goldsmith (d. 1774)
- A. E. Housman (d. 1936)
- Ted Hughes (d. 1998)
- Henry James (d. 1916)
- John Keats (d. 1821)
- D. H. Lawrence (d. 1930)
- C. S. Lewis (d. 1963)
- Henry Wadsworth Longfellow (d. 1882)
- Christopher Marlowe (d. 1593)
- John Milton (d. 1674)
- Wilfred Owen (d. 1918)
- Alexander Pope (d. 1744)
- Sir Walter Scott (d. 1832)
- William Shakespeare (d. 1616)
- Percy Bysshe Shelley (d. 1822)
- William Makepeace Thackeray (d. 1863)
- Dylan Thomas (d. 1953)
- Anthony Trollope (d. 1882)
- Oscar Wilde (d. 1900)
- William Wordsworth (d. 1850)

Westminster Abbey

People have been worshipping on the site of Westminster Abbey, yet another of London's distinctive icons, for more than 1,000 years—and counting.

Decade that building began on the first church on the site
The 1040s, by Edward the Confessor

Year consecrated 1065

Year the Abbey as we know it today was built Most of the Gothic church seen today was completed between 1245 and 1272

Height of the Towers 225 feet (69 m)

Number of people buried at the Abbey More than 3,200

Number of kings and queens buried in the Abbey 17

Last body buried at the Abbey The Unknown Soldier, who fell on a French battlefield during World War I, was buried here in 1920.

Number of kings and queens coronated at the Abbey Every one since 1066, except for Edward V and Edward VIII, who weren't officially coronated (see Monarchs, p. 17)

The one object with the most graffiti on it Amazingly, the Coronation Chair. In the 18th and 19th centuries, it wasn't considered bad form to etch your name for posterity's sake on one of the nation's icons.

Number of royal weddings at the Abbey 16, the most recent being the wedding of Prince William and Kate Middleton in April 2011

·Livery Companies of the City of London·

Since medieval times, crafts and trades have formed associations to protect their commercial interests, regulate business, maintain standards of workmanship, and mediate disputes. Originally, guilds also had a religious role, with patron saints and links to specific chapels and churches.

Each guild had a livery hall (few of which survive), where its members met and entertained guests. Each guild also had its own distinctive ceremonial clothing, badges, and emblems, called a livery,

The crest of the Clothworkers' guild, established in the 15th century

MY TRUST IS IN GOD ALONE

that guild members still wear today on official occasions.

Starting in the 18th century, the guilds' primary concerns shifted to charitable works. They focused more on caring for members who had fallen on hard times and built almshouses to provide housing for those in need.

In 1515, the Alderman of the City of London ranked the 48 livery companies then in existence, establishing the "order of precedence" (based on the guilds' power and influence). The first dozen on that list make up the influential Great 12 City Livery Companies:

1. The Mercers Originally purveyors of fine fabrics, the company gradually came to represent general merchants (the term "mercer" derives from the Latin for "merchandise"). Since they rank first in the order of precedence, the Mercers have the right to call themselves the "premier" livery company.

2. The Grocers Formed in the 14th century, the Grocers derive from an even older Ancient Guild of Pepperers, which regulated the sale of spices.

3. The Drapers The trade association for merchants of wool and cloth.

4. The Fishmongers For sellers of fish and seafood.

5. The Goldsmiths Representing goldsmiths, silversmiths, and jewelers.

6. The Skinners For traders of skins and furs, which was big business in the medieval world.

7. The Merchant Taylors Originally representing the City's tailors, the Merchant Taylors have been arguing with the Skinners for some 600 years about who should be sixth and who seventh on the list. To keep the peace, they alternate spots from year to year. Although probably apocryphal, this is commonly cited as the origin of the expression "at sixes and sevens."

8. The Haberdashers Representing sellers of cloth accessories (e.g., beads, ribbons, purses, gloves, pins, etc.) as well as those in the sewing trades.

9. The Salters For merchants of salt (critical for preserving meats and fish).

10. The Ironmongers Originally known as Ferroners, the Ironmongers regulated the City's smiths and iron trade.

11. The Vintners For the City's wine merchants.

12. The Clothworkers Representing those finishing (e.g., fulling,

---

FAST FACT

In 2013, the Company of Educators was added to the roster of livery companies, bringing the total number of active guilds up to 109.

shearing, and planing) cloth products.

A few additional interesting guilds (but, alas, not part of the big 12):

• **The Apothecaries** act for makers and dispensers of medicines and drugs. In 1673 the Apothecaries founded Chelsea Physic Garden, the oldest botanical garden in London, which they managed until 1899.

Traditional livery attire

• **The Wax Chandlers** and **the Tallow Chandlers** both represent candlemakers. Candles made from wax (beeswax) were used in churches and the homes of the wealthy, while tallow (rendered fat) candles had a less exclusive clientele. Every year, on September 14, the Wax

Chandlers still present St. Paul's Cathedral with their altar candles.

• **The Stationers,** formed in 1403, was originally a guild for printers. After 1557, its members had the right to seize books the Church of England or the Crown deemed offensive. In 1937 the Stationers

amalgamated and combined names with the Newspaper Makers' Company, and today mostly represents the communications and media industry.

• **The Coopers** were granted a Royal Charter by Henry VII. In addition to making and repairing wooden casks and barrels, the Coopers also were granted the right to inspect vessels used to store ale, beer, and soap.

• **The Coachmakers** built and regulated the building of coaches (there was also a separate company for wheelwrights). Today the Coachmakers promote excellence in all modern transportation industries (be it on the roads, on the rails, or in space).

FAST FACT

In 1342, Edward III decreed, "No taverner shall mix putrid and corrupt wine with wine that is pure and good." In 1364, taverner John Penrose fell afoul, and it was decided he "shall drink a draught of the same wine which he sold . . . and the remainder of such wine shall then be poured on [his] head."

·Unusual Small Museums·

Never mind the big hitters—the British, Natural History, V&A, and Science museums. London has a superb collection of often eccentric but compelling smaller museums.

• Bank of England Museum

Where does all that money come from? The collection of artifacts the Bank of England has accumulated during its 300-year history offers some clues *(bankof england.co.uk)*.

• Museum of Brands, Packaging and Advertising

It's all here: "the brands and packs, posters and ads, fads and fashions, toys and games . . . a kaleidoscope of images and iconic brands"— more than 12,000 items in all *(museum ofbrands.com)*.

• The BDA Museum

Don't like the dentist? The British Dental Association's museum won't help, but force yourself to visit anyway. Its 20,000 artifacts offer a fascinating account of all things dental, from the horrifying instruments of the distant past to the extraordinary technology of the present *(bda.org/museum)*.

• The Cinema Museum

Crammed with artifacts, equipment, and memorabilia, the museum celebrates all things cinematic *(cinemamuseum.org.uk)*.

• The Clockmakers' Museum, Guildhall

The world's oldest and finest collection of clocks and watches holds 600 English and European watches, 30 clocks, and 15 marine timekeepers, along with a number of rare horological portraits *(clockmakers.org)*.

• The Fan Museum

The only U.K. museum devoted to fans has more than 4,000 examples from across the globe, some dating from as far back as the 11th century *(thefanmuseum.org.uk)*.

• The Foundling Museum

Learn the fascinating story of the Foundling Hospital, created in 1739

A small selection of the Fan Museum's collection

to care for abandoned children, and of some of its major benefactors, such as the artist and satirist William Hogarth (1697-1764) and the composer George Frideric Handel (1685-1759) *(foundlingmuseum.org.uk)*.

• The Garden Museum
Beautifully set near the Thames in and around the previously abandoned church of St. Mary's, Lambeth, the museum is the burial place of John Tradescant (ca 1570-1638), Britain's first great gardener and plant hunter *(garden museum.org.uk)*.

• The Grant Museum of Zoology
London's last university-based zoological museum, founded in 1828 as a teaching collection, has more than 67,000 specimens, including skeletons, mounted animals, and creatures preserved in fluid—many of them very strange and long since extinct *(ucl.ac .uk/museums/zoology)*.

• The London Fire Brigade Museum
Here's one for children or adults who still secretly daydream about becoming firefighters *(london-fire.gov.uk/our museum.asp)*.

• The Royal London Museum
Never mind the historic surgical instruments and other displays at this hospital museum. Most visitors are interested in two things: the forensic section (the Jack the Ripper murders were committed just around the corner) and the displays devoted to Joseph Merrick, the "Elephant Man," who spent the last four years of his life in a specially adapted room in the building *(bartshealth .nhs.uk/about-us)*.

• V&A Museum of Childhood
This Bethnal Green offshoot of the main Victoria & Albert Museum in South Kensington is a treasure chest of toys, games, and exhibits relating to childhood. Many date back hundreds of years. Combine a visit with a trip through the toy-crammed rooms of Pollock's Toy Museum *(museumofchildhood.org .uk* and *pollockstoy museum.com)*.

• Whitechapel Bell Foundry
Britain's oldest manufacturing company, founded in 1570, made Big Ben and other historic bells. It has a small exhibition space and offers superb tours—but book early as spaces fill quickly *(whitechapel bellfoundry.co.uk)*.

FAST FACT

In 1752, the Whitechapel Bell Foundry cast the Liberty Bell, which rang in Philadelphia in July 1776 to summon citizens to hear the reading of the Declaration of Independence.

·Roman Ruins in London·

Here's something amazing to know and hard to imagine: As you walk along the streets of today's City of London (the old square mile), you're actually walking atop a gigantic man-made pile of rubble. The natural earth, roads, and foundations of the original Roman city of Londinium are buried beneath 10 to 13 feet (3 to 4 m) of landfill and detritus accumulated during 2,000 years of razings, fires, riots, and Blitzes, with constant rebuilding in between. If you fell that distance, you'd get hurt.

Although it's therefore unsurprising that the original Roman city—400 years in the making—is somewhat out of sight, out of mind, there are still several excellent places to see remnants of this once-flourishing society. You just need to know where to look.

Excavating part of the old Roman Wall

• **All Hallows by the Tower**
(Byward St., EC3)
One of the oldest churches in London, All Hallows was founded by the Anglo-Saxons in A.D. 675. An arch from that first church survives; below the arch traces of old Roman pavement can be seen, proving the site has been in use for 2,000 years.

• **The Bank of England**
(Bartholomew Lane, EC2)
A museum located within the bank displays Roman pottery, mosaics, gold, and coins discovered

when the building was rebuilt in the 1930s.

• **The City Wall**
The old Roman city wall was built at the end of the second century A.D. and stretched from Blackfriars in the west to the site of today's Tower in the east. It stood about two miles long, 20 feet high, and eight feet wide. You can still see the following:

• The most complete section stands just outside the Tower Hill Tube stop, EC3. (You can't miss it.)

• A less well-known segment (with bonus Norman and medieval add-ons) stands somewhat incongruously at the back of the parking lot fronting the Grange City Hotel, on Cooper's Row, a hundred yards or so north of the same Tower Hill Tube stop.

• At One America Square (at the juncture

of Crosswall and Cooper's Row, EC3), a fairly long wall section stands in the conference center basement and is visible through the window at street level from Crosswall.

• An extensive stretch of wall is hidden in the basement of Emperor House (35 Vine St., EC3), which houses a pub and a corporate office. Although the segment is not officially open to the public, you can ask to be shown the ruin.

A statue head is uncovered at the Temple of Mithras site, 1954.

• Other bits of the wall are visible near the Museum of London (whose address is, appropriately enough, 150 London Wall), which offers excellent walking tours, often with working archaeologists, to these and many other sites. (Included on their tour is a visit to the remains of the expansive stone fort that preceded the wall by nearly a century.) Check the website at *museum oflondon.org.uk*.

• **Guildhall Roman amphitheater**
(Guildhall, EC2, cityoflondon.gov.uk)
Underneath London's Guildhall lie the remains of the old Roman amphitheater, uncovered when the art gallery was being built in 1988. The amphitheater was Roman London's go-to site for gladiator fights and executions; its remnants are open to the public.

• **The London Stone**
(111 Cannon St., EC4)

FAST FACT

William Penn, founder of Pennsylvania, was christened at All Hallows by the Tower in 1644, and President John Quincy Adams was married there in 1797 while ambassador to England.

London Stone is most likely the central millarium (milestone) from which all Roman roads radiated and from which all mileage measurements were made. The stone is embedded in the exterior wall of a building that's currently a W. H. Smith newsagent, directly across from the Cannon Street train station. Last we heard it was still there, but there were plans afoot to move it into a corporate headquarters down the street.

• **The Museum of London**
(150 London Wall, EC2, museumoflondon.org.uk)
The museum houses hundreds of relics of Roman London.

• **St. Bride's Church**
(Fleet St., EC4)
In the church crypt you can see the foundation of a sixth-century Saxon church, as well as a portion of a decorated floor from an earlier Roman building.

• **The Temple of Mithras** *(EC4)*
In 1954, construction workers digging a building foundation on Walbrook unearthed the third-century A.D. Temple of Mithras, dedicated to the Persian god of light and sun. The ancient Roman temple was moved nearby so that construction could continue. Today it is accessible via Queen Victoria Street, but by 2016 it's scheduled to be returned to its original location.

Gun Salutes

Salutes are fired on special occasions in combinations according to protocol. They occur at the Tower of London (1 p.m.) using 25-pound guns from WWII and in Hyde Park or Green Park at noon (11 a.m. on the Queen's birthday) using 13-pounders from WWI.

- **Remembrance Sunday** (the second Sunday in November) One round at 11 a.m. and one more two minutes later to signify the end of the period of silence
- **Basic royal salute** 21 rounds
- **Basic royal salute in Hyde Park** 21 + 20 because it is a royal park
- **Tower of London basic salute** 21 + 20 because the Tower is a royal palace
- **Tower of London royal salute** 21 + 20 + another 21 for the City of London
- **Placing of the crown during the coronation service** 101 rounds

Only a handful of occasions merit an official gun salute. The most significant:

- **Feb. 6** (Accession Day)
- **April 21** (the Queen's birthday)
- **June 2** (Coronation Day)
- **June 10** (the Duke of Edinburgh's birthday)
- **The Queen's official birthday** (a Saturday in June)
- **Nov. 14** (the Prince of Wales's birthday)
- **The State Opening of Parliament** (usually November or December)
- **Royal births**

·Antiquated Traditions Still in Use·

The new Lord Mayor is elected and announced with great fanfare annually on September 29.

There'll always be an England. Part of the country's charm lies in its almost stubborn adherence to ceremonies, traditions, pomp, and pageantry that have their roots in the hazy distant past. We wouldn't have it any other way.

• **Beating the Bounds**

This charming custom underlies an actual antipathy between the Tower of London (the Crown) and the neighboring parish of All Hallows by the Tower. A marginal area of land surrounding the Tower and independent of the City was taken under the jurisdiction of the Tower in medieval times (All Hallows viewed this as an illegal land grab). The Tower reinforces its boundaries every three years on Ascension Day (the 40th day after Easter), when local children, armed with willow wands, proceed along the edge of the disputed land and beat the boundary stones. (All Hallows performs the ceremony annually from its side of the rift.)

• **The Ceremony of the Constable's Dues**

Every year, a large Royal Navy ship moors at the Tower of London for the Ceremony of the Constable's Dues, a nod to an ancient practice requiring all ships entering the port of London to stop to pay a toll of goods to the Tower's Constable.

Accompanied by an escort of Yeoman Warders in State Dress and a Corps of Drums, the Captain and his shore party escort march to Tower Green, where a keg of rum is delivered.

• The Ceremony of the Keys

The ritual locking of the Tower of London's gates has been performed nightly without fail for more than 700 years. The ceremony, led by the Chief Yeoman Warder (Beefeater) who carries the Keys of the Tower in one hand and a brass lantern in the other, takes place at exactly 9:53 p.m. and lasts for seven minutes.

• The Ceremony of the Lilies and Roses

This private ceremony occurs annually at the Tower of London on May 21, when the Provosts of Eton College and King's College, Cambridge, lay lilies and roses, their college emblems, on the spot in Wakefield Tower where Henry VI, founder of both schools, is said to have been murdered on that day in 1471.

• Changing the Guard

The colorful Changing the Guard happens at Buckingham and St. James's Palaces at 11:30 a.m. every day from May through July, and on alternate days the rest of the year. You can also watch the mounted Queen's Life Guard change guard at Horse Guards Parade daily at 11:00 a.m. (10:00 a.m. on Sundays).

• Election of the Lord Mayor and the Lord Mayor's Show

Each year on September 29, the senior members of each of the City's guilds—known as liverymen—are called to Guildhall to elect the new Lord Mayor. The festive garb of the guilds is on full display. On the day after the Lord Mayor takes office in November, London celebrates the Lord Mayor's Show, as the new mayor proceeds in a state coach along a 3.5-mile (5.6 km) parade route, accompanied by floats and bands, to the Royal Courts of Justice to swear allegiance to the Crown.

• Maundy Thursday

British monarchs long observed the Thursday before Easter by washing the feet of paupers, a reference to Jesus washing his disciples' feet at the Last Supper. The actual feet-washing is no longer carried out at the annual event; instead, the Queen gives elderly citizens purses of special coins. The number of annual recipients is determined by the monarch's age.

FAST FACT

In 1941, following a German bomb hit on the Tower, the Ceremony of the Keys was delayed by half an hour . . . but still took place.

Banqueting House hosted the service for centuries, but the venue now changes annually.

• The Quit-Rents ceremony

Every October, the City of London pays rent for a piece of land it rented in Shropshire in the days of King John and the Magna Carta. The rent is one blunt billhook (a small cutting tool) and one sharp ax. At the Quit-Rents ceremony at the Royal Courts of Justice, the City Solicitor tries (and must fail) to cut through a bundle of wood with the billhook. Then he must succeed in cutting through a similar bundle with the sharp ax. The tools and bundles are then presented to the Queen's Remembrancer (an officer of the Crown).

• Swan Upping

All swans on the Thames are owned by either the Queen or one of two city livery companies, the Dyers and the Vintners, who received their royal swan charters in the 15th century. Each year in the third week of July, the Queen's Swan Marker and the Swan Uppers of the Vintners and the Dyers corral groups of cygnets—baby swans—on the Thames. The guilds put identification rings on the swans' legs to mark them as their property; any unmarked swans are then known to belong to the Queen.

• Trooping the Colour

Another colorful bit of public pageantry is the annual Trooping the Colour ceremony that marks the official celebration in June of the Queen's birthday (though her actual birthday is April 21). The Queen proceeds in a carriage from Buckingham Palace to Horse Guards Parade, where she inspects her troops. The spectacle began in the early 1700s, when it was a practical event for soldiers to be shown the flags ("colours") of their battalions so that they could easily recognize and rally behind them in battle.

The ancient Ceremony of the Keys

·London Statues: A Miscellany·

Critics have often lamented that London is full of statues to old dead white men, and they may have a point, but it's also full of wonderfully eccentric statues with lively backstories.

Old Bailey's statue of Lady Justice lacks her usual blindfold.

• **Eros** in Piccadilly Circus does not represent Eros at all but, rather, his twin brother, Anteros, the Greek god of selfless love. It honors the philanthropic Seventh Earl of Shaftesbury (1801-1885), to whom the whole monument—the Shaftesbury Memorial Fountain—is properly dedicated.

• When depicted elsewhere, the famous allegorical statue of **Lady Justice** is invariably shown blindfolded to suggest that justice is objective, or "blind." But look again at the Old Bailey's—there's no blindfold.

• Sir Edwin Landseer (1802-1873) modeled the feet of his **bronze lions** in Trafalgar Square on the paws of a domestic cat.

• Bloomsbury's Queen Square, WC1, takes its name from the **statue of a queen** at its center: if only we could be sure which—Anne, possibly, or Mary, or Charlotte, wife of George III?

• In his statue outside Westminster Hall, **Oliver Cromwell** (1897-1899) is wearing his spurs upside down; **George IV** in Trafalgar Square (1843) is riding his horse without stirrups.

• The **four caryatids** on the north side of St. Pancras New Church (1819-1822) on Euston Road, NW1, were made too tall and a section had to be cut from the midriff of each to make them fit.

• The Savoy hotel is home to **Kaspar**, an art deco black wooden cat that is placed at the table of any party of diners that would otherwise total an unlucky 13.

• The statue of **William Huskisson** in Pimlico Gardens, SW1, commemorates a man known less for his achievements as a politician and more for the fact that he was the first person killed by a train. Sir George Stephenson's "Rocket" mowed him down in 1830 during a ceremony to open the Liverpool and Manchester Railway.

• **William III** died at Hampton Court in 1702 after complications arising from a fall from his horse when it stumbled on a molehill. His statue (1808) in St.

James's Square, SW1, portrays the king, his horse—and the molehill. His enemies raised a toast to "the little gentleman in the black velvet waistcoat."

London's Four Oldest Outdoor Statues

Every statue has a story, whether of the protagonists portrayed, the artists responsible, or the work's odyssey through the ages. These are some of the tales associated with London's four oldest outdoor statues.

1320 B.C.
An Egyptian basalt effigy of the lion-goddess Sekhmet guards the entrance to Sotheby's *(34-35 New Bond Street, W1)* in the heart of Mayfair. The effigy was sold by the auction house for £40 ($64) in the late 19th century but never collected by the buyer.

1395
The statue in Trinity Church Square, SE1, may represent King Alfred (849-899) and may date to the late 14th century; or it may have been sculpted in 1735 for Carlton House, which was demolished in 1825.

1586
The statue of Elizabeth I was removed from Ludgate in 1760 before being moved to the church of St. Dunstan in the West *(Fleet Street, EC4)*. Some date the statue to 1670-1699—the "1586" on the base possibly denoting the date Ludgate was restored. But, if original, it would be the only surviving statue of the Queen carved in her lifetime.

1638
Oliver Cromwell ordered the destruction of this equestrian statue of Charles I at the end of Trafalgar Square during the Interregnum—but the metalsmith hired for the job buried it instead; Charles II acquired the work at the Restoration of the monarchy in 1660.

·Statues of Americans in London·

London remembers and commemorates the contributions of the United States with monuments from different eras to U.S. presidents and outstanding American personalities.

Dr. King at Westminster Abbey

• Bush House
An American, Irving T. Bush, founded Bush House on Aldwych, home until 2012 to the BBC World Service. The two statues on the facade symbolize Anglo-American friendship; the building bears the inscription: "To the friendship of English-speaking peoples."

• Dwight D. Eisenhower
The statue was donated by the citizens of Kansas City and unveiled in 1989 in Grosvenor Square, W1, opposite the building (#20) where Eisenhower was based in World War II as Commander in Chief, Allied Force, and Supreme Commander, Allied Expeditionary Force.

• Martin Luther King, Jr.
Dr. King is depicted among the statues of ten 20th-century Christian martyrs in niches above the west entrance at Westminster Abbey. They were unveiled in 1998.

• John F. Kennedy
The bronze bust by Jacques Lipchitz was unveiled by his brothers Robert and Edward in 1965 at 1 Park Crescent, Marylebone Road, NW1.

• Abraham Lincoln
Situated in Parliament Square opposite the Houses of Parliament, this is a 1920 copy of a statue dated 1887 in Lincoln Park,

Chicago, by Augustus Saint-Gaudens.

• Ronald Reagan
Also in Grosvenor Square, this statue was unveiled on Independence Day, 2011. The Reagan Memorial Trust Fund met its reputed one-million-dollar cost; Westminster City Council waived its usual rule refusing permission for statues until ten years after the subject's death.

• Franklin Delano Roosevelt
This bronze (1948) by Sir William Reid Dick also stands in Grosvenor Square, W1. It was unveiled by Roosevelt's wife, Eleanor, and funded by private British public subscription; 160,000 donations were made and the sum required raised in just six days.

• Roosevelt and Churchill
"The Allies" (1995) has the two leaders sitting in conversation on a park

bench—with a gap for you between them—at the junction of Bond Street and New Bond Street, W1. It is the work of Lawrence Holofcener, a sculptor with dual U.S.-U.K. citizenship.

• **George Washington**
Outside the National Gallery, this statue donated by the state of Virginia is a copy of a statue (1921) in Richmond—and one of 20 replicas worldwide. The story goes that

Washington once said: "I will never set foot in London again!" When this statue was raised, soil from Virginia was placed beneath it, allowing the president to remain true to his word.

·London's Best Markets·

Most of London's markets, whether craft and antiques or traditional "fruit and veg," offer plenty of color and charm, but these are some of the best:

• **Alfies Antiques Markets, NW8**
(*alfiesantiques.com, lfm.org.uk*)
You won't find too many bargains here, but you will find plenty of tempting antiques, vintage fashion, and 20th-century design from the 100 dealers dotted around the five

floors of London's biggest covered antiques market. On Sundays in the same district, visit the 30 to 40 stalls of the **Marylebone Farmers' Market.**

• **Brick Lane, E1**
Brick Lane (*visitbricklane .org*) is a chaotic, vibrant, and multiethnic market—but one endangered by its own success as it has become overwhelmed by cheap goods aimed at tourists. Now it has spilled over into surrounding streets and buildings with, among other things, the

funky Sunday UpMarket in an old brewery (*sunday upmarket.co.uk*) and the Backyard Market (*backyardmarket.co.uk*). You'll find an incredible diversity of fashion, art, crafts, classic vinyl, and a cornucopia of old tools, CD players, and unmitigated but compelling trash. Food stalls cover every base, from cupcakes to Japanese yakisoba.

• **Camden Market, NW1**
(*camdenlockmarket.com, camden-market.org*)
Camden ranks with

Portobello as London's most popular market. Founded in 1972, it has expanded greatly to occupy several covered and adjoining street sites (Camden Lock, Camden Lock Village, Camden Stables, Inverness Street, and Buck Street). The range of art, crafts, foodstuffs, vintage clothes, and other goods is enormous. Weekends are very busy.

• **Columbia Road, E2**
Columbia Road (near Brick Lane and Spitalfields) is a good place to visit at any time for its 60 or so cafés; galleries; and vintage, antique, and garden stores; but it's at its best on Sunday *(8 a.m.-3 p.m.)*, when it hosts London's loveliest flower market *(columbiaroad.info)*.

• **Greenwich Market, SE10**
(greenwichmarketlondon.com)
Combine a trip to see the sights of Greenwich with a visit to one of London's lesser-known historic markets, which dates from 1737. It's a buzzy, eclectic place, best on weekends when most of the fashion, arts, and crafts stalls are open for business. Many stalls and specialty stores, though, are open daily.

• **Maltby Street & Spa Terminus, SE1**
Borough Market, SE1 *(boroughmarket.org.uk)*, and its range of small artisanal food and wine retailers used to be the destination of choice for London gourmet shoppers, but crowds and rising prices have taken the edge off the experience.

Brick Lane's vibrant market has something for everyone.

Some of the original retailers and food stalls have moved to nearby **Maltby Street** *(maltby.st)*; others, such as the outstanding London Honey Company and Ham & Cheese Co., have gone a little farther, to **Spa Terminus** *(spa-terminus .co.uk)*. Both are must-visit destinations for foodies.

• **Old Spitalfields Market, E1**
(oldspitalfieldsmarket .com, spitalfields.co.uk)
Spital Fields was just that in 1682 when Charles II granted this market its license—open fields on the edge of the city. The traditional fruit and vegetable market in the area moved to a new home in 1991, but following the recent revival of this once glorious period district, the market square and listed historic buildings of Old Spitalfields Market have become a popular destination, especially on weekends.

• **Portobello Road, W11**
Notting Hill's Portobello Road is one of London's most popular markets with visitors, making it very crowded on summer Saturdays. Fridays see fewer stalls but more room, with the bonus of a superb vintage clothes market under the Westway flyover. Otherwise, antiques cluster near the bottom (southern) end, fruit and veg in the central section, and the real junk (and bargains) in the stretch closer to Golborne Road *(portobelloroad.co.uk, portobellomarket.org)*.

· Eyewitness Accounts of the Plagues ·

Plague has ravaged London dozens of times, most notably the first major outbreak in 1348-1349 when at least a third of all Londoners died, and in 1665, when it made its last major appearance. Surviving contemporary commentaries of both outbreaks paint a woeful picture.

• "And there was in those days death without sorrow, marriage without affection, self-imposed penance, want without poverty, and flight without escape."
—Account of the 1348-1349 plague outbreak by John of Reading, a monk in Westminster

• "The year of our Lord 1349. A great pestilence reigning, this cemetery was consecrated in which . . . were buried more than 50,000 bodies."
—Inscription on stone cross, now lost, at the plague burial pit near London's St. Bartholomew's Hospital

• "7th September, 1665. Came home, there perishing near 10,000 poor creatures weekly; however, I went all along the city and suburbs from Kent Street to

St. James's, a dismal passage, and dangerous to see so many coffins exposed in the streets, now thin of people; the shops shut up, and all in mournful silence, not knowing whose turn might be next."
—*Diary entry of John Evelyn, a writer, gardener, and diarist as well as one of Charles II's key advisers*

The Black Death of 1348

• "So home and late at my chamber, setting some papers in order; the plague growing very raging, and my apprehensions of it great. So very late to bed."
—*Samuel Pepys's diary entry of July 21, 1665. Pepys lived in the parish of St. Olave Hart Street, on the eastern side of the city. Pepys, best remembered for his diary, was also an able naval administrator and later served as a Member of Parliament.*

• "That if any House be Infected, the sick person or persons be forthwith removed to the said pesthouse, sheds, or huts, for the preservation of the rest of the Family: And that such house (though none be dead therein) be shut up for fourty days, and have a Red Cross, and Lord have mercy upon us, in Capital Letters affixed on the door, and Warders appointed, as well to find them necessaries, as to keep them from conversing with the sound."
—*Extract from Rules and Orders published by the government to prevent the spread of the 1665 plague*

• "This day, much against my will, I did

FAST FACT

The 1665 plague was less devastating than the 14th-century outbreak, killing "only" 15 to 20 percent of the population. In both outbreaks, as is often the case, the poor were hit the hardest.

in Drury Lane see two or three houses marked with a red cross upon the doors, and 'Lord have mercy upon us' writ there; which was a sad sight to me, being the first of the kind that ... I ever saw."
—*Diary entry of Samuel Pepys, June 7, 1665*

• "The Bells seemed hoarse with continual tolling ... the burying Places would not hold the Dead, but they were thrown into large Pits dug in waste Grounds, in Heaps, thirty or forty together; and it often happened that those who attended the Funerals of their Friends one Evening, were carried the next to their own long Home."
—*Nathaniel Hodges's* Loimologia, *an account of the plague published in Latin in 1672 and in English in 1720. Hodges was a physician who remained, and survived, in London throughout the plague.*

A

JOURNAL
OF THE

Plague Year:
BEING

Obſervations or Memorials,
Of the moſt Remarkable

OCCURRENCES,
As well

PUBLICK *as* **PRIVATE,**
Which happened in

L O N D O N
During the laſt

GREAT VISITATION
In 1665.

Written by a CITIZEN who continued all the while in London. Never made publick before

L O N D O N :
Printed for E. Nutt at the Royal-Exchange; J. Roberts in Warwick-Lane ; A. Dodd without Temple-Bar ; and J. Graves in St. James's-ſtreet. 1722.

Defoe's *Journal of the Plague Year*

• "So the Plague defied all medicines; the very physicians were seized with it, with their preservatives in their mouths; and men went about prescribing to others and telling them what to do till the tokens were upon them, and they dropped down dead, destroyed by that very enemy they directed others to oppose."
—*Daniel Defoe's* A Journal of the Plague Year, *a fictionalized account of the plague published in 1722. Defoe was a native Londoner, born in the city in about 1660.*

• "The nights are too short to bury the dead; the long summer dayes are spent from morning into the twilight in conveying the vast number of dead bodies unto the bed of their graves."
—*Thomas Vincent's* God's Terrible Voice in the City by Plague and Fire, *published in 1667*

• "I commonly drest 40 soares in a day, held their pulse [and remained to] ... give judgment and informe myself in the various tricks of it ... I most commonly gave judgment whether people would live or dye at the first visit, almost always at the second ... [I] passed through a multitude and continuall dangers ... being engaged throughout the day until 10 at night, attending patients in one house after another."
—*William Boghurst's* Loimographia. *Boghurst was a physician working in the city at the time.*

London's Oldest Cemeteries

It's difficult to date many Roman, medieval, and other early burial places, but these are some of the capital's oldest documented formal cemeteries.

1657 Jewish Old Sephardi Cemetery, Mile End Road, E1

1665 Bunhill Fields, City Road, EC1

1692 Royal Hospital Chelsea Burial Ground, Royal Hospital Road, SW3

1697 Jewish Cemetery, Alderney Road, E1

1733 Jewish New Sephardi, Mile End Road, E1

1761 Jewish Cemetery, Brady Street, E1

1788 Jewish Cemetery, Lauriston Road, E9

1815 Jewish Cemetery, Fulham Road, SW3

1833 Kensal Green, Harrow Road, W10

1839 Highgate, Swain's Lane, N6

Bunhill Fields cemetery in the 19th century

·London's Famous Dead: Who's Buried Where·

Highgate Cemetery, final resting place of Karl Marx, Michael Faraday, and thousands more

Some of Britain's most famous—and many foreign notables, too—have lived, died, and been buried in London. St. Paul's Cathedral and Westminster Abbey contain the graves of many of the most preeminent, but others are scattered around cemeteries that are fascinating to visit for their own sake: vast areas of park, garden, and woodland filled with headstones and memorials that are grandiose and poignant by turn.

• **Brompton Cemetery, SW10** This contains the graves of Fanny Brawne (d. 1865), muse of the poet John Keats, buried as Fanny Lindon; Henry Cole (d. 1882), founder of the Victoria & Albert Museum and Royal Albert Hall; and women's suffragette Emmeline Pankhurst (d. 1928). Six of the most visited headstones are those of Messrs. Nutkins, McGregor, Tod, Jeremiah Fisher, Tommy Brock, and Peter Rabbett, whose names were adapted for use as characters by Beatrix Potter in her children's books. The writer lived nearby at 2 Bolton Gardens.

• **Bunhill Fields, EC1** Buried there are John Bunyan (d. 1688), author of *The Pilgrim's Progress;* William Blake (1827), painter, engraver, poet, and mystic; Daniel Defoe (d. 1731), author of *Robinson Crusoe;* and George Fox (d. 1691), founder of the Quakers.

• **City of London Cemetery, E12** Almost a million interments have taken place here since 1856; it holds more than 150,000 graves, the most of any cemetery in Britain, and includes exhumations from old graveyards and demolished churches. Two of the most-visited graves belong to Catherine Eddowes (d. 1888) and Mary Ann Nichols (d. 1888), victims of Jack the Ripper.

• **Hyde Park Pets Cemetery, W2** Some 300 interments took place between 1881 and 1903, including those of Ba-ba, Bibi, Chin Chin, Chips, Dolly, Drag, Fattie, Freeky, Sir Isaac, Orphie, Pomme de Terre, Pupsey, Jim, Minnie, Scam, Ruff, Scamp, Snap, Smut, Tally-Ho, Topper, and Wee Bobbit.

• **Kensal Green Cemetery, W10** Notables there include engineer Isambard Kingdom Brunel (d. 1859); mechanical "computer" pioneer Charles Babbage (d. 1871); playwright Sir Harold Pinter (d. 2008); novelists William Thackeray (d. 1863) and Anthony Trollope (d. 1882); and Major Walter Wingfield (d. 1912), the inventor of lawn tennis.

• **Highgate Cemetery, N6** Charles Cruft (d. 1938), founder of the dog shows; Douglas Adams (d. 2001), author of *The Hitchhiker's Guide to the Galaxy;* Karl Marx (d. 1883); novelist George Eliot (d. 1880)—the name on the grave is Mary Ann Evans; and chemist and physicist Michael Faraday (d. 1867) are all buried there.

• **St. Paul's Cathedral, EC4** The painter Sir Anthony van Dyck (d. 1641) is buried at St. Paul's; likewise, John Donne (d. 1631), poet; Sir Alexander Fleming (d. 1955), scientist; Horatio Nelson (d. 1805), Royal Navy flag officer; Sir Joshua Reynolds (d. 1792), painter; Joseph Mallord William Turner (d. 1851), painter; Sir Christopher Wren (d. 1723), architect; and Arthur Wellesley, First Duke of Wellington (d. 1852), soldier and prime minister.

• **West Norwood Cemetery, SE27** Those buried at this cemetery include Sir Henry Bessemer (d. 1898), inventor of the process for converting cast iron to steel; cookery writer Isabella "Mrs." Beeton (d. 1865); Sir Hiram Maxim (d. 1916), inventor of the first portable fully automatic machine gun; and sugar magnate Sir Henry Tate (d. 1899), who gave London the Tate Gallery.

FAST FACT

All *reigning* monarchs buried in London are buried in Westminster Abbey with the exception of Ethelred II (the old St. Paul's) and Jane, or Lady Jane Grey (the Tower).

Trafalgar Square

A few fun facts about Trafalgar Square, the 22.5-acre (1 ha) plaza generally considered, especially by tourists, to be London's central point:

Height of Nelson's Column (to the top of Nelson's Statue) 167 feet (51 m)

Height of Nelson's Statue 16 feet (5 m)

Battle for which the square is named The 1805 naval Battle of Trafalgar during the Napoleonic Wars. Lord Nelson commanded the British ships in a major victory over a combined French and Spanish fleet off Cape Trafalgar, Spain.

Pre–Battle of Trafalgar use of the real estate For hundreds of years, until the 1820s, the area that is today Trafalgar Square was part of the stables serving the king.

Craziest thing done at the top of the column Before Nelson's statue was affixed, the 14 stonemasons who worked on the column and statue had a refined dinner on the top platform, 150 feet (46 m) above terra (very) firma.

Country that donates the annual Christmas tree Norway. A Norwegian spruce has been sent by the city of Oslo each year since 1947, in thanks for Britain's support during World War II.

·The Lost Rivers of London·

The (now buried) Fleet River still enters the Thames at Blackfriars.

When you think of London's rivers, typically just the Thames comes to mind. And with good reason: Most of the city's other natural waterways have long since been buried, diverted, or, more ignominiously, channeled into the sewer system. Here are London's lost rivers:

• **The Effra**

The Effra makes its way through the South London neighborhoods of Dulwich, Herne Hill, and Brixton before entering the Thames near Vauxhall Bridge. Although the river is almost completely covered over by roads and buildings, remnants are still visible in Belair Park in Dulwich: The river supplies water for several of the park's ponds before descending into the sewer system.

• **The Fleet**

The Fleet rises in Hampstead Heath in north London before flowing south through Camden Town and Farringdon and into the Thames at Blackfriars. The river became a petri dish of muck, disease, and pollution in the Middle Ages; the open sewer was gradually covered over and buried.

FAST FACT

Put an ear to the street grating in front of the Coach and Horses pub (on the corner of Warner and Ray Streets, EC1) and you'll hear a lingering vestige of the Fleet River rushing beneath the city.

FIRST PERSON

❝The watercourse of Walebrook should be made free from dung and other nuisances.❞
~From a 1288 Royal Order of Edward I

• The Neckinger

With its origins in Southwark, the Neckinger once formed one of the boundaries of Jacob's Island, a notorious 19th-century slum, as it approaches the Thames. The river is now visible only where it empties into the Thames at St. Saviour's Dock, about a quarter mile (0.4 km) east of Tower Bridge.

• The New River

The short-lived New River was created by diverting another river in the early 17th century as a new freshwater source for London. Its route took it through Stoke Newington, where it ends today. By 1900 it had been built over and all but disappeared.

• The Tyburn

The Tyburn River flowed from Regent's Park through Marylebone before running along what is today Oxford Street. The river was harnessed in medieval times and diverted by a 3-mile-long (4.8 km) pipe to Cheapside, where it was used as a source of drinking water for the City's residents.

• The Walbrook

Thought to have been the first water source for Roman London, the Walbrook became very polluted throughout the centuries; by the end of the Middle Ages it had been covered over and mostly forgotten. It now runs 35 feet (10.5 m) below ground level, beneath its eponymous street, before emptying into the Thames near Cannon Street station.

• The Westbourne

The Westbourne rises in Hampstead and wends its way south before feeding into the Thames at Chelsea. The river used to be the water source for the Serpentine lake in Hyde Park, but planners found it more convenient to convert it into a sewer. The Westbourne can be glimpsed at the Sloane Square Tube station, where the river/sewer passes through the huge iron pipe running across the tracks above the District and Circle line platform.

The last visible trace of the Neckinger

·Five Great Occasions·

Crystal Palace, centerpiece of the Great Exhibition of 1851

Grand and significant occasions abound in London's long past—from the jubilees of queens Victoria and Elizabeth II to the wedding of Charles and Diana. In this list, the obvious and obscure mingle.

• 1470, The Earl of Warwick's Feast

A banquet prepared by the Earl of Warwick required, among other things, 62 chefs; 515 assistants; 1,000 waiting staff; 504,000 pints of beer; 174,720 pints of wine; 5,000 woodcocks; 4,000 ducks; 4,000 deer; 4,000 rabbits; 4,000 venison pies; 3,000 calves; 2,000 chickens; 1,000 rams; 1,000 egrets; 1,000 jellies; 600 fish; 400 herons; 300 pigs; 300 hogs; 200 cranes; 200 kids; 100 peacocks; 10 oxen; 8 seals; and 4 porpoises.

• 1851, The Great Exhibition

Or to give it its full title: The "Great Exhibition of the Works of Industry of All Nations," a prototype world's fair held in Hyde Park from May to October, 1851. Six million people—a third of Britain's population—attended, including 109,915 on a single day (October 7). Tickets ranged from a shilling (about £4.50/$7 in today's money) to £3 (now the equivalent of about £175/$280), and profits from the event helped found South Kensington's Science, Natural History, and Victoria & Albert museums.

• 1924-1925, British Empire Exhibition

This celebration of Britain's imperial dominion—56 colonies took part—was the world's largest exhibition up to that time; it drew 27 million visitors to the Empire Stadium (subsequently rebuilt as Wembley Stadium). Among the events was a historical pageant that involved 15,000 people, 1,000 doves, 730 camels, 500 donkeys, 300 horses, 72 monkeys, 7 elephants, 3 bears, and one macaw. The performance lasted three days.

• **1965, The Funeral of Winston Churchill**
Britain's wartime leader was honored with the largest funeral held anywhere up to then for a statesman. Representatives of 112 countries attended the service in St. Paul's Cathedral, and 321,360 people filed past Churchill's catafalque in Westminster Hall.

• **2012, XXX Olympiad**
As well as celebrating sporting prowess and, by general consent, London itself, the 2012 London Olympics required prodigious amounts of food for the participants. Deliveries to the Olympic Village included 19 tons of eggs, 21 tons of cheese, 82 tons of seafood, 100 tons of meat, 232 tons of potatoes, 360 tons of fruit and vegetables, and 25,000 loaves of bread.

•Can't-Miss Highlights of the Museum District•

This cute guy helped Alfred Russel Wallace develop his vision of natural selection.

London's bustling museum district on Kensington's Exhibition Road (off Cromwell Road) consists of the Natural History Museum (NHM), the Science Museum, and the Victoria & Albert Museum (V&A). The collections of these big three contain a wow-invoking figure of nearly 73 million pieces and artifacts. As a special favor, we've gone through them all (well ...

most of them, at least) and selected a list of essential objects and relics.

NATURAL HISTORY MUSEUM *(nhm.ac.uk)*
• **Audubon's** *The Birds of America* **book**
On show are select pages from a first-edition printing of John James Audubon's *The Birds of America*. Fewer than 200 copies of the 19th-century work of natural history art were ever printed, one reason *The Birds of America* is considered the most valuable book in the world.

• **Dodo skeleton**
A composite of bones from individual dodos, this unique skeleton depicts one of the famous birds that lived on an isolated island in Mauritius until the arrival of Dutch sailors in 1598. From there, the dodos fell victim to human and animal

A dodo model at the NHM

intrusion—the last dying off by 1700—living on in name only as a synonym for extinction.

• **Early bird fossil**
This skeletal fossil of the earliest known bird—the *Archaeopteryx*—helped prove that birds were in fact descended from dinosaurs. This was one of the first finds giving direct evidence in support of Darwin's (and Wallace's) theory of evolution.

• **Neanderthal skull**
This skull of a Neanderthal adult, discovered

in a Gibraltar quarry in 1848, was the first ever found and helped launch the study of our cousins on the evolutionary family tree, as well as other ancient humans.

• **Alfred Russel Wallace's insects**
Wallace traveled to Southeast Asia in the 1850s and 1860s, collecting insects to help develop—independent of Charles Darwin—the theory of natural selection. The museum displays specimens from Wallace's personal insect collection from the voyage.

SCIENCE MUSEUM *(sciencemuseum.org.uk)*
• **Babbage's Difference Engine No. 1**
A fascinating (very) early pre-computer, this large and complex machine was essentially a giant calculator that attempted to mechanically reproduce

---

FAST FACT

The classic, ungainly image of the dodo (as in the model pictured above) is most likely incorrect. In reality, dodos were less squat and chubby than originally and popularly depicted.

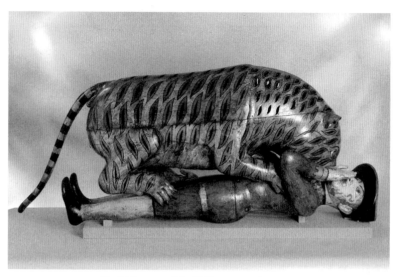
Tipu's Tiger, one of the V&A's most popular pieces

basic mathematical functions. Way ahead of its time when constructed in 1832, it encapsulated many of the concepts of the modern computer.

• **Crick and Watson's DNA model**
The famous double-helix molecular structure of DNA, one of science's most critical discoveries, was unlocked in the 1950s; this reproduction of their research model incorporates some of the original metal plates used by Crick and Watson to help determine

how DNA carries our cells' genetic information.

• **An early incandescent electric lamp**
This now simple-seeming 1879 artifact shows Thomas Edison's innovative genius in action: The lamp's carbon loop would glow when a current was passed through—the vacuum-sealed, oxygen-free bulb ensured that the filament could heat and light up without catching fire.

• **Fleming's penicillin mold**
In 1928, Scottish scientist

Alexander Fleming noticed that a mold he was working with halted the growth of bacteria—from there, the curative properties of penicillin were isolated and produced as a medicine, beginning in the 1940s. The museum displays a sample of the original mold from Fleming's London laboratory.

• *Puffing Billy*
The world's oldest surviving steam locomotive, *Puffing Billy* lived a functional life from 1814 to 1862, hauling coal from

the mines of northeastern England to waiting cargo ships.

VICTORIA & ALBERT MUSEUM *(vam.ac.uk)*
• Ardabil Carpet
The Ardabil Carpet, made for the Shah of Iran in 1539, is one of the oldest, largest, and most important carpets in the world. In every 10 square centimeters, the carpet contains an average of 5,300 colored knots (or 340 knots per square inch).

• Great Bed of Ware
Created in the 1590s as a curiosity to attract visitors to a pub in the town of Ware in Hertfordshire, the Great Bed is more than 11 feet long and 10 feet wide (3.3 m x 3 m). The bed gets a brief shout-out in Shakespeare's *Twelfth Night.*

• Gloucester candlestick
This richly detailed metal candlestick was crafted in the 12th century for the then abbey of Gloucester and is considered one of the finest pieces of early English metalwork.

• Mick Jagger's jumpsuit
Check out Mick's chest-exposing jumpsuit outfit from the Rolling Stones' 1972 world tour.

• James II wedding suit
This wool suit, with silver thread and lined with red silk, was made in 1673 for the future King James II's wedding to Mary of Modena.

• Plaster cast of "David"
This life-size model of Michelangelo's famous 16th-century statue had a specially produced and fitted fig leaf on hand to cover its vital parts during visits by Queen Victoria and other easily outraged female dignitaries.

• "The Three Graces"
One of the most recognizable works in the V&A, Antonio Canova's marble statue of Zeus's daughters was created in the early 19th century for Woburn Abbey's Sculpture Gallery.

• Tipu's Tiger
This mechanical organ is a longtime V&A favorite. The 1790 wooden piece, made for an Indian sultan, depicts a tiger attacking a poor supine European; a true multimedia work, an interior organ produces sounds akin to the tiger's growls and the man's moans.

• "V&A Chandelier"
Right above the main information desk in the entrance hall hangs Dale Chihuly's 2001 glass sculpture, nearly 30 feet in length and multicolored in "ice blue and spring green" (as taken from the piece's original name).

FAST FACT

The fig leaf created by the V&A to provide some modesty to the plaster cast of Michelangelo's "David" is no longer in use and is displayed next to the cast.

·London's Ancient Roman Roads, Then and Now·

Soon after the Romans established Londinium as their new provincial capital in the first century A.D., their famous roads began to radiate out of the city. These often followed the tracks of ancient British trails used as trading routes to important tribal towns. Some of today's busiest thoroughfares run along the exact courses of these old highways.

On the ancient Roman road that led to Stratford

• Akeman Street
An artery west, Akeman Street (a later Saxon name) began on what is today the Strand and ran 7 miles (11.3 km) through Westminster (and along Kensington Road and Kensington High Street) before joining the Silchester Road in Chiswick.

• The Colchester Road
This road ran from London to the Britons' chief city of Colchester, in Essex, and through to East Anglia. Its route within London isn't entirely known, but it's thought to have run along Eastcheap, out of the city at Aldgate, and northeast through Stratford and the Lea Valley (epicenter of the 2012 Olympics).

• Ermine Street
The main route north, Ermine Street extended from Bishopsgate, one of the Roman city gates (ca A.D. 200), along today's Norton Folgate, Shoreditch High Street, and Kingsland Roads—and onward ho to York.

• The Old Street–Stratford Road
This 5-mile-long (8 km) stretch of Roman road, built along a pre-Roman British track, ran east-west through the city. The westward route extended along today's Hatton Wall, Portpool Lane, across Gray's Inn Gardens, and past Red Lion Square in Bloomsbury. Its eastward reach ran through Bethnal Green and along today's aptly named Roman Road until it joined the Colchester Road near Stratford.

• The Silchester Road
This spoke of the wheel headed west, past the

town of Silchester in Hampshire and through to Exeter. The road ran along today's Oxford Street, Bayswater Road, Notting Hill, and Holland Park Avenue. (Imagine Roman soldiers and cart-wielding traders trundling down the road next time you're shopping along Oxford Street.)

• **Stane Street**
The route south of town, Stane Street appears to have branched off from Watling Street in Southwark, passing just east of today's Borough High Street. It continued south through the Elephant & Castle region for more than 50 miles to Chichester, then a tribal capital, in Sussex.

• **Watling Street**
This important Roman road connected Dover in England's southeast to London and St. Albans, and continued northwest toward Wales. Roman Watling Street's main branch ran northwest from today's Marble Arch along what is now Edgware Road, Maida Vale, and Kilburn High Road.

The Top 20 Languages Spoken in London

It's been many years since London was the exclusive reserve of native-born English speakers, as immigrants have been inexorably drawn to this most attractive of cities for centuries. This fact bears itself out in the 2011 census, when a count of the top 20 languages (other than English) spoken at home was tabulated.

1. **Polish** 147,816
2. **Bengali** 114,267
3. **Gujarati (India)** 101,676
4. **French** 84,191
5. **Urdu** 78,667
6. **Portuguese** 71,525
7. **Turkish** 71,242
8. **Spanish** 71,192
9. **Arabic** 70,602
10. **Tamil** 70,565

11. **Punjabi** 68,525
12. **Somali** 54,852
13. **Italian** 49,484
14. **Romanian** 39,653
15. **Persian/Farsi** 39,645
16. **Lithuanian** 35,341
17. **German** 34,712
18. **Greek** 31,306
19. **Russian** 26,924
20. **Tagalog/Filipino** 26,603

FAST FACT

A total of 1.73 million people, 22.1 percent of Londoners, listed a language other than English as their main language in the 2011 census.

·The City's Best and/or Most Important Paintings·

Georges Seurat's "Bathers at Asnières" (1884) hangs at the National Gallery.

London's trove of more than 300 galleries and museums makes the task of selecting its top paintings a tad subjective and necessarily limited (the National Gallery alone houses more than 2,300 works, many of them masterpieces). But select we shall: Here are some of the capital city's must-see paintings, some found in less obvious spaces. We'll list them alphabetically by location so you don't think we have the audacity to be ranking them ...

BANQUETING HOUSE
(Whitehall, SW1, hrp.org.uk)
•Sir Peter Paul Rubens's ceiling (ca 1636)
The massive panels on the ceiling of Banqueting House (the last remaining vestige of Whitehall Palace) were commissioned by Charles I to honor his father, James I. Rubens's four colorful eye-filling works cover an area of nearly 2,000 square feet (186 sq m).

COURTAULD GALLERY
(Somerset House, Strand, London WC2, courtauld .ac.uk/gallery)
• "La Loge" (Pierre-Auguste Renoir, 1874)
Renoir turns the theater

box into the stage and its socialite occupants into actors in this highly celebrated Impressionist work.
• "Self-portrait with a bandaged ear" (Vincent van Gogh, 1889)
As the title implies, this self-portrait was created after the troubled post-Impressionist lost his ear.

DULWICH PICTURE GALLERY
(Gallery Rd., SE21, dulwich picturegallery.org.uk)
• "A Girl at a Window" (Rembrandt, 1645)
A sensual portrait of someone often said to be a servant girl, though her gold chains and fine hat belie that theory.
• "Elizabeth and Mary Linley" (Thomas Gainsborough, 1771-1772)
Elizabeth was a particularly renowned beauty (no offense to Mary) as well as a highly regarded and popular singer.

THE IMPERIAL WAR MUSEUM
(Lambeth Rd., SE1, iwm.org.uk)
• "Gassed" (John Singer Sargent, 1919)
Sargent's disturbing work depicts soldiers in the aftermath of a mustard gas attack during World War I.

MUSEUM OF LONDON
(150 London Wall, EC2, museumoflondon.org.uk)
• "The Curds and Whey Seller, Cheapside" (unknown artist, 1730)
A window into the past: Sooty chimney sweeps buy (and perhaps steal) some food from a blind

Monet's "Water-Lily Pond" (1899)

street seller at the base of the old water conduit at Cheapside.
• "The Rhinebeck Panorama" (unknown artist, ca 1806-1807)
An intriguing bird's-eye view of London from above the Thames details everyday early 19th-century city life.

NATIONAL GALLERY
(Trafalgar Squre, WC2, nationalgallery.org.uk)
• "The Ambassadors" (Hans Holbein the Younger, 1533)
This Holbein double portrait incorporates the distorted image of a skull that's visible in correct proportions only when the painting is viewed at an extremely acute angle.
• "Bathers at Asnières" (Georges Seurat, 1884)
Young workers take a break on the banks of the Seine in Seurat's

post-Impressionist masterpiece.

• **"Sunflowers" (Vincent van Gogh, 1888)**
One of van Gogh's most recognizable paintings is part of a series intended to decorate a room the artist rented in Arles, France, while working with Paul Gauguin.

• **"The Virgin of the Rocks" (Leonardo da Vinci, ca 1491-1508)**
Originally the central panel of a Milanese church altar, its large size and excellent condition make it one of da Vinci's most important surviving works.

• **"The Water-Lily Pond" (Claude Monet, 1899)**
From the famous series of paintings of the Impressionist's pond in Giverny, France.

• **"Whistlejacket" (George Stubbs, ca 1762)**
This life-size portrait depicts the 18th-century champion racehorse Whistlejacket, in mid-rear.

NATIONAL PORTRAIT GALLERY
(St. Martin's Place, WC2, npg.org.uk)

• **"The Brontë Sisters" (Patrick Branwell Brontë, ca 1834)**
Patrick Branwell Brontë, the painting's artist and brother of the three authors, originally intended to include himself in this family portrait. After changing his mind, he tried to conceal his image by painting a white pillar where he had placed himself . . . but his ghostly outline has reappeared over time.

• **"Queen Elizabeth I" (unknown Dutch artist, ca 1575)**
This important portrait was probably painted from life; the image of Elizabeth's face became the model for the Virgin Queen's future portraits.

• **"J. K. Rowling" (Stuart Pearson Wright, 2005)**
A colored-pencil-on-paper portrait of the Harry Potter author. It's very popular with those who use the word "muggle" in everyday conversation.

Hans Holbein the Younger's "The Ambassadors"

❝With glassy countenance / Did she look to Camelot. / And at the closing of the day / She loosed the chain, and down she lay; / The broad stream bore her far away, / The Lady of Shalott.❞

~Alfred, Lord Tennyson, The Lady of Shalott

• **"William Shakespeare" (attributed to John Taylor, ca 1600)**
An oil-on-canvas that is thought to be the only portrait of the poet and playwright painted from life.

SIR JOHN SOANE'S MUSEUM
(13 Lincoln's Inn Fields, WC2, soane.org)
• **"A Rake's Progress" (William Hogarth, 1733)**
The intriguing series of eight detailed paintings chronicles the debaucheries and downfall of Tom Rakewell, who inherits great wealth but ends up in a London madhouse.

TATE BRITAIN
(Millbank, SW1, tate.org.uk)
• **"Caligula's Palace and Bridge" (J.M.W. Turner, exhibited 1831)**
The Turner classic depicts Caligula in a chariot crossing a bridge over the Gulf of Baiae. The picture received rave reviews when first exhibited in 1831.

• **"The Cholmondeley Ladies" (British School, ca 1600-1610)**
The painter and identity of the portrait's two women (holding babies in christening robes) remain a mystery. Some stories say the sitters, probably members of the aristocratic Cholmondeley family, were twins born and married on the same day.

• **"The Lady of Shalott" (John William Waterhouse, 1888)**
One of the original paintings from the bequest of Sir Henry Tate, the piece illustrates an 1832 poem by Alfred, Lord Tennyson, of the cursed Lady of Shalott of Arthurian legend.

TATE MODERN
(Bankside, SE1, tate.org.uk)
• **"The Snail" (Henri Matisse, 1953)**
Matisse created this work of cut, painted, and pasted paper (with the help of his assistants) after his failing health had limited his ability to paint.

• **"Swinging" (Wassily Kandinsky, 1925)**
An abstract painting highlighting the modernist artist's ability to convey movement.

WALLACE COLLECTION
(Hertford House, Manchester Square, W1, wallacecollection.org)
• **"The Laughing Cavalier" (Frans Hals, 1624)**
Neither laughing nor a cavalier, all that's known of the sitter of this famous Dutch baroque work is that he was 26 when the portrait was created.

·London's 11 Longest Running Shows*·

The Mousetrap, Agatha Christie's murder mystery, boasts the longest first run of any theatrical production of any type in the modern era, clocking up its 25,000th performance on November 18, 2012. It became the longest running West End show ever in 1958, after 2,239 performances. The sets, costumes, and props have been changed just twice, in 1965 and 1999.

The Mousetrap
Opened November 25, 1952, and is still running.

Les Misérables
Panned by the critics when it opened October 8, 1985, but it's still going strong.

The Phantom of the Opera
Opened October 9, 1986, and it's still running; it's also the longest running musical on Broadway and reputedly the highest-grossing single entertainment of any sort, anywhere, having earned an estimated £3.5 billon ($5.75 billion) worldwide.

The Woman in Black
Opened January 15, 1989, it's still running, making it London's second longest running "play"—as opposed to musical.

Blood Brothers
Opened August 27, 1988, it closed on November 10, 2012, after 10,013 performances.

Cats
Running from May 11, 1981, to May 11, 2002, *Cats* closed on its 21st anniversary after 8,949 performances, at the time a record for a British musical.

Starlight Express
It ran from March 27, 1984, to January 12, 2002, for a total of 7,406 performances.

FAST FACT

An enduring urban myth is that if you don't tip your London cabbie sufficiently when you arrive at the theater, he or she will tell you the ending of *The Mousetrap*.

No Sex Please, We're British
The show clocked up 6,761 performances between June 3, 1971, and January 6, 1987, but managed just 16 when it transferred to Broadway.

Chicago
The only revival on the list, it ran from November 18, 1997, to September 1, 2012, for a total of 6,187 performances.

Mamma Mia!
It has been performed 6,115 times since April 6, 1999, and is still going strong.

Buddy—The Buddy Holly Story
Saw 5,140 performances from October 12, 1989, to March 3, 2003, and was the first in a string of "jukebox" musicals.

* As of May 2014

FIRST PERSON

❝In London you have plays performed by good actors. That, however, is, I think, the only advantage London has over Philadelphia.❞
~Benjamin Franklin, *Letter, May 6, 1786*

Ten Oldest Theaters

The four oldest theaters on their original sites in London are also the four oldest theaters anywhere in the United Kingdom, though these and most others in the list have been rebuilt, some several times. The dates below represent the days on which the theaters opened for their first performances.

Theatre Royal, Drury Lane, May 7, 1663

Sadler's Wells, Rosebery Avenue, June 3, 1683

The Haymarket (Theatre Royal), Haymarket, December 29, 1720

Royal Opera House, Covent Garden, December 7, 1732

The Adelphi (formerly the Sans Pareil), Strand, November 27, 1806

The Old Vic (formerly the Royal Coburg), The Cut, May 11, 1818

The Vaudeville, Strand, April 16, 1870

The Criterion, Piccadilly, March 21, 1874

The Harold Pinter Theatre (formerly the Comedy), Panton Street, October 15, 1881

The Savoy, Strand, October 10, 1881

·A Tower Bridge Miscellany·

Tower Bridge is one of London's most immediately recognizable sights, distinguished by its Gothic towers and opening "bascules" (from the French for "tip up" or "tip over"), the lifting parts of the bridge. More than 50 designs were originally submitted for the bridge, and the winning entry, chosen in 1884, was by Sir Horace Jones—one of the judges. Construction started in 1886. The Prince of Wales, the future Edward VII, inaugurated the completed bridge on June 30, 1894.

• **The bridge cost** £1,184,000—or £114 million ($182 million) at today's prices.

• **More than 70,000 tons** of concrete were set in the Thames to provide piers for the two towers.

• **Eleven thousand tons of steel** provided the

Tower Bridge

framework for the towers, which are clad in Portland stone and Cornish granite.

• **The towers are 213 feet** (65 m) high, and the central span is 200 feet (61 m) wide.

• **The two 270-foot** (82 m) side spans are suspension bridges, which, with the walkways as ties, help spread the loads generated by the opening bascules.

• **Steam fed the six accumulators** needed to store the power to drive the bridge's hydraulics until 1974-1976, when oil

and electricity were phased in.

• **The bascules, or "leaves,"** weigh more than 1,000 tons each and take 61 seconds to reach their fully open angle of 86 degrees—though they are rarely opened fully.

• **The bridge once opened** as many as 50 times a day; now it opens infrequently. Ships wanting to pass must give 24 hours' notice.

• **The bridge's walkways were closed** in 1910 because of lack of use, the many suicides, and the large numbers of prostitutes and pickpockets the walkways attracted.

• **A surviving area in an arch** below the bridge is known as Dead Man's Hole, a mortuary where bodies thrown into the river from the Tower of London and elsewhere were collected and stored before burial.

• **Forty thousand motorists,** pedestrians, and cyclists cross the bridge daily.

• **Double-decker bus driver** Albert Gunton received a £10 ($16) reward in 1952 after being forced to jump his bus across the bascules as they began to open. He cleared a three-foot gap and made a six-foot drop to the still stationary northern bascule.

• **In May 1997, the opening bridge** divided the cavalcade of President Clinton, much to the consternation of his security staff. The president's lunch with Prime Minister Tony Blair had run late.

• **In August 1999, Jef Smith,** a Freeman (traditionally, someone able to trade freely) of the City of London led two sheep across the bridge, exercising a claimed ancient Freeman's right to take livestock across the four City bridges.

• **In 2012, the Chinese city** of Suzhou unveiled its own Tower Bridge, a decent enough copy except for the fact that it doesn't open.

Nine Unique Art Venues and Installations

Some are so cool they might have mysteriously disappeared when you go looking for them, so check ahead.

Banner Repeater
(Platform 1, Hackney Downs Railway Station, E8, bannerrepeater.org)
The unique feature of this popular exhibition space (with accompanying bookshop, reading room, and talk series) is that it's located right on Platform 1 of the Hackney Downs train station.

The Couper Collection Barges, Thames
(Riverside Walk, Hester Rd., SW11, coupercollection.org.uk)
Artist Max Couper created this waterborne gallery on a fleet of Thames barges two decades ago. In addition to his own work, exhibit spaces feature teenage artists, human rights themes, the river itself, and much more.

Crypt Gallery
(St. Pancras Church, Euston Rd, NW1, cryptgallery.org.uk)
The nicely moody underground crypt of St. Pancras Church has been hosting innovative art since 2002. Not a faux backdrop, the crypt contains the remains of more than 500 locals who were buried there in the 19th century.

Feliks Topolski murals

(150-152 Hungerford Viaduct Arches, SE1, topolskicentury.org.uk)

Feliks Topolski's murals depicting the 20th century's major political events stretch for hundreds of yards through viaduct arches on the South Bank. Seek out the Hungerford Bridge's arches—numbers 150, 151, and 152—near the Royal Festival Hall.

The Fourth Plinth

(Trafalgar Square, london.gov.uk)

Trafalgar Square's "Fourth Plinth" (the statue base in the square's northwest corner) has been used to display innovative contemporary artworks since 1999.

The Horse Hospital

(Corner of Colonnade and Herbrand St., WC1, thehorsehospital.com)

This art space for varying media (including film, fashion, literature, and music) is located in a two-story former horse stable just off Bloomsbury's Russell Square.

The Old Police Station

(114 Amersham Vale, SE14, theoldpolicestation.org)

This collective where many artists create and display their work is housed in an abandoned police station in South London's Deptford neighborhood.

White Cubicle Toilet Gallery

(George & Dragon Pub, 2 Hackney Rd., E2)

The ladies' restroom of a small, trendy, and often packed Shoreditch pub hosts rotating exhibits.

Windows 108

(108 Rosebery Ave., EC1, windowsoneoeight.com)

Artist Maggie Ellenby's window installations have been changing since she first started using a Victorian storefront on Clerkenwell's Rosebery Avenue as her canvas in 1993.

FAST FACT

Short-listed candidates for the Fourth Plinth's next artwork are displayed across from Trafalgar Square in the basement of St.-Martin-in-the-Fields church.

·London's Ten Worst Years·

A 15th-century illustration of the Peasants' Revolt of 1381

London has known plenty of grim days in its long history, but there have been several extended periods when it really would have been a good idea to be somewhere else altogether.

• **A.D. 60 Colchester,** in Essex, was the capital of Roman England, but Londinium was an important commercial center, and as such a target for the Iceni, a rebellious British tribe under the leadership of Boudicca (or Boadicea, d. A.D. 60 or 61). The Queen and her troops razed the city and forced the population to flee before Roman troops arrived to restore order.

• **851 Viking attacks** on London became commonplace earlier, but one of the worst occurred in 851, when more than 350 ships are said to have attacked the city.

• **1349 The Black Death**—bubonic plague—struck in November 1348, and by May 1349 had killed between a third and a half of the city's population.

• **1381 The Peasants' Revolt** of June brought

an army of rebels from Kent and Essex, under the leadership of Wat Tyler, to march on the city and capture the Tower of London.

• **1665 The Great Plague** was the last major outbreak of plague in London. Bills of Mortality issued at the time recorded 68,596 deaths. The actual number was probably considerably higher. During just one September week, 7,165 Londoners died.

• **1666 Fire broke out** on Sunday, September 2, and within four days consumed most of the medieval City of London—including 87 parish churches, more than 40 of the great livery halls, 13,200 houses, and the old St. Paul's. Officially only four people died in the fire, but its true toll was undoubtedly higher.

• **1683-1684 In December 1683, the Thames froze** to a depth of 11 inches (28 cm) for two months, allowing for an immense "Frost Fair" of temporary shops, inns, and entertainments on the frozen river (see Bygone Fairs, page 170).

• **1858 A hot summer** combined with the colossal volume of sewage flowing directly into the Thames produced the "Great Stink" that at last persuaded the government to initiate vast improvements to London's almost nonexistent sewers.

• **1940-1941 World War II's worst period,** for most Londoners, lasted from September 7, 1940, to May 10, 1941. An estimated 18,800 tons of bombs fell on the city, damaging 3.5 million buildings and killing more than 15,000 people—1,436 in a single night. According to London Fire Brigade call-out records for September 7, the Royal Arsenal in Woolwich was hit the hardest.

• **1952 Thick fogs known as "pea soupers"**— caused largely by huge numbers of coal fires—had been a regular feature of London life for centuries. But the toxic, pollution-laden fogs of December 1952, which were directly linked to 4,000 extra deaths, would lead to passage of the Clean Air Act (1956) to limit household and factory emissions.

FAST FACT

Although 1940–1941 was the peak of the Blitz, it was by no means easy sailing during the rest of the war. Here are the number of World War II air-raid warnings, by year, for one central borough: 1939 (3); 1940 (417); 1941 (154); 1942 (25); 1943 (95); 1944 (508); 1945 (22)

Red Buses

In 1907, London's largest private bus company, which until then ran buses in different colors, painted its vehicles red to make them stand out. The look caught on: The law now states that all London buses must be red.

First London "horse-drawn omnibus service" July 4, 1829; a 22-seat, three-horse journey from Marylebone Street to the Bank of England via King's Cross

First double-decker 1847

First motorized omnibus 1899

Last London horse-drawn bus service August 4, 1914

Bus stops introduced 1918-1919

Upper decks enclosed 1925

Routemasters The most iconic London bus of all— with the hop-on, hop-off rear platform—was in service from 1956 to 2005.

Routemasters built 2,876

Surviving Routemasters 1,280

Surviving Routemaster route Heritage, route #15 (Tower Hill–Trafalgar Square)

Number of buses today about 7,500

Passengers carried daily more than 6 million

Night-only routes 55

·London's Oldest Clubs·

The Oxford and Cambridge Club, a Pall Mall dignitary since 1830

London's traditional clubs were—and are—the domain of the great, the good, and the not so good. Most were—and occasionally still are—reserved for men. Many occupy outstanding historic buildings with grand interiors. The oldest evolved from coffeehouses, and many were given over to gambling. The most exclusive are still found in "Clubland"—the area around Pall Mall and St. James's Street—and are as popular, discreet, and difficult to join as ever.

• White's, 1693
(37-38 St. James's St., SW1)
London's oldest and most exclusive club has its roots in White's Chocolate House, founded by an Italian, Francesco Bianco (Francis White). An exception to the men-only rule was made when the Queen came to lunch to celebrate the club's 300th anniversary. A photograph recording the event was placed in the club's main lavatory. Prince Charles is a member.

• Boodle's, 1762
(28 St. James's St., SW1)
Men often belonged to more than one club, but Boodle's sacked any member who had the temerity to join White's. It took its name from a former headwaiter, and it is said to be the inspiration for "Blades Club" in the James Bond novels. Boodle's was the last club to retain chamber pots for use by members

"whose habits were formed before the days of modern sanitation."

• Brooks's, 1764
(60 St. James's St., SW1)
Brooks's grew out of a club founded by those blackballed—refused membership—by White's. It was once a byword for extravagant gambling, a place, according to one member, where "a thousand meadows and cornfields were staked at every throw." One member attended only to have his watch wound by staff.

• The Travellers Club, 1819
(106 Pall Mall, SW1)
The Travellers began as a point of reunion for travelers or those who wished to entertain people they had met on their travels: Its rules once stipulated members should have "travelled out of the British Isles to a distance of at least five hundred miles from London in a direct line." It still claims the odd bona fide traveler, but is otherwise one of the stuffier clubs.

• Athenaeum, 1824
(107 Pall Mall, SW1)
The club has a reputation for seriousness and intellectual vigor—though that hasn't prevented most British prime ministers from being members—and takes its name from the Athenaeum of ancient Rome, founded by Emperor Hadrian for the study of science and literature. It was one of the last major clubs to install a bar, nearly 150 years after its foundation. Winston Churchill and Charles Dickens were both members.

• Oriental, 1824
(Stratford Place, W1)
An 1837 account described its members as "persons who are living on fortunes amassed in India . . . it would be worth the while to count the number of times the words Calcutta, Bombay and Madras are pronounced in the course of a day." Staff included Alice, a waitress who arrived for work daily at 5:30 a.m. and was employed from 1916 to 1979, when she was 91, and three hedgehogs retained to combat beetles in the kitchen.

• Oxford and Cambridge, 1830
(71 Pall Mall, SW1)
Only in 1995 were female associate members allowed to use the club's main staircase and library, and only then upon payment of an extra £100. The introduction of newfangled gas lighting, and then

FAST FACT

To avoid confusing elderly members, staff at Pratt's Club (1857) all answer to the name George, with the exception of waitresses, who are known as Georgina.

electric lighting, were also resisted in their day. When the latter finally arrived, members insisted on a standing order that allowed a gentleman to call for a candle at his table: The order still stands.

• Garrick, 1831
(15 Garrick St., WC2)
The club was named after an actor and founded with the aim of tending "to the regeneration of Drama," though early members included a duke, five marquises, six earls, and 12 barons; today members from the worlds of television, stage, and law predominate. The club has a library of more than 10,000 volumes and owns thousands of prints, paintings, and artifacts connected with the stage. It clings to its male-only membership rule.

• Carlton, 1832
(69 St. James's St., SW1)
Leaders of Britain's Conservative Party have traditionally been offered full membership in the all-male Carlton Club, which presented a problem in 1975 when the leader was the future prime minister Margaret Thatcher. Rather than change its rules, the club effectively made Mrs. Thatcher an "honourary man." She remained the only woman entitled to full, rather than associate, membership until 2008.

Where to Get Traditional Straight-Edge Shaves

Combining the best of centuries-old ritual and 21st-century pampering, a few spots in town still offer a traditional straight-edge wet shave, complete with hot towels, a hearty bristled brush, and thick lather.

Austin Reed *(103 Regent St., W1, austinreed.co.uk)* has provided wet shaves and other face and body treatments in its lower ground floor salon since the 1930s.

Notting Hill's unusual **Carter and Bond** *(189 Westbourne Grove, W11, carterandbond.com)* is both a retail shop (with collectibles as well as a wide range of grooming products) and a barbering establishment.

In business for more than a century, **F. Flittner** *(86 Moorgate, EC2, fflittner .com)*, near Finsbury Circus, employs six barbers to see to your shaving needs.

Geo. F. Trumper *(trumpers.com)* has two locations in London—in Mayfair *(9 Curzon St., W1)* and St. James's *(1 Duke of York St., SW1)*. You can further your personal grooming education with a private shaving lesson at the Mayfair location to help ward off, as its website says, "common problems such as razor burn, bloodspots, ingrown hairs and redness."

There's no extra charge for sly humor at **Jack the Clipper** (*4 Toynbee St., E1, jacktheclipper.co.uk*), situated in the middle of Whitechapel, its semi-namesake's hunting ground. There is also a branch in Mayfair (*5 Shepherd Market, W1*).

Just off Theobald's Road, the **Legends Barber Shop** (*12 Lamb's Conduit Passage, WC1, thelegendsbarbershop.com*) offers both wet shaves (and other grooming options) and serious classes for prospective barbers.

Pall Mall Barbers (*27 Whitcomb St., WC2, pallmallbarbers.com*), near Leicester Square, is an independent establishment boasting more than 25 years of experience in the straight-edge shave business. And/or try out their second location (*45 Fitzroy Street, W1, southeast of Regent's Park*).

A high-end barber/self-styled gentleman's club, **Pankhurst** (*10 Newburgh St., W1, pankhurstlondon.com*) stands parallel to '60s mod Carnaby Street and is run by Vidal Sassoon–trained Brent Pankhurst.

A small barbershop in Maida Vale, **Peter & Minos** (*462 Edgware Rd., W2, 0207 723 0402*) has been providing haircuts and shaves to locals since 1968. The price can't be beat—it's only £8 ($13) for a standard hot-towel shave.

The Refinery (*the-refinery.com*) provides shaves as well as massages, manicures, and waxing (including a very detailed and entertaining selection of intimate waxing options that we're too shy to list; check the website). There are locations in the basement of Harrods in Knightsbridge and at 60 Brook Street, W1, in Mayfair.

Ted Baker (*tedsgroomingroom.com*) offers a traditional shave with all the finer amenities in six London locations.

In business for more than 200 years, **Truefitt & Hill** (*71 St. James's St., SW1, truefittandhill.com*) welcomed many a famous (and royal) head to its nearby Old Bond Street location for a trim and a shave. The company now has outlets all over the world.

·Famous London Animals·

London's a big place, chock-full of people and animals. Over the centuries, a few of the latter have become better known than most of the former.

• **Christian the Lion**
In 1969, two Australian friends bought Christian the lion cub on an impulse from Harrods' exotic pets department. The young lion lived with the men in their flat on trendy King's Road in Chelsea, later moving to the basement of the furniture shop where they worked. Cute, cuddly, and a local celebrity, Christian gradually became, as lions are wont to do, larger and in need of bigger surroundings. Christian then moved to Kenya and was gradually reintroduced into the wild. In 1971, the men were briefly reunited

Goldie the Eagle

with the by then semi-wild, full-size lion—the video of Christian recognizing, jumping on, and playing with his former owners has been seen by more than 100 million viewers worldwide on YouTube and TV.

• **Goldie the Eagle**
For nearly two weeks in 1965, everyone in London was looking for Goldie. Goldie was a golden eagle that escaped from the London Zoo, making periodic appearances in the treetops of local

neighborhoods and parks. After 12 days on the lam, Goldie was finally recaptured and taken back to his enclosure, much to the relief of the smaller animals of the city that were becoming increasingly prone to being had for dinner.

• **Guy the Gorilla**
Guy, a western lowland gorilla, was for 30 years one of the most beloved residents of the London Zoo. He arrived as a wee baby in November 1947 (on Guy Fawkes Day, hence his moniker) and, with his gentle ways, instantly became a huge hit. As an intimidating-looking adult—weighing in at more than 500 pounds (227 kg)—he was known to carefully hold and study little birds that had accidentally landed in his

FAST FACT

Jumbo the Elephant stood nearly 11 feet (3.4 m) in height and weighed 13,000 pounds (5,900 kg). His name gradually became synonymous with anything supersized.

enclosure before sending them flitting on their way. Guy died in 1978; a statue honoring the gentle giant was unveiled in 1982 and still stands near the zoo's main entrance.

• **Jumbo the Elephant**
Time was, a trip to the zoo meant a ride high atop Jumbo. Born wild in Africa in about 1861, Jumbo lived at the London Zoo starting in 1865. There the young pachyderm charmed crowds with his good nature and increasingly impressive stature. American showman P. T. Barnum bought the elephant in 1882 and took him to the United States for exhibition—over the objection of thousands of London schoolchildren, who wrote to Queen Victoria asking her to intervene. Sadly, Jumbo was killed in a train accident in Canada in 1885, but his memory lives on at Tufts University in Massachusetts, where he is the official mascot (P. T. Barnum was an early trustee of the university).

• **The Queen's Corgis**
If there's one thing we know about Queen Elizabeth II, it is that she loves her Welsh corgis. It's a family affair: Her parents also had several of the little dogs. Since taking the throne in 1952, the Queen has owned more than 30 corgis (a few notables over the years include Crackers, Sugar, Whisky, Sherry, Monty, Emma, Linnet, Willow, and Holly).

• **(The Real) Winnie the Pooh**
In a string of naming connections, A. A. Milne's lovable character Winnie the Pooh was based on his son's stuffed teddy bear, named Winnie. The teddy bear was meanwhile named after Winnie, a live bear that his son visited and befriended at the London Zoo in 1924. Winnie the actual animal was an American Black Bear that a Canadian lieutenant brought to England at the onset of World War I—he donated the bear to the zoo once he was deployed to fight in France. Winnie lived at the zoo from 1914 until her death in 1934.

London Zoo Q&A

Approximately how much food does the zoo purchase each year to feed its animals?

- **Hay** 52 tons (47 tonnes)
- **Bananas** 32 tons (29 tonnes)
- **Apples** 32 tons (29 tonnes)
- **Straw** 31 tons (28 tonnes)
- **Brown clover** 29 tons (26 tonnes)
- **Fish** 21 tons (19 tonnes)
- **Dairy pellets** 20 tons (18 tonnes)
- **Carrots** 14 tons (13 tonnes)
- **Meat** 10 tons (9 tonnes)
- **Oranges** 5 tons (4.5 tonnes)

·Itineraries If Money Were No Object·

Head to Cliveden House for a three-hour spa treatment and lunch.

This is a fantasy sampler of some of the many indulgent things London has to offer. The price tags may be a bit prohibitive, but dare to dream.

1. POSH AND PAMPERED

Daytime activity
The Pavilion Spa at Cliveden House
(Cliveden House, Taplow, Berkshire, SL6, clivedenhouse.co.uk)
Indulge in the Cliveden Retreat, a three-hour spa treatment that includes massage, facial, manicure, pedicure, body wrap, and lunch in the Conservatory (£225/$360).

Transportation
U.K. Chauffeurs
(13 Ditton Rd., UB2, 020 8150 6853, uk-chauffeurs .com)
Book a limousine for the ride to and from Cliveden House. U.K. Chauffers' Lincolns seat eight and start at £160/$256 the first hour and £70/$112 for each additional hour.

Dinner
CUT at 45 Park Lane
(45 Park Lane, W1, 45parklane.com)
Take your limo to Wolfgang Puck's first restaurant in Europe and indulge in an eight-ounce rib eye steak made of 100 percent Wagyu beef for £92/$147.

After-dinner drink
Salvatore's Bar at the

Playboy Club London
(14 Old Park Lane, W1,
playboyclublondon.com)
Try the Calabrese Legacy
cocktail. Each of the ingredients—cognac, kümmel,
curaçao, and bitters—is
more than 200 years old.
It's only £5,500/$8,800.

Accommodations
The Dorchester
(53 Park Lane, W1,
thedorchester.com)
Stay in the Harlequin
Suite, the largest (2,242
square feet/208 sq m)
of the hotel's three roof
suites, overlooking Hyde
Park: £9,320/$14,900.

2. ROYAL RIVER VIEWS
Daytime activity
Tour the city
berkeleychauffeurs.com
Berkeley Chauffeurs
will drive you to Lon-
don's most famous sites
in a luxury Mercedes
S Class car (£480/$770
for eight hours).
Pre-dinner activity

The Shard
(Joiner St., SE1,
theviewfromtheshard.com)
Stop at the Shard for
some of London's most
spectacular views
(£29.95/$48).

Dinner
River Café
(Thames Wharf, Rainville
Rd., W6, rivercafe.co.uk)
Have the chauffeur
drive you a half hour
west to this waterfront
restaurant along the
northern bank of the
Thames. Snag a mag-
num bottle of the 1990
Billecart-Salmon Grand
Cuvee champagne for
£900/$1,440 or (if you're
exceptionally thirsty
and rich) the five-liter
2000 Aldo Conterno
Barolo Granbussia for
£2,400/$3,840.

Transportation
from dinner
Chelsea Flyer
(thamesflyer.com)

Send the car home and
travel back east on the
water with the Thames
VIP Transfer. The
closed-cabin luxury boat
can pick you up near
the restaurant at Dove
Pier Hammersmith and
deliver you to Embank-
ment Pier near the Savoy
hotel for £599/$960 per
hour. Throw in a bonus
bottle of champagne for
£55/$88.

Accommodations
The Savoy
(Strand, WC2, fairmont
.com/savoy-london)
Sleep tight in the Royal
Suite. Among the nice-
ties: eight windows
with sweeping views
overlooking the river,
a dining room that
seats eight, a service
kitchen for those trav-
eling with a personal
chef, and a personal
butler on call 24 hours
a day (£10,000/$16,000
per night).

FAST FACT

**The Savoy hotel on the Strand reopened in October 2010 after
a three-year refurbishment. The extensive renovations cost a
whopping £220 million ($352 million) to complete.**

3. GENTLEMAN'S RETREAT

Morning activity
John Lobb Ltd.
(St. James's St., SW1, johnlobbltd.co.uk)
Have yourself fitted for bespoke shoes at this venerable London institution. We recommend the Crocodile Shoes for approximately £9,700/$15,500.

Transportation
Signature Car Hire
(signaturecarhire.co.uk)
Have Signature Car Hire meet you at the shoe shop with a Ferrari 458 Spider for you to get around today. The two-seaters have a minimum two-day rental and cost £1,695/$2,700 per day. (Remember, money is no object, so we'll pay for two days but only use it for one.)
Afternoon activity

The Grove
(Chandler's Cross, Hertfordshire, WD3, thegrove.co.uk)
Drive out to Hertfordshire, where a round of golf is in order at the Grove championship course. Green fees are £185/$295 on summer weekends, equipment costs £45/$72 to rent, and a personal caddy adds £50/$80.

Dinner
Restaurant Gordon Ramsay
(68 Royal Hospital Rd., SW3, gordonramsay.com/royalhospitalroad)
Then drive back to town to Gordon Ramsay's flagship restaurant for dinner. Order from the Menu Prestige (a fixed price of £135/$215) and enjoy a fine (three Michelin stars) meal. You might as well order a bottle of the 1920 Château

Mouton Rothschild 2ème cru classé (Bordeaux red) for £10,000/$16,000.

Accommodations
The Ritz London
(150 Piccadilly, W1, theritzlondon.com)
Ditch the car (you've been drinking wine) and taxi it to the Ritz, where your Prince of Wales Suite awaits. It's 1,990 square feet (185 sq m) of luxury at £10,200/$16,320 per night.

4. LIVE LIKE A QUEEN

Getting around is a breeze when your hotel includes a complimentary Rolls-Royce Phantom and chauffeur. Let's all thank the Lanesborough.
Shopping
Bond Street/Harrods shopping
(harrywinston.com, prada.com, alexander mcqueen.com)

FIRST PERSON

❝All guests at The Lanesborough Hotel are received as honoured guests … and cared for by personal butlers. Within the comfort of your own bedroom, your butler … will be on hand as and when required with complete discretion.❞

~From the Lanesborough Hotel website

Spend your afternoon shopping at Bond Street's high-end stores, such as Harry Winston, Prada, or Alexander McQueen.

Pre-opera dinner
The Ivy
(1 West St., WC2, the-ivy.co.uk)
Have an early dinner at the Ivy in the West End, once the haunt of all the celebrities and stars (and still the haunt of some celebrities and stars). Try the roasted Devonshire chicken (for two) for £44/$70.

Evening activity
Royal Opera House
(Bow St., WC2, roh.org.uk)
Then it's time for culture at the opera. Prices vary, but go for a box (four seats) at up to £230/$370 each.

After-theater drink
Chinawhite
(4 Winsley St., W1, chinawhite.com)
After the fat lady sings, head to Chinawhite nightclub near Oxford Circus. Order a Golden

Cocktail, made with Hennessy Paradis Imperial cognac and Luxor 24-karat gold leaf champagne. Don't gulp it down—the cocktail also includes a pair of handmade 18-karat gold rings at the bottom of the glass. Seems a steal at £2,012/$3,220.

Accommodations
The Lanesborough
(Hyde Park Corner, SW1, lanesborough.com)

Sporting your new rings, have the Lanesborough driver take you home for a well-deserved night's rest. Your sprawling 4,000-square-foot (380 sq m) suite—the aptly named Lanesborough—has floor-to-ceiling views across to Green Park, four bedrooms, five and a half bathrooms, butler service, and fresh fruit replenished daily (and for £18,000/$28,800 per night, it really should).

Sleep in style at the Savoy hotel.

ABOUT THE AUTHORS

Tim Jepson was born near the River Thames and grew up on the fringes of London, close to Amersham, the second-most outlying station on the city's Tube, or subway system. Since 1985, interspersed with periods living and traveling abroad, he has lived in London itself, first in Islington and latterly in Notting Hill. He has written six other books for National Geographic and is a guide and expert for National Geographic Expeditions. His travel articles have appeared in the *Daily Telegraph, Vogue, Conde Nast Traveller,* and other publications.

Larry Porges has been a book editor at the National Geographic Society in Washington, D.C., for more than a decade. He was born in New York and lived in London for five years, three of those in Maida Vale. Porges studied English history at Tufts University and the British and European Studies Group, London. He wrote the 2011 revision of the National Geographic guidebook to London, was a contributing author on the National Geographic e-book *Quintessential London,* and has been published in *National Geographic Traveler* magazine and other publications. Despite frequent trips back, he misses London, especially the *London Evening Standard,* Little Venice, and being surrounded by people who still think of Starburst as Opal Fruits.

ACKNOWLEDGMENTS

Tim Jepson would like to thank Margaret Jepson for instilling an early love of London and James Bishop for the generous gift of his library of books on the city. He is also grateful to the many friends and former colleagues who have shared tips and ideas, and to those who helped with research on the ground, notably Sarah Shuckburgh, Victoria Homewood, Dana Conley, Jane Lambert, Simon Horsford, and Gabriella Le Breton.

Larry Porges would like to thank the following people, who provided expertise, research, and/or advice: John Maloney, Dr. Jennifer Paxton, Jacob Field, Zack Sobczak, Anne Marie Houppert, Liz Young, Eva Absher-Schantz, Rose Davidson, Marlena Serviss, Abigail Cloft, Katherine McCutcheon, Ellen Dupont, Damien McCrystal, Noelle Weber, and Hannah Lauterback. Special thanks go to Barbara Noe and Caroline Hickey of National Geographic Travel Books for their flexibility, support, and caffeine during the course of this project; to all his friends for patiently listening to random facts about London the past year; and especially to his parents and siblings for nurturing a passion for all things London.

Both Larry and Tim would like to thank the team at National Geographic who helped make this book a reality: Elisa Gibson for her excellent design, Leslie Allen for her editing prowess, Judy Klein for expertly ushering the book through the various editing phases, Jane Martin for her photo research, Keith Bellows for his overall vision, and dozens of other critical people behind the scenes. Special thanks go to Alison Ince for her painstaking fact-checking and corrections.

BIBLIOGRAPHY

Ackroyd, Peter. *London: The Biography.* Chatto and Windus, 2000.

Ackroyd, Peter. *London Under: The Secret History Beneath the Streets.* Anchor Books, 2011.

Adams, Bernard. *London Illustrated 1604-1851.* The Library Association, 1983.

Ash, Alexander. *Top 10 of London.* Hamlyn, 2012.

Ash, Russell. *The Londoner's Almanac.* Century, 1985.

Bailey, Paul, ed. *The Oxford Book of London.* Oxford University Press, 1996.

Barker, Felix and Peter Jackson. *London: 2000 Years of a City and Its People.* Macmillan, 1974.

Baxter, R. *Reliquiae Baxterianae: or, Mr. Richard Baxter's Narrative of The most Memorable Passages of his Life and Times.* M. Sylvester, T. Parkhust, J. Robinson, J. Lawrence & J. Dunton, 1696.

Bayley, Stephen. *The Albert Memorial.* Scholar Press, 1981.

Beames, Thomas. *The Rookeries of London: Past, Present and Prospective,* 2nd ed. Thomas Bosworth, 1852.

Beddard, Robert A. *The London Frost Fair of 1683-84.* Corporation of London, 1972.

Bell, W. G. *The Great Fire of London in 1666.* John Lane, 1920.

Brooke, Christopher. *London 800-1216: The Shaping of a City.* Secker and Warburg, 1975.

Cannon, Jon. *Cathedral: The Great English Cathedrals and the World That Made Them.* Constable and Robinson, 2007.

Cawthorne, Nigel. *The Strange Laws of Old England.* Piatkus, 2013.

Davies, Hunter. *A Walk Round London's Parks.* Hamish Hamilton, 1983.

Davies, Philip. *Lost London: 1870-1945.* Transatlantic Press, 2009.

Defoe, D. *A journal of the plague year: being observations or memorials of the most remarkable occurrences, as well publick as private, which happened in London during the last Great Visitation in 1665.* Ed. L. Landa, Oxford University Press, 1969.

de Rapicani, F. *A foreign visitor's account of the Great Fire, 1666.* Transactions of the London and Middlesex Archaeological Society, 1960.

Diprose, Graham and Jeff Robins. *The River Thames Revisited.* Frances Lincoln, 2007.

Douglas, David C. *William the Conquerer.* Eyre Methuen, 1964.

Dryden, J. *Annus Mirabilis from John Dryden: a critical edition of the major works.* Ed. K. Walker. Oxford University Press, 1987.

Edmonds, Mark. *Inside Soho*. Nicholson, 1988.

Elborough, Travis and Nick Rennison. *London Quiz*. The Little Bookroom, 2010.

Evelyn, J. *The Diary of John Evelyn*. Ed. E. S. De Beer, 6 vols. Oxford University Press, 1959.

Fletcher, Geoffrey. *The London Nobody Knows*. Cassell, 1989.

Forshaw, Alec and Theo Bergström. *Smithfield Past and Present*. Hale, 1990.

Fowler, Peter, ed. *London's Bridges*. HMSO, 1983.

Frost, Thomas. *The Old Showmen, and the Old London Fairs*. Tinsley Brothers, 1875.

Gadd, I.A. and P. Wallis, eds. *Guilds, society and economy in London 1450-1800*. Centre for Metropolitan History, 2002.

Gatrell, V.A.C. *The Hanging Tree: Execution and the English People, 1770-1868*. Oxford University Press, 1994.

Gies, Francis and Joseph Gies. *Daily Life in Medieval Times*. Grange Books, 2005.

Glinert, Ed. *The London Compendium: A Street-by-Street Exploration of the Hidden Metropolis*. Penguin Books, 2003.

Guard, Richard. *Lost London: An A–Z of forgotten landmarks and lost traditions*. Michael O'Mara Books Limited, 2012.

Hahn, Daniel and Nicholas Robins, eds. *The Oxford Guide to Literary Britain & Ireland*. Oxford University Press, 2008.

Hall, Martin. *The Blue Plaque Guide to London Homes*. Queen Anne Press Ltd., 1976.

Hanawalt, Barbara A. *Growing Up in Medieval London: The Experience of Childhood in History*. Oxford University Press, 1993.

Hodges, N. *Loimologia, or, an historical Account of the Plague in London in 1665, With precautionary Directions against the like Contagion*. E. Bell and J. Osborn, 1720.

Hodgett, Gerald A. J. *A book of medieval refinements, recipes and remedies from a manuscript in Samuel Pepys' library*. Cornmarket Reprints, 1972.

Hollingshead, John. *Ragged London in 1861*. Smith, Elder, and Co., 1861.

Hollister, C. Warren. *Henry I*. Yale University Press, 2001.

Horn, Pamela. *The Victorian Town Child*. Sutton Publishing Limited, 1997.

Howard, Rachel and Bill Nash. *Secret London: An Unusual Guide*. Jonglez, 2010.

Jenkins, Simon. *A Short History of England*. Profile, 2012.

Johnson, Steven. *The Ghost Map: A Street, an Epidemic and the Hidden Power of Urban Networks*. Riverhead Books, 2006.

Jordan, Thomas E. *Victorian Childhood—Themes and Variations*. State University of New York Press, 1987.

Lawrence, Alistair. *Abbey Road: The Best Studio in the World*. Bloomsbury Publishing, 2012.

LFR Partnership. *London's Riverscape Lost*

and Found. Art Books International, Ltd., 2000.

Library Committee of the Corporation of London. *The Guildhall Miscellany, Volume IV.* October 1971-April 1973.

Long, David. *Bizarre London.* Constable and Robinson, 2013.

Long, David. *The Little Book of London.* The History Press, 2008.

Margary, Ivan D. *Roman Roads in Britain.* John Baker, 1955.

Marsden, Peter. *Roman London.* Thames and Hudson, Ltd., 1980.

Mayhew, Henry. *London Labour and the London Poor: The London Street-folk.* Griffin, Bohn, and Company, 1861.

Mayhew, Henry. *The Street Trader's Lot, London: 1851.* Reproduced by Stanley Rubenstein, Sylvan Press, 1947.

McNay, Michael. *Hidden Treasures of England.* Random House, 2009.

Mills, A. D. *A Dictionary of London Place Names.* Oxford University Press, 2010.

Moote, A. L. and D. C. Moote. *The Great Plague: The Story of London's Most Deadly Year.* Johns Hopkins University Press, 2004.

Norrie, Ian. *Walks Around London.* Deutsch, 1984.

Pepys, Samuel. *The Diary of Samuel Pepys.* Ed. Richard Le Gallienne. Modern Library, 2001.

Pepys, Samuel. *The Diary of Samuel*

Pepys. Eds. R. Latham and W. Matthews, 11 vols. G. Bell and Sons, 1970-1983.

Poole, Austin Lane. *Medieval England.* Oxford University Press, 1958.

Potter, Harry. *Hanging in Judgment: Religion and the Death Penalty in England from the Bloody Code to Abolition.* SCM Press, 1993.

Pottle Frederick A., ed. *Boswell's London Journal 1762-1763.* Yale University, 1950.

Quinn, Tom. *Eccentric London.* New Holland Publishers, 2005.

Riley, Henry Thomas, M. A. *Memorials of London and London Life in the XIIIth, XIVth, and XVth Centuries.* Longmans, Green, and Co., 1868.

Roberts, Clayton and David Roberts. *A History of England: Prehistory to 1714.* Prentice-Hall, 1980.

Rolle, Samuel. *London's Resurrection or the Rebuilding of London.* W.R. for Thomas Parkhurst, 1668.

Ross, Christopher. *Tunnel Visions: Journeys of Underground Philosopher.* Fourth Estate, 2001.

Ross, James Bruce and Mary Martin McLaughlin, eds. *The Portable Medieval Reader.* Viking Press, 1949.

Rubinstein, Stanley. *Historians of London.* Peter Owen, 1968.

Saunders, Ann. *The Art and Architecture of London.* Phaidon, 1984.

Schofield, John. *The Building of London: From the Conquest to the Great Fire.*

British Museum Press, 1984.

Sheppard, Francis. *London 1808-1870: The Infernal Wen.* Secker and Warburg, 1971.

Sloane, B. *The Black Death in London.* History Press, 2011.

Stow, John. *A Survey of London.* Clarendon Press, 1908.

Taswell, W. *Autobiography and anecdotes by William Taswell, D.D., sometime rector of Newington, Surrey, rector of Bermondsey, and previously student of Christ Church, Oxford, A.D. 1651-1682.* Ed. George Percy Elliott, Camden Soc., old series, vol. 55, 1853.

Timbs, John. *Curiosities of London, Exhibiting the Most Rare and Remarkable Objects of Interest in the Metropolis.* J. S. Virtue and Co., 1867.

Time Out London. Time Out, 2013.

Trench, Richard and Ellis Hillman. *London Under London: A Subterranean Guide.* John Murray Publishers Ltd., 1984.

Van Young, Sayre. *London's War: A Traveler's Guide to World War II.* Ulysses Press, 2004.

Victoria & Albert Museum. *Ham House.* HMSO, 1976.

Vincent, T. *God's Terrible Voice in the City.* G. Calvert, 1667.

Waller, Maureen. *1700: Scenes From London Life.* Four Walls Eight Windows, 2000.

Ward, Joseph P. *Metropolitan Communities: Trade Guilds, Identity, and Change in Early Modern London.* Stanford University Press, 1997.

Waterhouse, Edward. *A short narrative of the late dreadful fire in London.* W.G. for Richard Thrale and James Thrale, 1667.

Weinreb, Ben and Christopher Hibbert, eds. *The London Encyclopaedia.* Macmillan, 1983.

Whitfield, Peter. *London: A Life in Maps.* The British Library, 2006.

Williams, Penry. *Life in Tudor England.* B. T. Batsford Ltd. and G. P. Putnam's Sons, 1964.

Wiseman, Samuel. *A Short and Serious Narrative of London's Fatal Fire.* Peter Dring, 1667.

Wood, Anthony. *The Life and Times of Anthony Wood, Antiquary, of Oxford, 1632-1695, described by himself.* Ed. Andrew Clark, 5 vols. Clarendon Press for the Oxford Historical Society, 1891-1907.

Wright, Thomas, ed. *A Traveller's Companion to London.* Interlink Books, 2004.

Yapp, Peter, ed. *The Travellers' Dictionary of Quotation.* Routledge, 1983.

Illustrations Credits

Cover, Lavandaart/Shutterstock; 11, Londonstills.com/Alamy; 12, Jeffrey Blackler/Alamy; 16, Peter Barritt/Getty Images; 17, Georgios Kollidas/Shutterstock; 18, Classic Image/Alamy; 22, Mr William Terriss as Mercutio (gravure), English photographer (19th century)/Private Collection/© Look and Learn/The Bridgeman Art Library; 25, Alison Wright/National Geographic Creative; 26, Lawrence M. Porges; 28, Express/Stringer/Getty Images; 31, Redferns/John Hoppy Hopkins/Getty Images; 34, Jack Kay/Stringer/Getty Images; 35, Andy Stagg/VIEW/Corbis; 36, Charing Cross, London, ca 1900 (photo), English photographer (20th century)/Private Collection/The Stapleton Collection/The Bridgeman Art Library; 38, Harrods, showing the Coronation Tower being added to commemorate the coronation of King George V (color litho), English School (20th century)/Private Collection/© Look and Learn/The Bridgeman Art Library; 40, "The Great Fire of London in 1666" (oil on canvas), Verschuier, Lieve (1630-1686)/Museum of Fine Arts, Budapest, Hungary/The Bridgeman Art Library; 43, Bob Thomas/Getty Images; 46, Lonely Planet Images/Getty Images; 48, Richard Baker/In Pictures/Corbis; 51, Keenpress/National Geographic Society/Corbis; 52, Peter Adams/Corbis; 53, Glyn Thomas/Loop Images/Corbis; 54, Steven Morris/the food passionates/Corbis; 55, Peter Williams/Getty Images; 57, David Gee/Alamy; 59, Bon Appetit/Alamy; 61, Dutourdumonde Photography/Shutterstock.com; 63, Catherine Benson/Reuters/Corbis; 64, Courtesy London Landmark Hotel; 66, Richard M Lee/Shutterstock; 67, North Wind Picture Archives; 68, Catmando/Shutterstock; 69, catwalker/Shutterstock.com; 70, "Arsenal v. Sheffield, F.A. Cup Final, Wembley, 1936" (oil on canvas), Cundall, Charles Ernest (1890-1971)/Wingfield Sporting Gallery, London, UK/The Bridgeman Art Library; 72, John McKenna/Alamy; 73, Sunday Morning scene, Petticoat Lane Market, London ca 1900 (b/w photo), English photographer (20th century)/Private Collection/The Bridgeman Art Library; 74, Corbis; 76, Reading the Daily Courant, Jackson, Peter (1922-2003)/Private Collection/© Look and Learn/The Bridgeman Art Library; 79, Advertisement for the Floating Glaciarium (engraving), English School (19th century)/Private Collection/© Look and Learn/Peter Jackson Collection/The Bridgeman Art Library; 81, Robert Harding Picture Library Ltd/Alamy; 82, Woman counterfeiter of silver coins burned at the stake, Old Bailey, London, March 1789, for high treason, from a collection of chapbooks on esoterica & folklore (woodcut), English School (18th century) (after)/Private Collection/The Stapleton Collection/The Bridgeman Art Library; 84, Bill Sikes's House on Jacob's Island (w/c on paper), English School (19th century)/Private Collection/© Look and Learn/Peter Jackson Collection/The Bridgeman Art Library; 86, Views in the Rookery, St. Giles's (litho), English School (19th century)/Private Collection/The Stapleton Collection/The Bridgeman Art Library; 87, UIG via Getty Images; 93, r.nagy/Shutterstock; 95, Nick Ansell—WPA Pool/Getty Images; 96, Tim Graham/Getty Images; 100, Stapleton Collection/Corbis; 103, Florian Monheim/Arcaid/Corbis; 105, Kiev.Victor/Shutterstock.com; 106, Evening Standard/Hulton Archive/Getty Images; 107, Peter Kunasz/Shutterstock; 108, St. Antholin's Church, a View From the West along Watling Street, ca 1850 (w/c on paper), English School (19th century)/London Metropolitan Archives, City of London/The Bridgeman Art Library; 110, Lawrence M. Porges; 112, Bettmann/Corbis; 113, Lawrence M. Porges; 114, Mike Goldwater/Alamy; 116, Francesca Moore/Alamy; 119, GL Archive/Alamy; 122, A street in Whitechapel: The last crime of Jack the Ripper, from "Le Petit Parisien," 1891 (litho), Dete, Beltrand and Clair-Guyot, E. (fl. 1884)/Private Collection/The Stapleton Collection/The Bridgeman Art Library; 124, Leonard Lenz/Corbis; 125, Riot in Broad Street, June 1780 (engraving), Heath, James (1757-1834)/Private Collection/The Bridgeman Art Library; 126, Sir Oswald Mosley, 1967 (photo)/Private Collection/Photo © Mark Gerson/The Bridgeman Art Library; 127, Police at Bramley Road, Notting Hill, 1958 (b/w photo)/© Mirrorpix/The Bridgeman Art Library; 128, Avella/Shutterstock; 130, Lawrence M. Porges; 132, Lawrence M. Porges; 133, chrisdorney/Shutterstock; 134, Lee Torrens/iStockphoto; 137, © The Trustees of the British Museum. All right reserved; 138, Chess pieces, found in an underground chamber in the parish of Uig, Isles in Lewis, Outer Hebrides in 1831, ca 1135-50 (walrus ivory), Scandinavian School (12th century)/© National Museums of Scotland/The Bridgeman Art Library; 141, England, London, black cabs driving along street/ Dorling Kindersley/UIG/The Bridgeman Art Library; 142, Embalmed body of Jeremy Bentham as exhibited at University College/University College Museum, London, UK/The Bridgeman Art Library; 143, The Beadle of the

INDEX

The National Geographic Society is one of the world's largest nonprofit scientific and educational organizations. Its mission is to inspire people to care about the planet. Founded in 1888, the Society is member supported and offers a community for members to get closer to explorers, connect with other members, and help make a difference. The Society reaches more than 450 million people worldwide each month through *National Geographic* and other magazines; National Geographic Channel; television documentaries; music; radio; films; books; DVDs; maps; exhibitions; live events; school publishing programs; interactive media; and merchandise. National Geographic has funded more than 10,000 scientific research, conservation, and exploration projects and supports an education program promoting geographic literacy. For more information, visit www.nationalgeographic.com.

National Geographic Society
1145 17th Street N.W.
Washington, D.C. 20036-4688 U.S.A.

For information about special discounts for bulk purchases, please contact National Geographic Books Special Sales: ngspecsales@ngs.org

For rights or permissions inquiries, please contact National Geographic Books Subsidiary Rights: ngbookrights@ngs.org

Interior design: Elisa Gibson

Printed in the United States of America

14/QGF-CML/1